Basics of ...

BUSINESS
LAW

Basics of ...

BUSINESS LAW

An Introductory Course
For Everyday People

Albert L. Kelley, Esq.

Basics of ...
A Basic Knowledge Imprint of
ABSOLUTELY AMAZING eBOOKS

Basics of ...

is an imprint of
ABSOLUTELY AMAZING eBOOKS

Published by Whiz Bang LLC, 926 Truman Avenue, Key West, Florida 33040, USA

For information contact:
Publisher@AbsolutelyAmazingEbooks.com

ISBN-13: 978-0615977065 (Basics of ...)
ISBN-10: 0615977065

To my wife, Angie, who reminds me that life is more
than business.

Basics of ...
BUSINESS LAW

Table of Contents

WELCOME TO...1

BUSINESS LAW 101.......................................1

LEGAL BASICS..3

WHAT IS THE "LAW".................................3

DECIDING WHAT BUSINESS FORMAT TO USE...15

SUBCHAPTER S CORPORATIONS.......................33

LIMITED PARTNERSHIPS and LIMITED LIABILITY

CORPORATIONS 36

Limited Partnership 36

STOCK OWNERSHIP BASICS 40

CORPORATE CONTROL 46

NOT-FOR-PROFIT CORPORATIONS....................53

ENDING A..

NOT-FOR-PROFIT CORPORATION.......................59

CONTRACTS...64

BASICS 64

TYPES OF CONTRACTS 67

OFFERS 70

ACCEPTANCE 73

ABILITY TO CONTRACT 76

CONSIDERATION 79

LEGALITY 82

CONTRACT INTERPRETATION 86

THIRD PARTY BENEFICIARIES 91

TERMINATION OF A CONTRACT 94

BREACH OF CONTRACT 100

WHAT CAN YOU DO IF CONTRACT IS BREACHED?

.... 103

AGENTS 109

EMPLOYMENT 116

EMPLOYEE/INDEPENDENT CONTRACTOR 116

RISKS IN EMPLOYMENT LAW 120

HISTORY OF EMPLOYMENT LAWS 122

THE 125

CIVIL RIGHTS ACT 125

IS THERE DISCRIMINATION? 136

HANDICAP DISCRIMINATION 141

AGE DISCRIMINATION 152

THE EQUAL PAY ACT..155

SEXUAL HARASSMENT...158

INVESTIGATION OF SEXUAL HARASSMENT.....161

PREGNANCY AND FMLA 164

AFFIRMATIVE ACTION 167

PRIVACY RIGHTS..170

CONFIDENTIALITY OF EMPLOYEE RECORDS ..173

PRIVACY AND EMAIL..176

VARIOUS EMPLOYMENT LAWS 179

EMPLOYMENT CONTRACTS 185

LABOR..188

HISTORY OF UNIONS...188

WHAT THE UNION DOES FOR EMPLOYEES AND
EMPLOYER...191

PHASES OF LABOR RELATIONS 195

THE LEVELS OF UNIONS AND HOW THEY ARE
ORGANIZED 198

HOW DO YOU GET A UNION STARTED?...........201

THE STEPS TO SUCCESSFUL COLLECTIVE
BARGAINING..204

RATIFYING A LABOR AGREEMENT 208

DIFFERENCE BETWEEN A STRIKE AND A
LOCKOUT...211

LABOR GREIVANCES 214

WHY DISCUSS UNIONS?.................................217

ARBITRATION IN LABOR AGREEMENTS............219

EMPLOYEE DISCIPLINE 223

HANDLING LABOR DISPUTES NOT COVERED BY
THE COLLECIVE AGREEMENT 226

HIRING/FIRING PRACTICES................................229

EMPLOYEE REFERENCES...............................229

AT-WILL EMPLOYMENT 232

TERMNATNG AN AT-WILL EMPLOYMENT 236

LIMITATIONS IN EMPLOYMENT CONTRACTS..239

INTELLECTUAL PROPERTY 242

HISTORY OF TRADEMARKS COPYRIGHTS AND
PATENTS 242

COPYRIGHTS 245

TRADE SECRETS 249

TRADEMARKS...252

PATENTS 258

SALES 260

iv

A SALE: AN EXCHANGE OF GOODS AND SERVICES 260

FOCUS ON SALES AND THE UNIFORM COMMERCIAL CODE 263

'GOOD FAITH'...

IS A BIG PART OF A SALES CONTRACT 266

SHIPPING HAS A LANGUAGE OF ITS OWN.......269

REMEDIES FOR 272

SALE OF GOODS 272

FALSE ADVERTISING 275

RULES VARY WHERE LABELING, DISLOSURE PRICING CONCERNED 277

FINANCES 280

CREDIT CARDS 280

KNOW YOUR RIGHTS AGAINST DEBT COLLECTORS..283

COMMERCIAL PAPER AND NEGOTIABLE INSTRUMENTS..286

SURETY AND GUARANTEES...........................293

LETTERS OF CREDIT 296

BANKS AND 299

LARGE FINANCIAL TRANSFERS 299

v

SEIZING COLLATERAL 301

BANKRUPTCY...304

SALE OF BUSINESS 310

INTERNATIONAL TRADE 313

PROPERTY OWNERSHIP 318

BAILMENTS..321

COMMON CARRIERS..324

HOTELKEEPERS LIABILITY 327

INSURANCE 330

REAL ESTATE 333

CONDOMINIUMS...337

DEEDS 340

MORTGAGES 342

LEASES 349

EVICTIONS...352

RENTAL DAMAGES 357

COLLECTION OF RENTAL DAMAGES.............359

THIRD PARTIES ON PROPERTY 362

INVITEES 365

LICENSEES 368

TRESPASSERS...370

RESTRICTIVE COVENANTS.............................372

ZONING...375

ENVIRONMENTAL LAWS 378

FEDERAL 381

ENVIRONMENTALLAWS 381

LAWYERS' 386

SOURCES OF LAW...................................386

PRESS STATEMENTS 392

LAWYER'S OATH 396

TV COURTS 402

BUSINESS VALUATION 407

CIVIL RIGHTS DECEMBER HOLIDAYS 410

YEAR END 413

PA P E RWO R K...................................413

CLOSING 416

About the Author 417

WELCOME TO BUSINESS LAW 101

Welcome to Business Law 101. Please take a seat. If you're not supposed to be in this class, please turn the page. Just kidding.

Business Law 101 is a primer to help give readers a basic understanding of business law. It will cover issues such as contracts, partnerships, corporations, stocks, sales and intellectual property.

Let me begin by giving you my background. My name is Al Kelley and I am a lawyer, author, businessman, book publisher, film producer and college professor. I have been practicing law since 1990 focusing on business law, corporations, entertainment law, contracts, copyrights, and trademarks. I am a member of the Florida Bar, and the Trial Bar of the United States District Court for the Southern and Middle Districts of Florida. I also am the owner or co-owner of numerous companies. For three years I taught Business Law, Personnel Law and Administrative Law at St. Leo University. This book started because people often asked basic questions about business law. People are interested in business issues: why choose a partnership over a corporation or an LLC; when may they lawfully refuse to accept delivery of a shipment; when do they need worker's compensation; why should they register a trademark? While some questions are specific to one person's needs, many are standard business questions with uniform answers. I hope to provide you with the answers to the basic questions and let you know what questions to ask for the specific ones.

Now for the mandatory disclaimer. The information being provided in this book is not designed to be specific legal advice. It is offered for information purposes only. It is not oriented towards any specific issue and through it, I am not representing any person or entity. The principles presented are general business law, based primarily on Florida law (I am not licensed to practice in any other state and do not profess to be an expert on the laws of other states). If you have a specific business issue that you need advice on, consult with an attorney of your choice.

While you won't get college credit for reading this book, I hope to provide you with the same information that you would receive in an introductory business law course (and then some). We will begin by covering some basic legal information, such as sources of law, business organizations, etc. and get more detailed as we go.

I hope you find this book informative and entertaining, but mostly, I hope you find it useful. With that, welcome to class, hope to see you back on the next page. Class dismissed.

LEGAL BASICS

WHAT IS THE "LAW"

Newspapers are filled with business stories. It is common to read reports on the stock market, mergers, executives, and striking workers. It is a rare week that we don't see a headline about business law. Over the last few years we've had Imclone, Enron and Martha Stewart. More recently we have seen countless stories about banks and other financial businesses. At the core of all these stories lies the law. It is the guiding source as to what happens in business and why. Corporate lawyers are among the most in demand and among the most highly paid.

To understand business law, it is advisable to first understand some basic legal principles. There are numerous sources of law. The premier source is the Constitution. Not only do we have a Constitution for the United States, each state also has a Constitution. These documents are the cornerstone of all our laws. Their purpose is to set out the basic legal theories for their citizens and legislatures to follow. Therefore, they cannot be changed by statutes or the legislature; only by a vote of the people.

Next we have the statutes, both state and federal. These are the laws passed by the state and federal legislatures. These laws regulate the activities of the citizens of the states and their local governments. There are currently approximately 48 Titles in the Florida Statutes, covering nearly 1,000 chapters, and likely hundreds of thousands of laws. Many of the state statutes for business are the same for many states. These are called the Uniform Commercial Codes (UCC). The UCC was drafted by committees formed by representatives from each state and ultimately adopted by the legislatures of those states. We will discuss the UCC in detail later.

Related to statutes are ordinances. These are the laws passed by lower government agencies such as the City and County Commissions. They only apply to the citizens who live in their districts.

The next section of laws is the administrative regulations, such as the Internal Revenue Code. Administrative regulations are governed by the various administrative agencies such as the Securities and Exchange Commission, the National Labor Relations Board, and the Department of Business and Professional Regulation. These regulations have the weight of statutes but are enforced by the agencies rather than the Courts.

As for the Courts, they are our next source of law. Caselaw has the weight of statutes. When the Court publishes its decision on a case, that decision becomes the law for all similarly situated cases before that court and all lower courts. This is the theory of "stare decisis" (literally, to stand by the decision). Prior decisions set precedent for all future courts to follow until the decision is reversed by a higher court.

Next we have the common law. These are rules and

principles that derive their authority solely from custom and usage. The common law is not found in the statute books, but is still followed and can be enforced. As an example, a businessman who adopts a name for his store can prevent any other person from using the same name in the same locality, even if the name is not registered as a trademark. This "common law trademark" is fully enforceable in the court system.

COURTS

Here in Florida, our Courts are divided from lowest to highest in the following manner: County Court, Circuit Court, Appellate Court, Supreme Court. This is not true for all states and even the names do not have the same meaning (In New York, the Supreme Court is the lowest court, not the highest).

Each Court has its own requirements as to what cases may come before it. For example, in Florida, County Court can hear cases involving disputes of up to $15,000.00. Above that amount, the cases are heard by the Circuit Court. County Court hears landlord/tenant cases; Circuit Court hears cases to enforce real estate sales contracts. The Appellate Courts primary purpose is to review decisions made by the Circuit Court (the Circuit Court reviews decisions made by the County Court) and the Supreme Court reviews decisions rendered by the Appellate Courts (the Supreme Court also reviews all death penalty cases).

On the Federal level there are three court systems. The lowest are the Federal District Courts, followed by the U.S. Court of Appeals, and then the United States Supreme Court.

Just because a court can hears a certain type of case doesn't mean the Court can hear a specific case. There is a question of where in the state the case can be heard. This is referred to as "venue". Venue generally means where the

Defendant resides, where the details of the lawsuit occurred or, in contract cases, where a contract was signed last. The case must be filed in the proper venue.

Related to venue is the concept of jurisdiction. Jurisdiction means what type of cases a Court may hear, such as those indicated above. It also indicates when a court may hear a case. The court does not have jurisdiction unless the Defendant has been served. If a defendant is never served with a lawsuit, the Court does not have jurisdiction over them and cannot hear the case. Or, if I have a dispute with someone from New York and I file in the case in Nevada just to make it more difficult, the Court has no jurisdiction because Nevada has no involvement with the details of my dispute.

We are going to cover contracts later, but one thing you need to know is that almost anything legal can be done by contract. This includes determining what law will apply to a contract and what Court can hear disputes involving the contract. What this means is that you can state that a contract will be governed by the laws of the state of Florida. You can also state in the contract that, in the event of a dispute, litigation may only be filed in a particular location, such as Key West. This can be a convenient issue as many contracts involve numerous parties from different places and could otherwise be enforced in many places. If you use your home city as the dispute forum it can provide many benefits such as reducing litigation costs, and allowing more familiarity with the laws that govern your contract.

Your contract can also require that all disputes go to some form of alternative dispute resolution, such as mediation or arbitration. Mediation essentially is an attempt to resolve a dispute by asking a disinterested third party to moderate the discussions and try to facilitate a settlement of issues; arbitration uses a disinterested third party (or panel) to actually make a decision which is generally binding on the parties to the dispute. If a contract calls for one of these forms of alternative dispute resolution, litigation is improper until the contract requirement is complied with. Any lawsuits filed can be placed on hold until the alternative dispute resolution is attempted. Unfortunately, what started as a way to reduce the cost of resolving disputes has in many cases become more expensive than simple litigation, although the resolution is usually quicker and reduces the backlog on the Court system.

LEGAL REGULATIONS

There are many reasons for the various regulations placed upon business. First and foremost is the safety of the public. Regulations help prevent dangerous products from being sold. The second and actually more encompassing reason is the prevention of unfair competition.

We live in what is called a free enterprise society. This doesn't mean free from regulation; it means that businesses are free to enter the market, subject to certain regulations. If a company takes action to prevent another from doing business it is called a restraint of trade and is illegal.

What is regulated? To some extent, everything. The Food and Drug Administration (FDA) regulates the sale and safety of foods and drugs. The Federal Aviation Administration (FAA) regulates the airlines and their maintenance. The various state bar associations regulate who can practice law and how. The Department of Business and Professional Regulation regulates numerous occupations such as cosmetologists, contractors and chiropractors.

State agencies set out their regulations in their Administrative Code. However, in addition to these agencies, the State and Federal legislators can also place regulations on business through the statutes. As an example, banks must follow regulations under the Financial Institutions Reform, Recovery and Enforcement Act (FIRREA). The Uniform Commercial Code regulates certain financial transactions and the sale of goods. Consumer Collection Agencies must follow the rules set out in the Unfair Debt Collection Act.

The government can also regulate competition, especially unfair competition. The Federal Trade Commission Act made illegal certain unfair methods of competition, such as disparaging competitor's products, discrimination of customers, spying on competitors and misappropriation.

The government can also regulate prices. Laws have been passed which prevent a business from price discrimination, if the purpose is to lessen competition or create a monopoly. Price discrimination doesn't mean that the business demands a higher price from one group of people over another. It means that the business cannot sell items at an artificially low price to shut down other businesses. This used to occur when the large supermarket chains moved into small towns. They would sell their items below costs to drive the Mom-and-Pop business out. Once the supermarket had taken over the territory, they could then raise their prices to astronomical levels as there was no competition.

The idea that business cannot use certain tactics to gain control of the market creates an interesting situation. The Sherman Antitrust Act states, "every person who shall monopolize or attempt to monopolize or combine or conspire to monopolize any part of the trade or commerce among the several states or with foreign nations shall be deemed guilty of a felony". Yet, isn't this exactly what every businessman is trying to do? Isn't this the dream of every business - to be so well liked by his customers that he puts his competitors out of business?

Bill Gates was very successful at marketing his operating systems and selling it below market value (even often giving it away), and through his efforts, Microsoft eliminated nearly all of their competitors. Indeed, because they were so successful, the Justice Department considered a demand that Microsoft be broken up into three or more separate companies, just to open the opportunities for others to enter the field. Microsoft even created a division to promote their largest competitor, Apple Computers, to lessen the appearance of Microsoft being a monopoly.

Price discrimination is allowed in certain situations. When there is a difference in the grade, quality or quantity of goods, costs of transportation, a good faith effort to meet competition, differences in methods, deterioration of goods, or close out sale on a certain line of goods, price discrimination will be permitted.

Regulation of prices also includes interest rates. The various states have what are called usury laws. These regulate what percentage a business may demand as a finance charge.

Punishment for violating regulations can be very costly. As an example, violations of OSHA regulations often exceed $100,000.00 and a violation of the Sherman Antitrust Act can cause corporations to be fined up to one million dollars and an individual up to $100,000 and/or three years incarceration.

BUSINESS ETHICS

Business ethics- almost an oxymoron, but they do exist. Business ethics is a balancing act of profits and the needs and desires of society. Generally, this is not something that can be easily governed by law. It is more a question of morals.

Often, business people will look to the law as a beginning to ethical questions. If it is legal, it is moral. This is called the positive law theory of business ethics.

Others look to natural law for their ethical standards. This is a belief that standards exists universally and cannot be changed by the law. A classic example was slavery. While it was legal at one point in time, many people refused to own slaves because they felt it was a violation of natural law.

A third view is what is referred to as situational ethics. This is the line of thought that ethical behavior depends on individual circumstances.

A fourth view is the stakeholder theory. This requires businesses to consider what would be in the best interest of all those with an interest in the company. This includes not only shareholders, but also the employees and surrounding community.

Why do we have business ethics? Wouldn't it be sufficient if each business just did what was best for that business? Isn't this the true meaning of competition?

The first reason for business ethics is simply a matter

of trust. Businesses and customers both need the ability to have trust in who they are dealing with. They need to know that contracts will be honored and that products will meet the standards they were advertised with. Employees need to have faith that their employment will be continued each day.

Another reason for business ethics is financial performance. Studies indicate that those companies that have a strong value system tend to perform better than their counterparts. These studies tend to focus on high standards for product quality, employee welfare, and customer service.

Behavior will change based upon what theory of ethics a business follows. Consider a business ethics decision that arose several years ago. Cigarette manufacturers developed a cartoon character with an eye toward attracting young smokers. Under a positive law theory (at the time), this was a proper decision as it was legal, and thus moral (although this law has since changed). Under a natural law theory, this decision was improper as it attracted teens and young adults to a dangerous and addictive habit. The decision would be questionable under a situational ethics standard, as it could be argued that while it was not appropriate to attract teens to smoking, they were already being attracted to smoking through peer pressure and this was no more than a clever marketing campaign. The decision would be debatable under a stakeholder theory since, while it appeared to be a good financial decision for the shareholders and employees, the business must consider the negative ramifications to its reputation for trying to attract young smokers.

Recognizing a business ethics question is often easy; resolving it is usually not. There are three models for trying to reach a resolution. First is the Blanchard and Peale Three Part Test. This test asks first: Is it Legal? Then: Is it balanced? Then: How does it make me feel? The first question is one of positive law. If the idea is legal, move on. If not, the analysis is over. The second question is one of natural law. Is the action fair? The last question is more situational, allowing the manager to consider how he or she feels in that particular situation.

The second type of test is the "Front Of The Newspaper Test". This simply requires managers to consider how their actions would be described in a critical front-page article in a newspaper. This is almost purely a stakeholder theory test.

Third is the Laura Nash model. This is a series of questions: Have you defined your problem accurately? How would you define your problem if you stood on the other side of the fence? How did this situation arise in the first place? What is your intention in making this decision? How does the intention compare with the probable results? Whom could your decision or action injure? Can you discuss your decision with the affected parties? Are you confident that your position will be as valid over a long period of time as it appears now? Could you discuss your decision with your supervisors, coworkers, officers, board of directors, friends and family? This approach reflects part of all the ethical theories and gives the broadest level of evaluation. But the decision is still yours.

BUSINESS ENTITIES

DECIDING WHAT BUSINESS FORMAT TO USE

When trying to decide what form of business to use, a number of issues need to be taken into consideration.

1. Nature of the business. Certain businesses traditionally use certain forms. For years, lawyers, doctors and accountants generally operated as sole proprietorship, general partnership or professional service corporation. They cannot be formed as limited partnerships, however, today many are forming as limited liability corporations. These formats allow for personal control of the business and management of the daily operations. Manufacturing is generally run as a corporation due to the ability of shareholders to participate in the management of the business without requiring any specialized skills. Marketing is also generally run as a corporation. Many small businesses operate as sole proprietorships or general partnerships to avoid the legal hassles of a corporation. Large retail businesses and brokerages are run as corporations in order to bring in highly specialized personnel to run the various aspects of the business. Since the Nineteen nineties, many of these businesses are choosing to form limited liability corporations to gain tax benefits without sacrificing a basic corporate format.

2. Nature of assets. What assets will the business hold? Real Estate investments are often run through a limited or general partnership with the title held in a land trust. While this can also be done through a corporate format, there are potential problems because when the value of the land goes up, the shareholders may be hit with double taxation when the property is later sold or large capital gains tax when the stock is sold. Sometimes the business may want to set up a separate business to lease the property or manage the property. To do this the land can be held in a partnership to purchase the land and then form a corporation to handle the management of the property. You can also form a corporation to actually lease the property from the partnership. This may be done to further limit liability, as injuries that occur on the property will be the liability of the corporation, not the partnership and can shield the property from seizure. This format also allows for single taxation when the property is sold, while giving a tax break for leasehold expenses. The partnership can write off much income for improvements and maintenance, while at the same time taking depreciation on the property. Another format for real estate holdings is the limited liability company. This allows an easier method of selling land by simply transferring the ownership of the LLC. While this used to be a successful method of avoiding doc stamps on the transfer, some states are now treating a transfer of the LLC as if it were a new deed. In Florida, if the LLC is transferred within three years of purchasing the property, the transfer of the LLC will be taxed at the same rate as the doc stamps on the real property.

3. Personal Liability. The only forms of business that allows an avoidance of personal liability are the corporation, limited liability corporation, and for some members, a limited partnership. Personal liability cannot be avoided in a sole proprietorship or general partnership. Why is this important? Let's say the business is having financial problems. In a sole proprietorship, the business owner (or in a general partnership, the partner) is personally responsible for the bills of the business. However, in a corporation, the business alone is responsible for the bills. The shareholders are not personally responsible for the payment of the bills. The corporation can file bankruptcy without affecting the credit of the shareholders. Another situation arises if a person is injured on the premises or by an employee working for the business. If the injured person obtains a judgment against the business, they can seize property of the sole proprietor or partners, but cannot seize any property of shareholders (with limited exceptions to be discussed later). In a corporate setting, the judgment holder can only seize assets of the corporation or in an LLC, only assets of the LLC.

4. Centralization of management. If the business is going to be small with few employees, a sole proprietorship or partnership may be acceptable. If, however, the business will be larger, with multiple managers, you generally want a corporate or LLC structure to centralize management into specific officers.

5. Noncompetition agreements. Partners may enter into noncompetition agreements; however, these agreements are generally not enforceable against

shareholders unless they are also employees.

6. Ease of formation- a sole proprietorship is the easiest organization to form- nothing is required but a business license and perhaps a fictitious name. A general partnership also can be formed with no official actions, however, it is highly recommended to put the partnership agreement in writing. A limited partnership must be filed with the State and must file annual reports to continue its existence. Corporations are the most formal of the organizations. It requires Articles of Incorporation (or Articles of Organization for LLC's), Bylaws (Operating Agreements for LLC), stock certificates, documentary tax stamps, and an annual report every year. It may also require a shareholder's agreement, a small business tax election and must hold a meeting of the shareholders and directors each year (There is no annual meeting requirement for LLC's but they are recommended).

7. Management and control- In a sole proprietorship, the owner makes all the decisions and controls the business. In a limited partnership, the general partner makes all decisions. In a general partnership, however, unless there is an agreement to the contrary, each partner has an equal right to control the business. In a corporation, the management and control are exercised by the Board of Directors and the officers. Shareholders have the right to ratify certain actions of the Board but are not generally involved in the day-to-day activities. In LLC's, management is controlled by Managers.

8. Credit and Capital requirements- a sole proprietorship is limited in its start-up capital to the personal assets of the proprietor. Partnerships can have

greater capital as there are more owners to contribute. Corporations and LLC's have an additional benefit, in that not only do they have the initial owners' capital, but they are able to raise additional capital through the sale of stock. Generally, corporations can raise up to one million dollars through a private stock sale, however. For larger stock purchases, the corporation must register with the SEC and comply with the state's blue sky laws (laws regarding corporate investments).

9. Continuity of life- a sole proprietorship dies with the sole proprietor. The same is true with a partnership. In addition, a general partnership ends with the withdrawal of any partner and a limited partnership ends with the death or withdrawal of the general partner. A corporation or LLC continues its existence indefinitely unless dissolved by the State, the Court or a vote of the shareholders (members).

10. Conveyance of interest- For a sole proprietorship, the owner can sell the business, at any time to whomever he or she wants. In a general partnership, the partners cannot transfer their interest without a written agreement to that effect between the partners. For corporations, absent a shareholders agreement to the contrary, stock certificates are freely transferable to any one at any time. To restrict the sale of stock, a written shareholder's agreement must be drafted and signed by all shareholders and language must be added to the face of the certificates informing purchasers of the existence of the agreement.

11. Probate problems- a sole proprietorship can only be operated for a period of four months after the appointment of the personal representative when the

owners dies, unless there is a will authorizing continuation during probate. A partnership ceases to exist on the death of a partner, but a partnership agreement can be drafted that allows the surviving partner to buy out his partner's interest and continue operations. For a corporation, there is no effect on the death of a shareholder. The corporation continues to operate, even while the shares are in the probate process (If a director or officer dies, the shareholders or surviving directors may name a replacement).

SOLE PROPRIETORSHIPS

For the next few sections we will be focusing on the specifics of various business formats. The first is the sole proprietorship. The majority of businesses in this country are sole proprietorships. It is the simplest and least expensive of the various business organizations to start up.

A sole proprietorship can be started simply by beginning to do business. Because the business is owned and operated by an individual it is not necessary to open a separate bank account for the business (though this would be advisable to keep better track of income and expense). As with any business, the sole proprietor will still need to apply for and obtain an occupational license (city and county).

If the business is to be run under a name other than the name of the owner, the proprietor must file a fictitious name application with the Department of State. It is required that the business first run an ad in the local newspaper of the intent to use a name. While you may do business under any name that has not been trademarked either through state or federal law, you should make sure that you don't choose a name that is already in use in that locality. This could cause a violation of a common law trademark and require you to change the name later. The name must not contain the words "Corporation" "Company" or Incorporated" or any of their abbreviations.

Once the business is started, all assets of the business will belong to the business owner. This includes the licenses, the equipment, the furniture and the leases. The owner of the sole proprietorship is also the controller of the business. He (or she) can hire managers and employees to assist with the operation, but the proprietor is always in control. However, the proprietor also has full liability for the business. That is, if an employee causes an accident while acting in the course of his or her business duties, the sole proprietor shall be personally responsible for the damages.

The sole proprietor shall also be legally responsible for all decisions made by the employees and managers. For example, if a manager hires employees based on sexual discrimination, the owner will subsequently be responsible for his wrongful act, even if the owner wasn't aware of it or hadn't authorized discriminatory practices.

The sole proprietor also has full personal responsibility for the business financial status. If the business cannot pay suppliers of employees, they can sue the individual owner and attempt to seize his personal assets to satisfy any judgment they receive. Business creditors can go both against the business's assets and the owners' assets.

One of the greatest problems with a sole proprietorship is the continuity of the business. A sole proprietorship only last as long as the owner is alive. Under Florida's probate laws, the owner's personal representative can only operate the business for up to 4 months while they attempt to wrap up the affairs of the business. The assets and liabilities then become part of the owner's estate.

A sole proprietor will be taxed for all income under applicable individual tax rates. The income and expense will be included on the individual tax statement; there need not be a separate tax filing for the business. The proprietor may also be responsible for paying self-employment tax.

Another problem with sole proprietorships is the lack of available startup capital. The new business owner is limited to his or her personal savings or any loans he or she is able to obtain.

While the startup costs are less expensive than with a corporation or even partnership, those costs are borne solely by the proprietor. Other business organizations can turn to shareholders for an influx of capital.

PARTNERSHIPS

A partnership is created by an agreement between two or more persons to act as co-owners of a business. The partners are considered the agents of the partnership, not employees. As such, each partner has the authority to bind the partnership and each is liable for the debts of the partnership.

The partnership does not require a written agreement, but it is highly advisable. Even in the absence of a written agreement, the formation and operation of the partnership will fall under the requirements of the Uniform Partnership Act of the Florida Statutes. A partnership does not need a trade name though they are common. If they use one, it must be registered with the Department of State. In addition, a partnership generally may not use the words "company", "corporation", or "incorporated" in their name.

A partnership may be a general partnership formed to operate a continuing business, or it may be a special partnership formed for a single transaction only. It is also not required in most circumstances for a partnership to register its existence with the Department of State, however, registration is available and advisable. Because a partnership does not have to be registered, the identity of the partners may be kept confidential, unless required to be disclosed by law. Anyone who can legally enter into a contract may become a partner, including minors. A partnership may also be created even if the partners don't design it as such. The issue is how the relationship appears, not what it is called.

To determine if a partnership exists, look at the following factors: control, sharing of profits and losses, co-ownership of property, contribution of property, contribution of efforts, among other things.

Property purchased with partnership assets becomes property of the partnership. Each partner has the right to use partnership property for partnership purposes. The property is not divisible, so the partners cannot exclude the other from using the assets. Upon the death of a partner, the rights of the partnership assets transfer to the remaining partner rather than to his heirs. A partnership is a voluntary agreement and is personal between the partners. No one can be forced to be a partner with someone they don't want to be a partner with.

Partnerships can be terminated by a number of methods. It may occur by agreement of the partners, by expulsion of a partner, by a withdrawal of a partner, by the death of a partner, by bankruptcy of the partnership, or by court order based on insanity, incapacity, misconduct, impracticability, failure, and equitable circumstances such as fraud. The partners must be given notice of the dissolution, unless it is clearly shown. After the dissolution, the partnership may continue for a reasonable period for the sole purpose of winding down its affairs. During this period, the partners cannot continue with business activity, but only take those actions necessary to wind the business down. At the winding down, creditors get first priority of payment, and then the partners divide the balance. This is done by first reimbursing the partners for their contributions to the partnership, then dividing the capital of the business and lastly dividing the assets.

What can partners do? Each partner may do the following in the furtherance of the partnership business: enter into partnership contracts, sell goods, purchase property in the partnership name, borrow money, obtain insurance, hire employees, pay claims, make admissions of liability, and accept notice of service on behalf of the partnership.

What can't a partner do? Without consent of all other partners, a partner cannot: enter into a contract that ceases partnership business (such as selling all assets of the partnership), submit controversies to arbitration, confess judgments, or assign property to creditors.

Partners have certain duties to the partnership and to the other partners. These duties include a duty of loyalty and good faith (a partner cannot take actions that would be detrimental to the partnership, nor take a benefit for himself that would rightfully belong to the partnership), a duty of obedience to the partnership agreement, a duty to use reasonable care, a duty to provide information to the partnership for any issue that may affect the partnership, and a duty of accounting for all expenses of the partnership.

CORPORATIONS

A corporation is basically a fake person controlled by a group of real people, and considered separate from the real people.

The corporation is a legal entity, with the same rights as a person. This means the corporation can be held liable as if it were a person; it can sue and be sued; it can commit crimes and be punished; it can enter contracts and own property; it can incur debts and borrow money. And none of these actions will create liability in the shareholders, outside their investment in the corporation. One of the few differences between a corporation and an individual is one of representation. While an individual is allowed to represent himself or herself in court, a corporation must be represented by an attorney (except in small claims court)

Because it is a separate and legal entity, ownership may be transferred without affecting the rights and obligations of the company or other shareholders. In other words, let's say I start a corporation. As the sole shareholder, officer and director of the company, I am authorized to enter into contracts in the corporate name. If my company enters into a contract with John Smith and then I sell my stock to Bob Jones, the contract with John Smith is still valid. John cannot cancel the contract simply because I am no longer involved. The contract is with the company, not with me. The company still exists, even though I have sold my stock to another person.

A corporation is a creature of statute. It is created by filing Articles of Incorporation with the Department of State (this is true for nearly all states). These Articles set fort certain information that controls the activity of the company until changed. It includes the name of the company, the physical and mailing address for the company, who the incorporator is (the person who is filing the Articles), and how many shares of stock the corporation may issue. The name of a corporation is important. Only one corporation may register under a specific name (as opposed to a fictitious name that may be registered by countless people).

There are several types of corporations:

Public Corporations: local governments are public corporations. They are established to run governmental purposes. Cities are public corporations; towns are not.

Quasi-public corporations: private companies that provide public utilities, for example, many power companies are Quasi-public corporations.

Public Authority: government created companies to provide services to the public, such as a Housing Authority.

Private corporations: Most other corporations are private corporations. These are companies that are operated for private gain of their shareholders. These can be publicly traded on one of the stock exchanges, such as Microsoft or Xerox, or closely held corporations which are owned by small groups of shareholders and not traded on the open market.

Private corporations can be divided into many

categories:

Domestic corporations: Any corporation formed in the state where it is doing business is considered a domestic corporation.

Foreign corporations: Any corporation formed in one state and doing business in another. As an example, I used to be shareholder in a software company called Royal Software. The company was formed in Florida, but held an office in Hawaii. In Florida we were a domestic corporation; in Hawaii we were a foreign corporation.

Special service corporations: formed to provide a special service, such as banking, insurance or transportation. These corporations are usually subject to special codes and statutes.

Subchapter-S corporations: this is a special creature of the internal revenue code. It allows small corporations (those with less than 100 shareholders) to avoid double taxation. We will discuss this in a later article.

Professional corporations: corporations to provide professional services such as lawyers, doctors or accountants.

Non-profit corporations: not to be confused with tax-exempt corporations. Non-profit corporations are organized for numerous purposes, but are not intended to earn a profit for shareholders.

All of the above areas of law must be reviewed and considered in making a business decision. Unfortunately, it is not always easy to find the law. Many can be located on-line; some are found in libraries. Some laws, such as trademark/copyright caselaw, are available only in specific libraries. Some laws can be found in multiple locations.

Also, because the Court makes decisions every day, the law changes every day. For these reasons, researching the law can be difficult.

A corporation has no right to do business in a foreign state. While under the U.S. Constitution all individuals are granted the privileges and immunities of all the states, corporations are not. A state may exclude foreign corporations, or may charge special fees for a foreign corporation to do business in that state.

The main benefit of a corporation is the protection of liability. In most cases, the shareholders' only liability is the extent of their investment in the corporation. This is not absolute. There is legal doctrine called "piercing the corporate veil" which allows a court to disregard the existence of a corporation and chase after the individual shareholders. This requires that the court make special findings to show that the corporation is really just a sham to hide assets of the owner. This court can do this by determining whether the corporation maintains adequate records, whether there has been a co-mingling of funds, whether there has been a diversion of the corporate assets by the shareholders, whether the corporation was created to evade a debt or to perpetrate a fraud, or if it would be inequitable to recognize the corporation.

What happens when two companies want to join together, or one company wants to take over another? There are a few ways to handle this.

First is a consolidation. This is where the two companies cease to exist and a new company emerges. Think back to the labor wars. There were two major labor unions - the American Federation of Labor and Congress of Industrial Organizations. These two groups consolidated to form the AFL-CIO.

Second is a merger. This is where one company becomes part of another company. Several years ago there was a merger between NationsBank and Barnett Bank. NationsBank was the surviving company and Barnett Bank no longer exists.

Third is the conglomerate. This is where a larger company makes a smaller company a subsidiary. Both companies continue to exist, but one dominates over the other. An example is Pizza Hut and Pepsi. Several years ago Pepsi bought Pizza Hut. While both companies continue their existence, Pepsi is considered the parent organization of Pizza Hut.

Another way companies can join is through an asset sale. This is where one company buys another company's assets, but does not take over the company's debts. This allows the purchaser to operate the new business free and clear. In some states, such as California, asset sales are governed by bulk sale laws that require notices to be given to creditors and debtors of the company to ensure payment of debts before the transfer is concluded. Failure to make proper notice can create liability in the buying corporation. In other words, if the transaction doesn't comply with the requirements of the bulk sale law, the buyer may be liable for all the debts of the selling company, even though he only purchased the assets. This can be a very costly proposition. Currently, Florida does not have a bulk sale law.

There are some transactions that simply aren't allowed. In the computer wars it would have made sense for Microsoft to buy out Apple, but this could not happen. It would have given Microsoft a monopoly on computer sales. Thus the merger would not be allowed by the Securities Exchange Commission.

SUBCHAPTER'S CORPORATIONS

The Subchapter-S Corporation (also referred to as an S-Corporation) is derived from Section 1244 of the Internal Revenue Code. S-Corporations are formed to save taxes. How does this happen? By bypassing the corporate tax.

Under general tax rules, when a company makes a profit, it is taxed on that profit. The remaining profit is then often distributed to the shareholders as a dividend. The shareholders are then taxed on the dividend. This means that the IRS has taxed the profits of the corporation twice, and in states with a state income tax, this may amount to nearly 70% of the profits. Because this is very onerous to small businesses, the Internal Revenue Code created the Subchapter-S provision that benefits small businesses. With a Subchapter-S corporation, the profits of the corporation are passed directly to the shareholders (as are the losses) so that the profits are only taxed on the individual level. Let's give an example. Let's say a corporation has a before tax profit of $10,000.00. Under general tax laws, using an estimated federal income tax of 25% and an individual rate of 20%, the corporation would pay $2,500.00 in federal income tax. The remaining $7,500.00 is then paid to the shareholders as a dividend. If we use an estimated tax rate of 20%, the shareholders pay $1,500.00 in individual tax on this dividend. This leaves a balance of only $6,000.00 of the original $10,000.00. In states outside of Florida that have a state income tax, this amount would be even lower. However, if the corporation falls under the provisions of Subchapter-S, the profits are passed directly to the shareholders. Therefore, the company would pay no income tax and the full $10,000.00 is passed directly to the shareholders. The shareholders then pay tax on the dividend of $2,000.00, leaving a balance of $8,000.00. By filing as a Subchapter-S corporation, the shareholders/corporation saved $2,000.00 (or 20%) in taxes.

Some business people believe they can avoid this tax by simply not paying dividends, however general corporations (called C-corporations) are subject to an accumulated earnings tax if they amass more than $250,000.00 in retained earnings. Also, if the assets are sold, the shareholders will be taxed on the dissolution of the business.

There are many benefits to Subchapter-S Corporations. First, corporate income tax is usually higher than individual income tax. Also, shareholders may be able to reduce taxes even more by shifting income to family members who may be in lower tax brackets. Another benefit arrives for shareholders that are also employees of the corporation. Salary income is subject to both income tax and social security tax, however, dividend income is subject only to income tax. Therefore, by taking a smaller salary and the balance as a dividend, the shareholder/employee can reduce the amount of social security tax they pay.

Another advantage to S-corporations occurs when the corporation has a loss. As with income, losses are passed directly to the shareholders. The shareholders can then use these losses to offset income in other areas.

There are certain requirements to forming a Subchapter-S corporation. First, this election is only for small businesses, so there can be no more than 100 shareholders. Also, all shareholders must be either U.S. citizens or legal resident aliens. Finally, the company cannot derive a substantial portion of its income by investing in other businesses. Formation of a Subchapter-S corporation requires the filing of an application (IRS Form 2553) which requires all shareholders to consent to the Subchapter-S election. This application must be filed within 75 days of the first business activity, or by March 15 of any calendar year.

LIMITED PARTNERSHIPS AND LIMITED LIABILITY CORPORATIONS

There are two final business types to discuss: limited partnerships and limited liability companies. Both combine aspects of partnerships with aspects of corporations, and both create lower liability for some members.

Limited Partnership

A limited partnership allows for the development of a partnership with lower levels of liability for certain members of the partnership. It is run by a general partner who has full authority over the partnership and full responsibility for the affairs of the partnership. The partnership also has what are called limited partners, who are more like shareholders. Their liability for debt of the partnership is limited to their investment in the partnership. However, the limited partners can have no control over the day-to-day operations of the partnership. Their participation is in their investment. Unlike a general partnership, the personal assets of a limited partner are protected from judgments against the partnership. Also unlike a general partnership, a limited partnership requires more effort to start up operations. The limited partnership must follow the language in the Revised Uniform Limited Partnership Act. This Act requires the Limited Partnership to register with the Department of State and identify all partners, their classification and interest. Some states allow the limited partnership to keep the names of the limited partners confidential. If the requirements of the RULPA are not fully complied with, the partnership may be deemed a general partnership and each member, including the limited partners, will be fully liable for all debts of the partnership.

Limited Partnerships allow limited partners to make additional contributions without losing their limited protections, so long as they do not exercise any control over the partnership business. What can limited partners do? Limited partners may consult with the general partners, act as employees or independent contractors for the business, and vote on certain matters without losing their protections. The limited partner may also file suit against the partnership if the general partners fail to act in a manner consistent with the goals of the partnership. The name of the limited partner cannot be used in the name of the Limited Partnership. In other words, if I was a limited partner, the name of the partnership could not be "Albert L. Kelley Limited Partnership".

Limited Liability Companies

Limited Liability Companies have been around for several years. In fact, Florida was the second state in the country to recognize LLC's. However, they went relatively unknown until the early 2000s when the tax code was changed to make them more favorable. Today, LLC's are among the fastest growing business entities.

Limited liability companies, like LLP's are combinations of partnerships and corporations. They provide all the tax benefits of a Subchapter-S corporation, without the limitations of a Subchapter-S corporation. The owners of the LLC can opt to be taxed either as a corporation or as a partnership (If there is only one member, he can chose to be taxed as a sole proprietor). By choosing the partnership option, the LLC receives the same tax pass through benefit of a Subchapter-S corporation. In other words, the profits pass through the LLC directly to the members. The LLC itself would not pay corporate tax. If the owners desire to treat their income as a C-corporation, they can make that option as well. Some LLC's will ask to be taxed as a corporation and then elect Subchapter-S status. This allows them to gain the tax pass-through benefit, but also allow them to save money on the social security taxes. Unless they have chosen to be taxed as a Subchapter-S company, a limited liability company may have more than 100 shareholders, there are no restrictions on nationality of members and there is no restriction on sources of income.

Limited liability corporations are formed similarly to a corporation, but the terminology is different. Rather than having Articles of Incorporation, they have Articles of Organization; instead of Bylaws, they have an Operating Agreement. Instead of shareholders they have members, and instead of directors, they have managers.

The LLC has certain advantages over the LLP. First, all

members are allowed to retain control over the business, while also keeping their limited liability protection. Second, a Limited Partnership requires a general partner who has full liability; a limited liability corporation protects all its members. No member has liability outside of his or her investment.

The LLC also has benefits over a corporation. The primary benefit is in liability. In a corporation, shareholders have stock which is deemed a personal asset. If the individual shareholder is sued, their stock can be seized to satisfy their judgment. However, LLC's are more like clubs that you are a member in. A creditor cannot take your membership, only those dividends actually paid. The exception is for a single member LLC. In a recent Florida Supreme Court decision, it was held that in a single member LLC, the ownership could be treated the same as stock in a corporation.

In a single member LLC there is an additional advantage. Because the income of the LLC is taxed as a sole proprietorship, the LLC is not required to file a tax return. All income and expense will be included in the Member's personal tax return (For a multimember LLC, the LLC will have to file a tax return but all taxes are paid by the members based on their individual K-1 forms.

STOCK OWNERSHIP BASICS

The last few sections have concentrated on various types of business organizations. Now we are going to spend a little more time specifically on corporations.

The major difference between corporations and other business organizations is stock issuance. This is what makes a corporation what it is. It can issue stock. This allows it to raise capital and to easily transfer ownership.

If you invest in the stock market and buy a share of stock in IBM, you become an owner of IBM, albeit, a very minor one. However, as an owner, you will receive copies of their annual report and be invited to attend their annual meeting to vote on who the corporate directors will be. You also will get to vote on certain salary issues and bonuses, mergers and acquisitions. You get the right to inspect the company books. You get the right to receive dividends when distributed. You get the right to receive assets if the company is dissolved. And most importantly for some, you get the right to file a shareholder's derivative suit.

A shareholders derivative action is a lawsuit filed by a shareholder to force the directors and officers of a corporation to take action that would benefit the corporation. It also allows the shareholder to sue for damages caused by them to the corporation if they act improperly. It can also be used by minority shareholders to challenge actions of the majority shareholders and to ask for involuntary dissolution of the company.

How much stock can a corporation issue? As much as it wants, under certain restrictions. The articles of incorporation set out the number of authorized shares a company can issue. It does not have to issue all the shares that are authorized. If a company wants to issue more shares, it merely amends the Articles of Incorporation to allow for additional shares (I'm purposefully simplifying the process. More detailed discussions will be saved for later). As an example of what a company can do, as of June 30, 2013, McDonald's Corp. (yes, the burger people) authorized 165 million shares of preferred stock, but had not issued any and authorized 3.5 billion shares of common stock, but only issued 1,660,600,000 shares. Each one of these shares represents an ownership interest.

Stock has essentially three values: par, book, and market. Before investing in any company, it is important to know the definition of these values to understand what you are buying. Par value is the same as face value for the initial issuance of stock. It is the amount that the share is mandated to be initially issued for. Not all stock has a par value. While par value was required several years ago, it no longer is. However, many companies, especially small ones, still use par value as a way of fixing the initial value for later tax purposes. McDonald's Corp. set a par value on its common stock at $0.01.

Book value is derived from taking the value of all the assets of the corporation, divided by the number of shares issued by the company. For McDonald's, in 2013, its total value was listed at $34,453,400,000.00. This gives a book value of roughly $20.75 per share.

Market value is what the shares actually sell for. As of September 15, 2013, McDonald's shares traded for $97.35 per share; however, their 52-week low was only $83.31, while their 52-week high was $103.70.

I mentioned above two types of stock, preferred and common. Common stock is just that - common. It usually means that the owner (also called holder or bearer) gets to cast one vote for each share he owns and that he shall get no preferential treatment over any other shareholder. Preferred stock is usually non-voting stock, but it gets priority when it comes to receiving dividends or a division of assets upon dissolution of the company. That means that the preferred shareholders get paid first; the common shareholders only get paid if there is money left.

Usually, stockholders can sell, trade, give or bequeath their shares to anyone. Occasionally, stock is restricted so that transfers are only allowed after certain procedures have been followed, such as offering to sell to other shareholders first. Once a share of stock has been purchased, possession of the share is not enough. The shareholder needs to ensure that the transfer has been registered in the corporate records. Only those shareholders listed in the corporate register will be allowed to vote or participate in corporate issues.

Now we're going to talk about trading or selling stocks. State statutes that restrict the selling of stocks are called Blue Sky laws. They usually require stockbrokers to be licensed, prohibit fraudulent practices, and require a registration of certain securities (I will use the words stocks, shares, and securities interchangeably, unless otherwise indicated). In addition to state regulations, there are federal laws as well. The federal security laws cover the trading of stocks, bonds, and even investment contracts. Some key points:

The Securities Act of 1933 was passed to regulate the initial offering of stock by a company. Before a security can be sold publicly in interstate commerce, a registration statement must be filed with the Securities Exchange Commission (SEC). This statement discloses certain financial information about the securities. The seller must also provide a prospectus to each potential investor. This is to ensure that there is full disclosure of information about the company to the buyer so they can make an informed decision to invest. Small businesses may avoid some of the requirements by filing under a Regulation A offering. This allows a business to raise up to $5 million in a year by using a simplified process. There are other exemptions from registration. A Rule 505 exemption allows offerings of less than $5 million to less than 35 non-accredited purchasers; however, these must be non-solicited and non-advertised sales. A Rule 506 exemption allows companies to raise an unlimited amount of money by private placement of shares. This exemption generally involves investment houses that advise their private investors where to invest their funds. A Rule 504 exemption allows companies to raise $1 million without any registration or regulation. Aside from the allowed exemptions, serious penalties lie for those who violate the SEC rules. Violators may be charged both civilly and criminally.

The Securities and Exchange Act of 1934 is like the follow-up to the Securities Act of 1933. While the first Act covered the initial offering of stock, the 1934 Act covers the resale of stocks (thus the word "Exchange"). The Securities Exchange Act of 1934 includes the rules that govern the major trading houses, such as NASDAQ and the New York Stock Exchange. It requires companies that are listed on the major exchanges with over $3 million in assets to file numerous financial statements. Recently, this issue has been in the news as many companies have used creative accounting to make these financial statements appear to increase the company's income or assets, while decreasing the debt or liabilities. Companies who use non-standard accounting practices may be held liable, both civilly and criminally, as can their officers who participated in the fraudulent activity.

The Securities Exchange Act of 1934 also restricts certain trading practices. The most well-known, and most highly publicized of these rules is the rule against insider trading. Companies must take steps to ensure that information that may affect the value of their stock is kept confidential until it is released to the public as a whole. Those who obtain the information in advance cannot use their knowledge for personal gain. Violators may be forced to pay up to three times the profits gained or lost in an insider trade. An insider is not just an employee or officer of the corporation. It includes anyone involved with the company and anyone who learns confidential information from someone who is involved with the company, who makes security transaction on that information. A few years ago, the secretary of a company leaked information to her husband, who in turn gave half a dozen people the stock tip. All were arrested on insider trading and had to return their income plus pay heavy fines. To diminish insider trading, owners of companies making an initial public offering are restricted from selling shares for a period of time. In addition, shareholders with at least 10% share of the company must register their shares with the SEC, as must corporate officers and directors.

CORPORATE CONTROL

Now that we have discussed types of corporations and shareholder issues, we need to look at control of the corporation. There are three levels of control in any corporation: Shareholders, Directors, and Officers. Surprisingly, the owners of a corporation actually have little to do with the day-to-day control of the business. The Shareholders control is very limited; they get to vote on major issues such as mergers and acquisitions. They vote on whether or not to sell off the assets of the business. But their strongest control issue is the election of directors. By law, shareholders of a company must meet once a year to discuss the status of the corporation and to elect directors for the next year. Often, these meetings are a mere formality, but notices of the meeting must be sent out timely so every shareholder can attend. There must be a quorum present either in person or by proxy, and if a shareholder cannot attend in person, they may appear by telephone or computer, so long as they can hear and participate in the meeting.

The Directors are elected to manage the business for the benefit of the shareholders. They do not have to be shareholders themselves, although they usually are. The directors are the long-range planners of the company. They make the decisions on where the company should go and they ratify all long-term contracts and plans. The directors have a fiduciary relationship with the company, meaning they must act with the best benefit of the company in mind. They cannot take actions to benefit themselves that would hurt the company. They also cannot take advantage of opportunities that should go to the company. If the directors have acted in good faith with adequate information and with the belief that their action was in the best interest of the company, the courts will generally not interfere with their decisions. This is known as the Business Judgment Rule. If, however, the decision was made improperly or with fraud or illegality, the Court can overturn the directors' decisions. Like the shareholders, the directors are required to meet once a year to ratify the prior actions and to elect the Officers of the company.

The Officers run the day-to-day business of the corporation. Like directors, they do not have to be shareholders, but again, they usually are. There are no statutory requirements as to how many officers a company must have nor what their titles must be. As a general rule, a company usually has at least a President, Vice-President, Secretary and Treasurer. In addition, there may be a Chief Executive Officer. I have heard of companies who used more unusual titles for their officers, such as "Captain", or even "Top Dog". The important aspect is for the officers to have the needed authority to run the business.

The role of the officers differs from corporation to corporation, but some issues generally remain the same. The President is in charge of the administrative functions of the company. He can hire and fire employees and he must make sure that the wishes of the Board of Directors are carried out. Unknown to many, often the President does not have the authority to take long-term actions. As a general rule, though not often followed, the President does not have the authority to enter into long-range contracts and he cannot settle claims against the company. He also cannot sell off the assets of the company. These actions belong to the Board of Directors. However, in order to streamline operations, the Board will often appoint a Chief Executive Officer, who has the authority to take these larger actions on the Boards behalf.

The job of Vice-President varies by company. In some it is merely a back-up position; in others it is a divisional management position. The Secretary is the officer responsible for the paperwork of the corporation. It is the Secretary's job to ensure all corporate records are maintained and to send out notices, minutes and agenda for meetings. The Secretary is often considered the company records custodian and therefore may be called to testify in litigation matters. The Treasurer of the company is responsible for the financial records of the company. Even if the company hires accountants to keep the books and gives the President the authority to sign checks, the Treasurer must still be familiar with the company's financial status as they can be called to testify if there are any questions about the company's finances.

Like directors, officers have a fiduciary relationship to the corporation. While officers and directors are not personally responsible for the debts and liabilities of the company, they may be held liable for their actions in the corporation, if they act improperly or against their by-laws. If their decisions are considered criminal, the officers and directors authorizing those decisions may be tried, and if found guilty may be ordered to pay fines or even be jailed.

BUSINESS NAME

Does a business need a name? Absolutely. Aside from the obvious reason that people need to be able to find the business in the phone book, a name is needed to get an occupational license.

What are the requirements for a business name? For a sole proprietorship (a non-incorporated business owned by a single person) the business name can simply be the name of the business owner. For example, a doctor who wants to open a small family practice may simply use his name as the business name - Dr. John Smith. He can do this automatically without the need to register the name. If, however, he chooses to use a name other than his own, he must register the name with the Department of State.

If the business is to be incorporated, the corporation must have a name. Under Florida law, every corporate name must be distinguishable from every other corporate name. In other words, only one corporation may use a name. If you desire to name your corporation XYZ, Inc., you must first check to learn if there is already a corporation called XYZ, Inc. If there is, you must choose a new corporate name (You also cannot use the name if there is a XYZ, LLC). Even if a corporation is involuntarily dissolved, their name cannot be used for a period of one year, allowing the corporation to reinstate its status without losing its name.

All corporation names must include either the words

"corporation", "company", or "incorporated" or the abbreviations "Corp.", "Co." or "Inc." If the business is to be run by a Limited Liability Corporation, the name must contain the words "Limited Corporation" or the abbreviation "LLC". The corporate name may not simply use the word "Limited" as that is reserved for limited partnerships. Once a corporation has a name, it may use the corporate name also as a business name with no additional filing requirements. However, if the corporate name and the business name are to be different, the business name must also be registered with the Department of State as a fictitious name, also known as a d/b/a.

Partnerships are not required to register their existence with the Department of State unless they are set up as Limited Partnerships. However, if the partnership will be doing business as an entity, it needs to register its name as well. There are no requirements for the name of a general partnership (it does not have to use the word "partnership")

Before registering a fictitious name the name it should be advertised in a newspaper of general circulation in the area where the business is to be located. Many states now allow fictitious names to be registered electronically. If registering by electronic filing the fee must be paid by credit card.

There are numerous penalties for failing to register a fictitious name. The business may not file suit or defend a lawsuit in court under the name unless registered. More importantly, failure to register a business name is a misdemeanor criminal offense, punishable by a fine of up to $500.00 and/or jail time of up to six months.

NOT-FOR-PROFIT CORPORATIONS

What is the difference between a profit corporation and a not-for-profit corporation? This seems obvious, but many do not truly understand the difference.

Most companies are organized "for profit". This means that the corporation's purpose is to have its income exceed its liabilities so that ultimately the shareholders will see a benefit either through dividend payments or through increased value of their stock shares. With a not-for-profit corporation, the goal may still be to have income exceed expenses, however, the ultimate purpose is for the excess to be used for some public benefit, not to benefit shareholders. In fact, a not-for-profit corporation does not have shareholders. Instead they have members. These members cannot receive dividends and have no ownership interest in the corporation or its assets. Often these memberships are honorary.

Like with profit corporations, not-for-profit corporations have a board of directors. This Board has as its purpose the overall control of the corporation. While a profit corporation may have a single director, a not-for-profit corporation must have a minimum of three directors. Directors for the company may be any natural person over the age of 18. Also like profit corporations, a not-for-profit corporation may have officers. These usually, but not necessarily include a President, Vice Presidents, Secretary and Treasurer. A not-for-profit corporation cannot use the word "Company" in its name.

Another misconception about not-for-profit corporations is that the offices and directors are not paid. This is not necessarily true. While many Boards ask Officers and Directors to serve voluntarily, there is no law requiring this. Indeed, Directors and Officers may receive a salary for their service and the directors are even authorized to set their own salary level. Unless the corporation falls under certain restrictions, there is no requirement even that the salary be reasonable. In other words, some not-for-profit corporations may pay their officers and directors salaries that are clearly excessive. Even members may receive compensation for services they actually provide to the corporation.

A not-for-profit corporation is formed much the same as a profit corporation. Formation begins with the filing of Articles of Incorporation with the Florida Department of State. The Articles must set forth the name and street address of the not-for-profit corporation, must state the specific purpose of the corporation, tell how the directors are elected or appointed, and provide the name and address of the registered agent. Like with profit corporations, the registered agent must sign a statement that they are familiar with the duties of a registered agent and that they agree to serve in that capacity.

Once the not-for-profit corporation has been formed, it is up to the members, directors and officers to run it. Running a not-for-profit corporation is similar to running a profit corporation in many ways. The frequency and place of meetings of the members should be set out in the by-laws for the corporation. While a failure to hold an annual meeting can be fatal to a profit corporation, it has essentially no effect on a not-for-profit corporation, unless the voting power is deadlocked and the corporation has failed to elect new directors after the term of office has expired.

Also, unlike the shareholders of a profit corporation, members of a not-for-profit corporation have no inherent power to vote on issues affecting the corporation. The members only have those rights to vote as set out in the corporation's articles of incorporation or by-laws. If the Articles or By-laws fail to give the members voting power, the right to vote rest solely with the directors of the corporation. The corporation may, but is not required to give membership certificates to their members. They must, however, keep a membership book listing all members in alphabetical order.

Notices must be sent to all members prior to a meeting, unless the members waive notice either before or after the meeting. However, if a member appears at a meeting without receiving notice, it will be presumed that they received notice, unless they object prior to any action being taken.

When members are allowed to vote, they may do so in person, or by proxy. Proxies will only be deemed valid for a period of 11 months after they have been signed. Also, if allowed by the by-laws, elections for directors may be done by mail, rather than require a separate meeting. If a corporation is a member of a not-for-profit corporation, the chairperson or an officer may vote the corporations interest on behalf of the corporation.

The statutes also authorize cumulative voting by the members, if allowed in the Articles of Incorporation. Cumulative voting allows a member to cast all of their votes for a single candidate rather than spread them out over several candidates. As an example, if a not-for-profit corporation has five director positions open, a member may vote for five separate candidates (one for each position), or may cast five votes for a single candidate. Cumulative voting allows members to increase their voting strength to obtain the representative they want on the board.

Like shareholders in a profit corporation, the members of a not-for-profit corporation are not personally liable for the acts of the corporation. The member may, however, become liable to the corporation for dues, assessments or other fees the corporation may require.

Finally, while it is very difficult for a shareholder to lose their interest in a profit company, the Articles of Incorporation or By-laws may set out situations in which membership in a not-for-profit corporation may be terminated (such as when membership is tied to property ownership or some other attribute).

Officers of a not-for-profit corporation are elected annually unless the Articles or Bylaws state differently. The officers are elected by the Board of Directors, however, the Bylaws may authorize a duly appointed officer to appoint other officers. While the statutes do not specify what officers are required, traditionally, a corporation has at least a President, Vice President,

Secretary and Treasurer (The statute does require the Board or the Bylaws to designate one officer for the purpose of taking minutes and certifying records. Usually, this is the job of the Secretary). The job of the officers should be set out in the Bylaws. Unless specifically stated, neither the Secretary nor the Treasurer may act on behalf of a corporation. These are merely ministerial officers who have no authority to bind the corporation without the approval of the President or Board of Directors.

Officers may resign at any time by serving a notice on the corporation. The notice is effective upon its receipt, unless a different date is specified within. Once the resignation is received, the Board or other officer may appoint a successor, so long as the successor does not take office until the resignation is effected.

The Board may also remove an officer at any time for any reason, with or without cause. Appointment to an officer position does not confer any contract rights to the office. If the officer was appointed by another officer, they may also be removed by that officer.

Officers that serve without compensation are immune from liability for any monetary damages that result from any vote, decision, statement or failure to act unless there is some breach or failure to perform their duties, if the breach or failure constitutes a criminal violation, confers an improper benefit on the officer or is a reckless act or omission committed in bad faith.

An officer may enter into contracts with the corporation to obtain a personal benefit or for the benefit of a corporation the officer is related to, so long as the relationship or personal interest is known to the Board of

Directors and members authorizing the transaction, and if the contract is fair and reasonable. Although profit corporations may make loans to their officers and directors, not-for-profit corporations are precluded from doing so. Authorizing such a loan is considered a violation of their duty to the corporation of any director or officer who voted for the loan and may lead to personal liability to the officer or director.

ENDING A NOT-FOR-PROFIT CORPORATION

Not-For-Profit Corporations can be terminated for many reasons. If they were formed for a specific goal and that goal is achieved, the corporation has no further purpose and should be dissolved. Similarly, if the goal becomes unattainable, the corporation should be dissolved. Not-for-profit Corporations can also be dissolved for failure to follow administrative rules, or when the members or directors feel that it is in the corporation's best interest to dissolve. While certain aspects of dissolution of a not-for-profit Corporation are similar to a profit Corporation, there are some crucial differences.

There are three methods of dissolution of a not-for-profit Corporation. The first is voluntary dissolution. This occurs when the corporation or its members and directors determine that the corporation has reached its goals or cannot reach its goals, and decide to simply close the corporation. If this decision is made before the corporation actually begins operations, it may be dissolved by the incorporator or directors. If the corporation has begun operations, and the bylaws allow for members to vote, then the decision to dissolve must be voted on by the members, at a duly noticed meeting.

Before the corporation has begun operations, dissolution is basically an administrative process. The corporation must file Articles of Dissolution with the Department of State, listing the corporation name and date of incorporation, stating that the corporation has not yet begun conducting business, that there are no unpaid debts, and that the dissolution was approved by the incorporator or a majority of the directors. The Articles of Dissolution must be signed by the incorporator, or the chairman of the Board of Directors.

After the corporation has started operating, dissolution becomes a little more difficult. The decision to dissolve must be made by a majority of the Board of Directors, or if members are allowed to vote, by a majority of all the members. Next, the corporation must file with the Department of State a Plan of Distribution of all the corporations' assets. This is not required for profit corporations, as their assets are divided among the various shareholders after paying all debts. With not-for-profit Corporations, the members cannot receive any assets. Therefore the Plan must provide for distribution in ways that will not violate the statute. The Plan of Distribution must provide for the payment of all the corporations liabilities and obligations. Second, it must allow for the return of any assets held under a contractual agreement, such as a lease. Third, the plan must provide for a disposition of those assets held for charitable, religious, eleemosynary (related to giving of alms), benevolent, educational or similar purposes. These assets must be given to organizations that are engaged in activities that will further these purposes. Next, the plan must allow for the distribution of assets that are specifically set out in the Articles of Incorporation or Bylaws. Finally, the plan must allow for distribution of all other assets.

Once the plan is completed, Articles of Dissolution must also be filed with the Department of State, showing if a membership vote was necessary, that the number of votes cast for dissolution was sufficient. If no membership meeting is necessary, the Articles of Dissolution must state how many directors the company has and specify the vote tally of the directors.

Aside from voluntary termination, not-for-profit Corporations can also be terminated administratively by the Department of State for many reasons. Some of the reasons include: (a) failure to timely file their annual Uniform Business Report (UBR) along with the payment of the annual filing fee, (b) the failure to have a registered agent or registered office for more than 30 days, (c) the failure to notify the Department of any change, resignation, or discontinuation of registered agent for more than 30 days, (d) failure to provide full and truthful answers to interrogatories propounded by the Department of State, (e) expiration of the corporation's period of existence as set out in the Articles of Incorporation.

If the Department of State determines that any of the above grounds exists, they must provide the corporation with written notice of the intent to dissolve the corporation, and provide the corporation with a 60 day period to correct the deficiency. If the corporation fails to correct the problem, the Department shall issue a certificate of dissolution. The corporation may be reinstated by filing an application for reinstatement that sets out the name of the corporation and date of dissolution, a statement that the grounds for dissolution either did not exists or no longer exists, that the corporation name complies with Florida law (that is, that no other corporation adopted their name during the period of dissolution), and a statement that all fees have been paid. If the dissolution was for failure to file a UBR, the corporation may merely file a corrected UBR with all required fees to reinstate.

A dissolved corporation may not transact any business or activity except those necessary for the winding up of the corporations business and adopting a plan for distribution of assets. The directors, officers and agents may be held personally liable for any debt or obligation the corporation incurs while dissolved, due to an act of that director, officer or agent. This personal liability may be discharged by reinstatement of the corporation.

Upon dissolution, the name of the corporation shall be reserved for a period of one year. In other words, no other corporation may adopt the name until one year has passed from the date of dissolution. This allows the corporation to file for reinstatement within one year without the risk of losing their corporate name or identity. The dissolved corporation may waive this time period in order to allow another corporation to immediately assume use of the corporate name.

A not-for-profit corporation may also be dissolved by Order of Court. The Circuit Court for the county where the corporation has its primary office (or its registered office if the corporation is not located in Florida) has jurisdiction to dissolve corporations for various reasons. The Department of Legal Affairs can request the Court to dissolve a corporation if the corporation obtained their Articles of Incorporation by fraud. A member of a corporation may request dissolution if there is a deadlock in the management of the company that cannot be broken. A judgment creditor may request the corporation to be dissolved if the corporation is insolvent.

Finally, if the not-for-profit corporation is a church or religious society, the Court may dissolve the church if they fail to maintain religious worship, if they fail to use their property for religious worship, or if the membership has diminished to the point where the church cannot maintain worship or protect their property for a period of two years. If the Church is dissolved, their property must be held in trust by the Court or transferred to another church of the same domination.

CONTRACTS BASICS

Now we are going to start discussing contracts. We will start with the basics. What is a contract? A contract is a legally enforceable agreement between two or more entities. It may be verbal or written, it must be entered into freely, and it must create an obligation on all parties. It must also be for a lawful purpose. A contract to commit a crime is not enforceable.

Often in the legal field, when dealing with contracts, the parties are referred to by various terms. They may be called the promisor and promisee, or the obligor and obligee. These are not only confusing, they are misnomers. In a contract, both sides have an obligation. If there is not an obligation on one side, the contract is merely an unenforceable promise. In a contract, there must be a promise on both sides to do some act. Usually, one side promises to provide a good or service and the other side promises to pay money. To be clear, the contract should use the names of the parties, or a recognizable segment of their names, rather than ambiguous terms.

Any legal entity may enter a contract. This includes individuals, corporations, partnerships, even governments. Contracts may involve adults or children, although contracts with children present special problems we will deal with later. Often contracts will involve three or more parties. As an example, several years ago I was involved in contact negotiations involving four separate parties. Because of the structure of the deal, all four were named in the contract and all four had obligations under it. You see this often in real estate transactions where there is a buyer and seller, as well as real estate agents.

A contract arises based upon an offer and acceptance. Let's say I offer to sell my car for $10,000. This is not a contract because no one has accepted it. Or, if Ron offers to buy my car for $50.00. Still, there is no contract because I have not accepted the offer. A contract does not arise until both sides agree on the substantial terms of the deal. What about newspaper ads? Example: Sears advertises in the newspaper to sell a shirt for $10.00. John picks up the paper and takes the ad to Sears. Are they obligated to sell him the shirt? No. By a quirk in the law, Sears has not made an offer. They have merely made an indication of what offer they would accept. Whenever you go to the store, you are making an offer to buy, which the store can accept or reject. This is how they can refuse to sell to certain customers.

Now let's go back to my car. I tell Bob I want to sell my car and he says he wants to buy it. Is there a contract? No. We didn't agree on the price. What if we agree to determine the price later? Still no contract. The price is a substantial term. This is essentially a contract to enter into a contract, which is unenforceable. All the substantial terms must be clear and agreed to in order to have a valid and binding contract.

If the parties realize that they did not agree on the terms of a contract the contract becomes voidable. This happens when language is unclear or items in the contract are either left out or vague. As an example, if Bob and I agreed on a price for my car, there may still be questions. Perhaps Bob thought I would accept payments and I wanted a single payment. Or maybe Bob thought he could pay next week and I want the money now. If these are substantial terms, there is still no contract.

Offers and acceptances must be clear. If an offer is clearly not made in good faith, an acceptance won't make a binding contract. For instance, if my car breaks down and out of frustration I yell, "I will sell this to the first person that gives me $10!" That is not a good faith offer. Similarly, an acceptance that is not clear is invalid. If I say I want to sell my car for $500.00 and Bob says: "Sounds good", is he accepting the offer or merely commenting on my idea?

It is important to keep your contracts clear and complete to stop disputes from arising.

TYPES OF CONTRACTS

Contracts come in many different styles and are divided by many different names.

Formal Contracts - These are contacts that are executed (signed) under special formalities to authenticate them. An example of this is a Contract Under Seal. What is this? Simply your signature or corporate signature, followed by some mark indicating a legal seal. This may be a wax impression of a signet ring as back in olden times, or it may be simply an impression of a corporate seal. The purpose of the seal is to ensure the authenticity of the signature. Today, seals are rarely used and are not required for most contracts. Another example is a Contract of Record. These are simply contracts that have been recognized by the Court, such as settlement agreements in a lawsuit. Finally are Notarized Instruments, such as mortgages, and Negotiable Instruments such as promissory notes. These often require additional formalities such as witnesses.

Informal Contracts - all contracts that are not Formal Contracts, whether written or verbal.

Express Contracts - actual communication between the parties of the terms of the contract, whether written or verbal. This may sound unusual, until you read the next section.

Implied Contracts - This is not a contract by words, but by deed. It arises where an agreement is shown by action. As an example, where Bob provides goods or services to Steve who accepts them without objection, it can be implied that a contract has arisen where Steve must pay Bob the fair market value for the goods or services.

Quasi-Contracts - These are not true contracts, but rather, contracts that the law creates. It is often referred to as Unjust Enrichment. If one person gains a benefit and it would be inequitable to allow them to keep the benefit at someone else's expense, the Court can deem that this is a quasi-contract and require the party to pay for the benefit.

Valid Contracts - any contract that is binding and enforceable.

Voidable Contracts - contracts that are binding and enforceable, but due to certain circumstances may be rejected by one of the parties. The best example of this is a contract with a minor. People under the age of 18 may enter into contracts, however, with few exceptions, at any time before the minor turns 18 they may reject the contract and demand the return of their money, or other consideration. This is true, even if the minor cannot return the item purchased or if all parts of the contract have been completed.

Void Contracts - not binding and not enforceable. Any contract for an illegal action is void. You cannot have a contract for prostitution services or for the sale of illegal drugs. You cannot have a contract to kill someone.

Executed Contracts- a contracted where all parties have completed their mutual obligations under the agreement.

Executory Contract - a contact where one or more parties still have obligations to perform under the agreement; an unfinished contract.

Bilateral Contract - A contract that obligates both parties to perform some action; i.e. I will provide service, and you will pay $X.

Unilateral Contract - Only one party is obligated to act. This is distinguished from the above in that one action is only required if another occurs; i.e., If someone does X, then I will do Y.

Option Contract - This is an agreement to do something at a later date. The primary place you see this is in real estate leases with an Option to Buy. Here the tenant can at some point in the future decide to buy the property at a pre-set price. If the tenant exercises the option, the Owner must sell at that price.

Right of First Refusal - This is similar to an Option, however, the action starts with the Owner. If the Owner decides to sell, the Owner must offer the property to the Tenant first. Likewise if a third party makes an offer to the Owner to purchase the property, the Owner must allow the tenant to match the offer before accepting it.

OFFERS

Let's go into more details about contracts. For the purposes of this section we will use sales contracts as our examples, though these principles apply to nearly all contracts.

First is the agreement itself. As mentioned before, there are two parts to an agreement: an offer and acceptance. It starts with an offer. There must be an intention to make an offer. If a person makes an offer in jest, it is not a valid offer. The determining factor is whether a reasonable person would think that a valid offer had been made.

The first statement is not necessarily an offer. It could merely be an invitation to start negotiations. This is what I mentioned about retail stores putting ads in the paper. They are not making an offer, but inviting you to come to their store to negotiate. You do not have to pay the price the store is asking. You are free to offer a lower price. While this is common in many countries where they expect you to negotiate, it is not common in the United States.

Contracts are only acceptable while they are valid. That is, once terminated, a contract cannot be accepted. Most contracts are revocable at any time before acceptance. Any action or words sufficient to put the other on notice that the offer is revoked is sufficient. Thus, if I offer to sell my car by putting a "For Sale" sign in the window, the removal of the For Sale sign is an indication that the offer has been revoked. It is crucial that the revocation be communicated to the buyer, just as it was crucial that the offer was communicated. The revocation is not valid unless the buyer knows about it. Once I have communicated the revocation, the buyer cannot hold me to the contract.

Here's a question for you. An offer is made. Last week, Bob offered to sell me his Mercedes. I thought about it for a few days and on Monday sent him a letter accepting the offer. Unbeknownst to me, on Saturday, Bob had sent me a letter revoking the offer. Is there a contract? This is an example of the mailbox rule. It says that an acceptance of an offer is valid upon mailing, but a revocation is valid only on receipt. Therefore, Bob would be required to sell the car.

There are exceptions to the policy that a contract can be revoked at any time before acceptance. An Option Contract is an agreement to keep a contract open for a specified period of time. The option itself is a valid contract that can be enforced. Similar is a firm contract. This is an agreement that the offer will be irrevocable for a period of time. Finally, if the offeree would be harmed if the offer was allowed to be withdrawn, the Courts will often require the offer to remain open.

If the person accepting the offer changes the terms of the offer, there is a "counter-offer" which nullifies the original offer. If I offer to sell my car for $100 and Sue says she'll give me $50 for it we do not have a contract. Sue has made a counter-offer which I would then have to accept. Sue's counteroffer terminated the original offer; therefore she cannot then accept my prior offer and force me to sell the car for $100. Likewise, if you reject an offer, it cannot later be accepted.

If an offer contains a time element, such as "If you buy my car by next week, I'll sell it for $100", and the time period passes without acceptance, the offer is dead. If the offer does not contain a time period, then the Court will imply a reasonable time. After the lapse of a reasonable time, the contract is dead. What is a reasonable time? That depends on the contract. If I offer to sell a bushel of apples, a reasonable time may be a couple of days or hours. If I offer to sell my car, a reasonable time will probably be a couple of weeks. If I offer to sell a business, a reasonable time may be a couple of months.

If the offeror or offeree dies or becomes incapacitated, the offer is terminated. Likewise if the offer becomes illegal, the offer is terminated. Examples might be the sale of a designer drug. If the drug is not illegal, I can make a contract to sell it. But if Congress then makes it illegal, my contract will be terminated.

ACCEPTANCE

An acceptance agrees to all of the terms of an offer. It is not conditional- that would be a counteroffer. Most times, the offeree is free to accept or reject an offer. Laws may restrict this freedom in certain circumstances (As an example, a store is free to reject offers from any customer they choose, unless the store rejects the offer due to race, religion, handicap or sex).

There are no formalities to the acceptance of an offer, unless required by the offeror. An offer can be accepted by taking any action that manifests an intent to accept. This includes saying "We have a deal" or by shaking hands, or passing over money or goods. However, the offer may explicitly state that it can only be accepted in certain ways. The offer may say "This agreement may only be accepted by saying "Uncle" while standing on your head in Times Square." Only if the offeree travels to Times Square, stands on their head and says "Uncle" is there a binding contract. If the offer restricts the manner of acceptance, the offeree must follow that restriction.

Usually an acceptance must be communicated to the offeror. But as with everything else in law, there are exceptions. Although not common now, the major music companies used to have record clubs, where n a monthly basis, the company would offer you a new record or CD. These companies often had an agreement in their memberships that required a response to reject a contract, but not to accept one. If you failed to respond to their offer, it was deemed an acceptance and you must pay for the CD. However, this is due to the terms of initial agreement. In the ordinary case, if a company sends you an offer in the mail your silence equals a rejection (If a company sends you an unsolicited item in the mail without a prior agreement, they have just given you a gift. You have no obligation to return it or pay for it).

We discussed the mailbox rule for offers. There is also an exception to the mailbox rule for acceptance. If the acceptance must include the payment of money or if the offer requires the acceptance to be received to be valid, then the acceptance will not be valid until the offeror actually receives it (as opposed to the traditional rule that holds an acceptance is valid as soon as it is placed in the mail).

I also want to discuss auctions here, as they have some special rules. An offer at an auction is not placed by the auctioneer; it is placed by the person placing the bid. The auctioneer is the one accepting the offer. The offer is good until the auctioneer bangs the gavel, however, it may be withdrawn at any time before the auctioneer closes the bidding. An auction may be with or without reserve. Reserve means the auctioneer reserves the right to withdraw an article if the bids are too low. If the sale is without reserve, the auctioneer must sell, regardless of how low the bid is. If the sale is with reserve and the auctioneer is not satisfied with the amount of the bids, he can reject all offers by simply saying "no sale". Once the gavel has fallen on a successful bid, there is a binding contract and the bidder must buy the item.

The terms of a contract must be definite. If the primary terms are uncertain, there is no contract. Third parties must be able to reasonably determine what the intent of the parties was at the time of offer and acceptance. There are times when the terms are not specified but can be determined from things other than the language of the contract. The contract may incorporate the terms of another document, Often lawyers will refer to an existing document when drafting a subsequent agreement. Second, you can imply terms in some circumstances. This applies primarily when there is a standard practice in an industry or trade. You can also look at prior dealings between the parties. If portions of the contract are deemed too vague, it doesn't necessarily invalidate the entire contract. If the vague terms are unimportant, the remaining portions of the contract may still be valid. The contract may also hold that the vague terms are simply excised from the agreement, regardless of their import. Finally, a contract may have a vague term which is valid. As an example, a landlord may lease a rental space "when it becomes available". While this is a vague term, it is a definite one. Once the space becomes available, the landlord must rent it to the tenant. Because the term is definite, it is valid, even though vague.

ABILITY TO CONTRACT

One of the most important issues to consider before entering into a contract is the ability of the party to enter into a contract. Everyone is presumed to be able to enter a contract unless it is proved otherwise or unless they don't have capacity due to their status.

The primary status for incapacity is non-age. In most states, 18-year-olds are legally able to enter into contracts. This is not to say that those under the age of 18 are not able to enter contracts; they can. But they have the special power to void them. In other words, minors are authorized to nullify their contracts at any time, until they turn 18 and for a short while thereafter. Once voided, the other party must return all items given him by the minor, even if the minor cannot return the money paid, or the item they received.

Various statutes remove the non-age disability for various reasons, including: employment; loan contracts for educational purposes; contracts signed by married minors; contracts to perform or render artistic or creative services; to render services as a player or participant in professional or semi-professional athletics; to endorse a product or service; to use the minor's image for publicity purposes; to sell, lease, purchase or license or otherwise exploit literary, musical or dramatic properties; to receive compensation for services as a coach, trainer, manager or agent.

Generally, minors can void contracts for things such as food, clothing or lodging, but if they do, they still must pay the reasonable value for the items. In other words, if a minor enters into a lease agreement, they can cancel the lease at any time, but the landlord gets to keep the rent.

The ability to void a contract exists even if the other party is unaware that the minor has not yet reached the age of majority. If the minor presents a fake identification card, it is not a defense to the power to void the contract. In addition, parents are not usually liable for the contracts of their children. Therefore, when dealing with minors, it is often a wise move to make their parents part of the contract.

Another category of incapacity is incompetent parties. Incompetents are those who are mentally deficient. Because of their lack of mental acuity, their contracts may also be voided. The rule is if the person is so incompetent that he cannot understand the contract is being made, the contract is voidable. However, if he understands that concept, even if he is mentally disabled, the contract will be valid.

Intoxicated people are not considered incompetent and their contracts are valid, so long as they were aware they were entering into a contract. Later regrets will not void the contract. However, if they were so drunk that they did not know they were entering into a contract, the contract will be voidable.

A contract may also be voided if the parties made a mistake. If the mistake was unilateral (that is, if only one person made a mistake) there is no effect. In other words, if a party misquotes a price in a contract and the other relies on that price, the contract is valid at that price. If, however, both parties are in error, the contract is void - not just voidable.

If one party deceives the other, the contract may be voidable. If the issue is nondisclosure, there is often no liability. Then there is outright fraud. Fraud has several components: a false statement of fact, with knowledge of the falsehood, with the intent that the listener will rely on it, and because of that reliance there is some type of damage. All of the elements must be present for fraud to exist. Fraud is different than opinion. If the seller is merely stating an opinion, there is no fraud.

Where one party can exert their will over the other party, the contracts are voidable. A key type of situation is where a highly educated person is contracting with an uneducated person. Or where an aged person is entrusted to the care of a doctor, nurse, child or attorney and then contracts with that person.

CONSIDERATION

Often in contracts you will see the word "consideration". This does not mean you have to be nice to the other party. Consideration has a special meaning in contract law. Consideration is what each side gives and receives as the price for the contract.

There must be an obligation on both sides of a contract. This is what we call a mutuality of consideration. Each side to the contract must give up something. Often the consideration is minor. You will frequently see a contract state: "For $10 in hand paid". That is the consideration. It means that one side paid the other $10 in order to get them to enter into the contract. The other side's consideration is the service or merchandise they surrender. In other words, if we agree that for $10 I will clean your carpet, your consideration is the paying of $10 and my consideration is the service of cleaning the carpet.

Consideration does not have to be money, a service or an item. It can be another promise. The key is the obligation. If there is no obligation, there is no contract. Consideration can also be a promise not to do something. A waiver of a right is a valuable consideration. For example, a contract which states "I will pay you $10,000 if you do not smoke or drink in the next month" could be a valid contract, so long as the party is old enough to smoke or drink. If they are not yet old enough, the contract is invalid because they have no right to smoke or drink and therefore are not giving anything up. Likewise, if the consideration is a promise to do an act you are already obligated to do, there is no consideration. This is why police officers are generally unable to collect rewards for criminals they capture. They are already obligated to capture criminals and therefore there is no special consideration for their act.

What about when a party uses a prior act as consideration? As an example, John offers to pay Bob $10,000 because Bob helped John put out a fire in his building. This does not make a binding contract. Since the act already occurred, there is no obligation on Bob's part to do anything further. John has merely offered Bob a gift which is not binding and not enforceable. The consideration must be an obligation created by the agreement.

If there is no consideration, the contract is not binding. A contract without consideration is nothing more than a non-binding promise. If the consideration is another promise and that promise is not kept, the contract has no consideration and is not valid. The consideration must be sufficient. It may not be out of line with the value of a promise, but if it is valuable, it will usually be allowed.

In some cases there may be a dispute as to the amount of the consideration owed. If there is a dispute, and one side presents a partial payment, is there a contract? If the other side cashes the check, yes there is. If the amount is disputed, the acceptance of a partial payment fixes the amount.

There are some exceptions to the consideration rules. First is the adequacy of consideration. The court will generally only look at the adequacy of consideration if there is a question of undue influence or fraud. Therefore, even if consideration is grossly unequal (such as $100 for a 1999 Rolls Royce), the Court will not throw out the contract for want of consideration. Also, there are some contracts that don't require consideration. These include pledges to charities, certain contracts under the Uniform Commercial Code, and in some places, sealed agreements.

LEGALITY

Occasionally a court will find portions of a contract illegal or invalid. If only portions of a contract are held illegal, the contract still may be valid if the illegal portions can be excised without destroying the basics of the agreement.

If a contract is unfair or unconscionable - this is, the terms are so egregious that it shocks the conscious, the courts may determine that the contract is invalid. In other words, if the terms are too harsh to one party, the court may relieve them from the obligations of the contract. Usually, these contracts arise because one party has power over the other party, or some other unfair advantage in the negotiations. However, it only applies if the contract is clearly out of line. That a party makes a bad bargain is not sufficient grounds to find the contract unconscionable. Also, later events that may make the contract a bad bargain are not grounds to make it unconscionable. It must have been unconscionable at its formation.

A contract against the public welfare is generally not binding. This is true even if the contract is not illegal. For an example, a contract that offers a reward to police officers for catching a specific criminal or to the fire department for prompt service to a particular house is invalid. Aside from the fact that they already have a duty to do these jobs, the reward may divert them away from other issues that the public needs protection from.

Another area where this issue comes up is dealing with unlicensed people in certain areas. For example, unlicensed lawyers, doctors, realtors, accountants, etc. Any contract hiring an unlicensed professional is invalid and cannot be enforced. Any agreement to restrain trade violates public policy, such as an agreement between two stores to drive a third store out of business. In certain circumstances, a contract not to compete may be against public policy.

Finally, contracts cannot be made where interest is charged in excess of amounts allowed by statute. These are called usurious contracts. In Florida, Statute 687 allows for interest up to 18 percent (though there are some statutes that allow up to 30 percent in certain circumstances). These rates usually do not apply to credit cards.

Next, I want to cover the Statute of Frauds, Florida Statutes 725. This has nothing to do with fraud as most of us know it. The statute states that in certain circumstances a contract must be written to be valid. Generally, in Florida the contracts covered under the Statute of Frauds include any contract made in consideration of marriage; any lease for longer than a year; any guarantee or assurance made by a health care provider as to the results of any medical, surgical, or diagnostic procedure performed by any physician, osteopathic physician, chiropractic physician, podiatric physician, or dentist; for any contract that cannot be completed within one year; any contract for sale of land; and any contract where one person agrees to pay the debts of another person, living or dead. If any of these contracts are made by verbal agreement, they are not enforceable. The writing required by the Statute of Frauds doesn't require a formal written agreement, signed and notarized. It may be merely a memorandum stating the terms. So long as it is signed by the party it is being used against and contains all of the terms of the agreement, it may be sufficient.

A Statute of Frauds contract is generally voidable, not void. It is what we call an affirmative defense. In other words, it must be specifically pled as a defense at the beginning of a lawsuit or it cannot later be raised. As an affirmative defense, it does not deny the debt or obligation; it just says the debt cannot be enforced.

There are some ways to get around the Statute of Frauds. If there has been partial performance of the contract, the court may disregard the writing requirement and also if a party has detrimentally relied on the oral contract the court may enforce it. Here you must generally show that substantial injury will occur and that the other party will be unjustly enriched. This is especially true when a party acts on an oral agreement with the belief that it will be reduced to writing.

Oral statements come up in one other context and that is the parole evidence rule. This rule states that verbal statements cannot be used to modify or contradict the terms of a written contract. If the agreement is in writing, any modifications must also be placed in writing and signed by the parties.   Since the parties to a contract must have thought through the agreement when putting it in writing, they are now not allowed to allege that it doesn't say what they want it to. Further there is a policy that the last writing is controlling, so all prior agreements, both verbal and written, are merged in the final written contract. They cannot be enforced on their own.

The exception to the parole evidence rule is when verbal statements are used to clarify unclear portions of the agreement. That is, if the agreement is incomplete or vague, parole evidence can be used to complete it. Parole evidence may also be used to prove the existence of an agreement or to prove that the agreement was illegal.

CONTRACT INTERPRETATION

There are two decision makers in a court of law. The judge sits as the trier of law, and the jury is the trier of fact. If there is no jury, the judge sits as both. When there is a question as to the meaning of the language of a contract, both decision makers have a job.

If the language of the contract is not in question, the only issue is how the law affects the contract. This is a question for the judge. If the language is ambiguous, the jury must decide what is intended by the parties when they drafted the contract.

As we mentioned before, parole evidence (or verbal evidence explaining the contract) cannot be used to modify the terms of a contract. It can, however, be used to clarify the contract when the language of the contract is ambiguous.

The court will not, in most cases, rewrite the contract. The words of a contract are given their ordinary meaning, unless there is proof otherwise. As an example, the word "lift" will be interpreted to mean "to raise up" rather than the British meaning of "elevator" unless the court has evidence that the British meaning was intended.

If the word has special meaning in a trade, that meaning will be interpreted. Another example: if a lawyer agrees to prepare a "brief," the court will not interpret that term to mean that they are going to sew a pair of underwear. In legal terms, a "brief" is a legal document, so the court will interpret the contract to mean that the lawyer is going to draft a legal document.

The court will look at what a reasonable person would think the parties intended, based upon the experiences of the parties and the circumstances surrounding the contract.

When you buy software, it usually comes in an envelope with writing on the outside. This is called a "shrink-wrap license" and is a contract between the software company and the purchaser. The purchase of the software does not give you the right to use it any way you want to. You must agree to follow the language written on the outside of the envelope as well. Likewise, when you purchase a new car with a warranty, you will receive a user's manual for the car. That user's manual contains a maintenance schedule. This schedule is part of your warranty.

If a contract makes reference to another document, that document may become part of the contract. Conversely, if the contract states that it contains the full agreement, no other documents will be allowed to modify the terms.

There is a problem in this area regarding employee handbooks. I will discuss employment law later, but since we're on contracts and supplemental material, I want to touch on this briefly now. If you have a job and the employer gives you a handbook, that handbook may or may not be a part of your employment contract. And it may not depend on the intent of the employer. The courts will look at how the manual is treated. This is important in that, if it is part of the employment contract, it can only be modified if both the employer and employee agree. However, if it is just a statement of the policies of the employer, the employer may change it at will, whether the employee approves or not.

When the court is trying to interpret a contract, it begins by looking at the full contract to determine the intent. If the contract can be divided into separate obligations, the court may separate it into its component parts and interpret the various parts as separate contracts. This is especially true if the consideration is divisible as well.

In some cases, contracts may be conditional. This is also referred to as a contingency. The contract will not be valid unless certain conditions occur. This is the case with most contracts to purchase real estate. In the Florida Association of Realtors contract for Sale and Purchase (known as a FAR/BAR Contract), the contract states that it is contingent upon the buyer obtaining proper financing. If the buyer applies to the bank for financing and is refused, then the contract becomes null and void and the seller must return any deposit money to the buyer. If the contract is cancelled for any other reason, the Seller keeps the deposit as liquidated damages.   Many contracts state that they are contingent upon an attorney reviewing and approving the terms.

If the condition arises before the contractual obligation, it is termed a condition precedent; if it arises after the obligation, it is a condition subsequent. Condition subsequent are usually things that cancel contracts, whereas conditions precedent prevent the contract from forming.

What language prevails in a contract? When you have contradictory terms, the court is often asked to determine which is controlling. As a general rule, handwritten provisions in a contract take precedence over typewritten provisions, and typewritten provisions take precedence over preprinted provisions. If the conflict is between numbers that are expressed in both words and figures, the words prevail.

When resolving ambiguous terms, courts will construe a contract against the party who drafted it. That is, if you hire a lawyer to write the contract and there is an unclear term, the court will read that term in the light most favorable to the other party. For this reason, many contracts now have the phrase that "Ambiguous terms shall not be construed against the drafting party."

The court can also insert certain terms, without changing the contract. If the contract does not have a clause regarding when an act is to be performed, the court will imply that a reasonable time controls and can insert a date they deem reasonable.

If the contract is one that is covered by statutory law and there is an ambiguity as to that portion of the contract, the court will imply the statutory language and can redraft the contract to fit the statute.

If the parties have a particular pattern of conduct or custom of dealing with each other, the court can look to the prior dealing to interpret the language of the contract. In other words, if I have a tenant who routinely pays his rent three weeks late, and I accept the rent without objection, there may be problems if I try to evict him later. The court may decide that the contract has been redrafted to change the payment date. This is problem that many landlords get into.

When you enter into an agreement with someone, you have an obligation to act in the manner most favorable to carrying out the terms of the contract. If a person takes action to prevent the other side from performing its obligations under the contract, even though not precluded by the contract, that person might be found in breach of the agreement, or the other side might be excused from performing, though the contract remains.

Remember, however, interpretation issues only arise when the contract is vague, unclear or ambiguous.

THIRD PARTY BENEFICIARIES

Third party beneficiaries are people who are not parties to the contract, but receive the benefit from it. Because they are the recipients of the benefits, they are entitled to enforce the contract including being able to file a lawsuit on it.

The perfect example of a third party beneficiary contract is a life insurance contract. The person who contracts with the insurance company can't enforce the contract - they're dead! It can only be enforced by the person that the money is owed to (usually referred to in the contract as "the beneficiary.")

Generally, the parties who enter a third party beneficiary contract can change the terms to modify or destroy the interest of the third party, if the interest has not yet vested. In other words, using the life insurance example, a person is free to change the beneficiaries of their insurance contracts at any time before they die. They also are free to let the policy lapse. However, once the rights have vested, the contract cannot be modified without the consent of the beneficiary.

Just because a person may benefit from a contract, they are not necessarily allowed to enforce the contract. In many contracts, third parties may benefit even though they are not the intended beneficiary. If I agree to buy a car from a new car dealer, the manufacturer benefits as well. However, the manufacturer is not a third party beneficiary; the purpose of the contract is not to benefit the manufacturer. If I renege on the contract and don't complete the sale, the manufacturer cannot sue me to require performance. They are what we call an incidental third party beneficiary. Incidental third party beneficiaries receive indirect benefits but cannot enforce the contract.

Assignees to a contract are treated differently. Generally, an assignment is only a transfer of rights, not obligations. The assignment itself is not a contract and thus no consideration is necessary. The underlying contract may require that an assignment must be in writing, must be approved by the other party, or may not allow assignment at all.

As a general rule, when a contract is for the performance of personal services, the contract may not be assigned. The question is how personal the contract is. If the service is very personal, the contract cannot be assigned; if less personal, it may be assignable.

With the assignment of a contract, the question of delegation of duties arises. It is possible to assign a contract, but not delegate duties. For instance, a tenant may assign his rights in a lease to another person, but still be responsible for paying the rent. If the new tenant doesn't pay the rent, the landlord can look to the original tenant for the money.

If you assign the rights and delegate the duties it essentially changes the parties to the contract. Again, and even more so than with assignations, if the contract is for personal services, the duties are rarely delegatable. This is because the reason for the contract is to have a specific person perform the services. If you contract to have someone specific cater your wedding, you probably don't want them to delegate their duties to another person, such as McDonald's or Kentucky Fried Chicken.

While assignments are generally allowed unless otherwise stated in the agreement, delegation of duties are not allowed unless specifically stated. The exception is a contract that falls under the UCC for the sale of goods, which we will discuss later.

Generally, you do not need to tell the other party of an assignment, however, as a practical matter it would be a wise move. After all, how are they to know where to send the check if you don't tell them.

TERMINATION OF A CONTRACT

How do you end a contract? It depends on why it is ending. In most cases the contract ends because the parties have finished their mutual obligations. In some cases it ends because time has passed. In some cases it ends because a party has excused the other's performance. In some cases it ends because there has been a breach of performance.

The performance of a contract takes numerous forms. Once the agreement is in place, if a party offers to complete his obligations, it is said he made a tender to perform. As an example, let's say I hire someone to mow my lawn on a regular basis. If they show up on Monday with their equipment, that is a tender. Or if you order 25 chairs from a furniture company and it has a delivery truck show up at your business on Friday, that is a tender.

When the performance is the payment of money, then the person can tender payment by submitting cash only. A check or a money order is not sufficient as it cannot be spent and only represents money. It is not money itself. What if the check bounced? It would open all sorts of new legal problems. Often time, the contract will state that payment may be made in the form of a check or money order. Also, the tender must be for the full amount. A partial payment is not sufficient tender. In some cases, a refusal of the tender is an excuse of performance. Generally, if there are no extraneous circumstances, the tender must be accepted.

Let's look at a rental situation. If you rent an apartment, the tender issue is crucial to know. If the tenant is late with the rent, under Florida law chances are the landlord will post a three-day notice on the apartment door. Upon the posting, the tenant has three days to tender payment of the late rent. During the three-day period, the landlord MUST accept the rent. If the landlord refuses to accept the tender during this three-day period, the tenant has a valid defense to an eviction action. However, if the tenant misses the three-day period, the landlord is not required to accept the tender and the lease is over.

When a contract requires performance within a specific period of time, the contract ends upon the expiration of that period of time. If there is no time specified, the courts will imply a reasonable time. If a reasonable time has passed and there has been no performance, then the contract is in breach. If the contract states that there must be performance within a specified period, that time period controls and if there has been no performance, again the agreement is in breach. Often time, the contract will state that "Time is of the essence." This means that the parties have a right to insist upon strict compliance with the time deadlines. Any deviation from the deadlines may result in a breach. This is usually what is called boiler-plate language as it is routinely added to the contract for no specific reason (especially in preprinted contracts).

To be in compliance, the performance must be adequate. This does not mean perfect or exact, but usually the word used is substantial. In other words, if a party completes the vast majority of his obligation, so that all that remains are extremely minor issues, the courts may hold that he "substantially" complied with his obligations and thus the contract will be complete. The other side must pay the full contract amount (minus the cost of completing the minor issues). Of course, if performance is exact, there is no question here. Further, if the terms of the contract state that full compliance is required, then substantial performance will not be a defense.

Some contracts state that performance must meet the other party's "satisfaction". These contracts are not favored as they do not have a great deal of specificity, but they do occur and substantial performance is often not possible, because the outcome is judged by a subjective taste.

A contract may be discharged by agreement of the parties. If the deal just isn't working out, the parties may agree to end the relationship.

Sometimes the contract will allow either party to terminate it upon providing notice to the other party. On continuing contracts with no set expiration term, the contract may be terminated by either party at will, or at his or her discretion. A notice may, however, be required by law, even if it is not mentioned in the lease. For instance, in a landlord/tenant situation, if the lease doesn't have a notice requirement, then the Florida statutes spell out what notice is required. If it is a month-to-month lease, 15 days' notice must be given to validly terminate the lease.

If the contract is for services for a certain period of time, such as employment for a one-year period, the contract is considered complete at the end of that term and notice is not generally required to terminate it.

A contract may be terminated if the parties decide to replace the agreement with another agreement. The second contract can act as a nullification of the first. However, if the new contract does not state that it is a replacement of the first, the court must look at the purpose of the agreements. If they are contradictory, the second one will be treated as a replacement of the first. If not, both contracts can be enforced. A contract also may be ended by replacing the outcome. As an example, let's say I contract to sell four red chairs. When time to perform arises, I offer to provide four blue chairs. If the offer is accepted, it is called an accord. Once I have actually turned over the four blue chairs, there is an "accord and satisfaction" and the agreement is complete.

How else can a contract be ended? By impossibility. If something happens that makes performance impossible, the contract is over. Let's say I agree to rent you a house. The week before you are to move in, lightning strikes and the house burns down. The contract is over because it would be impossible for me to comply. If there is a mere inconvenience, the contract still is valid. An inconvenience would be if a company's delivery truck breaks down so it cannot deliver the goods. The shipper must simply find other ways to make delivery.

Death or disability of one of the parties will end a contract. I have agreed to mow your lawn, but on my way I'm in a car accident and lose my legs. I can't perform and therefore the contract is over. If the law changes so the purpose of the agreement becomes illegal, the contract is over.

In the law we have something called the bad bargain rule. This rule states that if a person made a bad bargain, the court will not overrule it. We must live with our agreements. There are a few times when the court says a person made such a bad bargain that he shouldn't be stuck with it. Usually these are when things occur that you have no control over. During the oil embargo of the 1970's, people went from paying 25 cents a gallon to paying $1 a gallon in a matter of weeks. This economic change caused a lot of problems for people who made contracts and included in their deal the cost of oil or gas. When circumstances change the outcomes of the contract, it may be terminated.

Finally a contract may be ended by an act of law. If you file for bankruptcy, certain contracts are ended, or may be ended. If you have not performed and the other side doesn't institute suit within a specific period of time, the statute of limitation will run and there is no further requirement on the contract.

(In Florida, there is a five-year statute of limitation on a legal or equitable action on a contract, obligation, or liability founded on a written instrument; a four-year limitation on a legal or equitable action on a contract, obligation, or liability not founded on a written instrument, including an action for the sale and delivery of goods, wares, and merchandise, and on store accounts; a two-year limitation on an action to recover wages or overtime or damages or penalties concerning payment of wages and overtime; and a one-year limitation on an action for specific performance of a contract.)

BREACH OF CONTRACT

Breach of contract is defined as failing to act as required in the contract. This can be a failure to do an act that was agreed to be done; failing to pay money owed; or doing an act that was agreed not to be done.

All terms of a contract are important. The parties must follow the terms. Any variation may be considered a breach. If the contract states an act must occur on Monday, and it is performed on Tuesday, that is a breach. Payment that is short by 1 cent is a breach.

Often the breach is committed before any action is required under the contract. This is called an anticipatory breach. An anticipatory breach may be committed by words or actions. If a landlord enters into a lease with a party to start in a month and then before the month begins signs a lease with another person, this is a breach of the agreement. It is called anticipatory because the time for performance hadn't yet arrived. Another example is when a party to a contract simply tells the other party that, "I'm not going to do it." This too is an anticipatory breach. The act or statement must clearly show that the party has no intention of carrying out their portion of the agreement. A repudiation or anticipatory breach may be corrected if the party realizes his or her error, unless the other party has changed their position because of the repudiation. If there has been an anticipatory breach, the aggrieved party generally does not have to wait until the time of performance to bring suit. Once a party has taken action to show he is not going to act, he may immediately be sued for breach of contract.

Anticipatory breaches do no always end in lawsuits. If one party calls and says she isn't going to perform, and the other side agrees, then we have a waiver of the breach. Waivers also can occur with standard breaches of contract. A common example is when a party to a contract makes a late payment. This is a breach because the payment wasn't made when required. If however, the late payment is accepted, there is a waiver of the breach. At that time, no suit is allowed because the breach was with permission.

At times the breach is only to a portion of the contract, but not to the main part. In this situation the waiver of the breach doesn't end the contract - it just waives that portion. The rest of the contract is still in effect.

Waivers can be dangerous. If they are frequent, they can modify the contract. If you make a habit of accepting payments late, this may become a modification of the contract so that all payments may be made late. Often landlords realize this only after the defense is raised in court and they find their contracts have been modified without their knowledge. For this reason, many contracts now include a clause that one or more waivers will not be deemed to be a modification of the original agreement. You also can accept a breach, but reserve your rights to sue on the breach. This only is allowed when there has been some damage or where there should be some set-off. This can also only be done with notice to the breaching party that you are reserving the right to proceed on damages.

The language of the contract can limit what happens as a result of a breach. There may be limitations requiring notices before the breach is recognized, or opportunities to cure when a breach has occurred.

WHAT CAN YOU DO IF CONTRACT IS BREACHED?

When a party breaches a contract, and the breach has not been waived by the other party, there are several remedies and/or penalties that should be looked into. First, you can file suit for damages. Damages are the money that you lose due to the breach. It may be due to a reduction in value, or the failure of a party to provide goods after payment. The theory for damages is that we want to put the plaintiff, or the innocent party, in the same position that he would have been in if there had been not breach.

If the contract was performed, but improperly or insufficiently, a suit for damages still may be allowed, however, it would be limited to the cost of correcting the improper or insufficient actions. This occurs when there is a sales contract and not all the items are delivered, or in a construction contract where the work is not fully performed and another contractor has to finish it.

There are three types of damages: compensatory, nominal and punitive.

Compensatory damages are the amount necessary to compensate the plaintiff for his loss. They equal the amount actually lost by the plaintiff or the amount needed to put the Plaintiff in the position he would have been in if there had been no breach.

Sometimes the court feels that the plaintiff should recover something, but there is no actual monetary loss, or the loss is extremely minimal. The court can award what are called nominal damages. These are usually small awards, often only $1 and are basically awarded just to give the plaintiff a moral victory.

Punitive damages are awarded to the innocent party to punish the wrongdoer. Punitive damages are awarded in excess of the actual compensatory damages. As a general rule, punitive damages are not allowed in contract actions. The reason for this is that in a capitalist society there are often business reasons to breach a contract (perhaps a cheaper supplier is found, or a contract will take too long to complete and another person can complete it faster). Because we live in a business society, we don't want to punish people for trying to improve their business.

Damages also can be divided into direct and consequential damages. Direct damages are those that spring directly from the breach itself. A consequential damage is one that is related to the breach, but not because of the breach alone. In other words, it is not necessarily a foreseeable damage. Let's go with an example. I buy a new car and the brakes fail the next day. That is a breach of contract, because the car wasn't in the condition it was warranted for. I can recover damages for the repair of the brakes. These are direct damages, as they are directly related to the breach of contract. If because of my brake failure, I get into an accident and there are other damages to the car, I might be able to get recovery for this as well, as these damages are foreseeable and arise directly from the breach. What if because of the brake failure and subsequent accident, the stress gives me a heart attack? This is not reasonably foreseeable and leads to what is called a consequential damage. It also is generally not compensable in a contract action. (This doesn't mean it wouldn't be covered under a product liability case or a personal injury action. Just not a breach of contract action.)

Generally, a party has a duty to mitigate damages if possible. This means that you have to take action to minimize the amount that the other party must pay. Let's say I have a two-year employment contract and am wrongfully fired from my job after just one year. I have a cause of action against my former employer for the salary I would have earned for the second year. However, I can't just sit back and sue without doing anything. I must try to obtain new employment in the same field at approximately the same salary. If I succeed in getting a new job, the award of damages will be reduced by the income of the new job. I would not, however, be required to accept a job that is substantially different or that pays substantially less than my previous job.

If a person fails to attempt to mitigate damages, the Court can refuse to award any damages. Generally, the only time you do not have to mitigate damages is when there is no way to reasonably mitigate them.

We already have covered monetary damages, but there are other remedies.

RECESSION
Rather than a lawsuit for damages, there may be a suit

for recession of the contract. Recession is where you ask the court to reverse the contract. This occurs when there is a material breach such that the contract should not be enforced. If a party has paid money toward this contract, they can ask to have the money returned. If the parties cannot be restored to their original position, recession cannot be granted, as it must fully reverse the contract.

SPECIFIC PERFORMANCE

If one party has fully performed its obligations under the contract, it can file an action for specific performance. This asks the court to order the other party to perform its portion of the agreement. This is a rare remedy, because the courts don't favor ordering people to do things. Usually, it is only allowed when the issue is unique, and money damages don't provide sufficient remedy. An example is a contract to purchase land. Land is always considered unique and therefore, if a buyer comes forward ready to buy, he can ask the court to order the seller to comply with the purchase and sale agreement. If the contract is to sell something rare or something where the sale is rare, specific performance can be ordered. Consider the sale of an airliner like a Boeing 747. This is not a rare item, but the sale is fairly rare. Airlines don't purchase many 747, rather preferring to repair the ones they already have. If the buyer refuses to complete the contract, the plane may not be sold to another buyer for months or years.

INJUNCTION

This is an order by the court either preventing or

requiring a party to do an act. If the contract states that the person is not to take a certain action, an injunction is the proper remedy.

LIQUIDATED DAMAGES

A contract may contain a clause that guarantees a specific amount to be paid as a liquidated damage in the event of a breach. Liquidated damages are allowed when actual damages cannot be readily discerned. The amount of the liquidated damage must not be excessive. If it is too large, the court may look at it as a penalty, and it will not be allowed.

SPECIFIC CLAUSES

You can add clauses to your contract that limit damages. Many common carriers will do this. When you ship a package with a major carrier such as FedEx or UPS, the contract will usually have a line that says essentially "Unless the value of the property is stated, the liability of the carrier is limited to the amount of postage."

You can also put a clause stating that the party breaching the agreement will not be liable for the breach. This is not favored by the court and must be clear and unambiguous to be enforced.

ATTORNEY FEES

Finally, and what most people are interested, in are attorney fees. Attorney fees are generally not considered damages in a contract action, and unless stated in the contract will not be awarded. As a general rule in a breach of contract lawsuit, each side is responsible for its own attorney fees. You need to review the language of your contract and the state statutes to see if your case will allow an award of fees.

AGENTS

When you have authorized someone to act on your behalf, you create an agency situation. You become what is called the principal and the person you retain becomes the agent. But what does this really mean?

An agent is not an employee, although employees can be agents. An agent is authorized to actually represent the employer and act on his behalf. An employee generally does not represent the employer. An exception is salespeople. They generally can be considered agents of the company they work for because they are authorized to enter into sales contracts for the employer.

Likewise, an agent is not an independent contractor. As independent contractor is contracted to perform a certain function for the company. An independent contractor works at his own direction, whereas an agent is controlled by the principal.

Lawyers are not always agents, but often serve that purpose. For instance, if you hire a lawyer to sue someone, the lawyer is your agent for the purposes of drafting the lawsuit and filing it. Most lawsuits do not require the party to sign the complaint, so long as the lawyer signs it. However, the Florida Bar does not allow lawyers to settle cases without their clients' knowledge, approval and signatures. In this sense you could say lawyers are agents for starting lawsuits, but not always for ending them. Many corporate lawyers are agents of their companies, negotiating and executing contracts for the business. Also, many lawyers become agents for certain clients. This includes sports agents, entertainment agents and literary agents. Their job is to negotiate contracts for their clients.

There are three basic types of agency. A special agent has been retained to perform a specific function. Once that function has been performed, the agency ends. An example is if the principal appoints an agent to negotiate a contract with a specific vendor. The principal may choose to do this because the agent has a better relationship with the vendor than the principal and can get a better deal for the company.

A general agent is one appointed to do anything that needs to be done in regards to a certain time, place or business. If a business hires a manager of a store and gives him full power to run the store, he is a general agent.

A universal agent has full power to do anything the principal might do. Thus, if the principal is leaving the country for a while, he can give full power of attorney to someone to take care of everything while he is gone. This would be running his business, caring for his house, maintaining his car, etc. The agency would last until the principal takes some action to revoke it.

The easiest way of creating an agency is by an express written agreement. An agency does not have to be in writing, but it really should be. A simple power of attorney will work for doing this. If you become an agent under a power of attorney, you become what is called "an attorney in fact," and you should write those words when signing any document (The proper way to sign a contract under a power of attorney is to sign your name, not the principal's name, and signify that you are signing as their agent. The signature should appear something like: "Bob Smith, as attorney in fact for John Jones.").

An agency relationship also can be developed by the conduct of the parties, even if the principal doesn't mean to create one. If an employee acts as an agent, and the principal doesn't object, an agency is created.

If a principal takes some action to make it appear that another person has the authority to act on his behalf, when the person does not actually have the authority, we call that "apparent authority." While this does not actually create an agency relationship, the principal will not be allowed to challenge it and he will be bound to any agreements that resulted. Thus, if you jokingly say "Talk to Carol, she handles all these things for me," she just might.

If someone enters into an agreement as an agent without proper authority, actual or apparent, the principal may either ratify the agreement or ignore it.   The ratification must be actual. That is, the principal must intend to ratify the action, must have been able to authorize the act when it occurred and when he ratified it, and he must have full knowledge, or should have full knowledge of all the facts before ratifying. The action must also be ratified before the other side withdraws the offer.

An agency may be terminated be either the principal or the agent. It also may be terminated by its own terms or in some cases by law. If the agency agreement specifies that it is only for a specific purpose, once that purpose is over the agency is over. If the agreement states that the agency is for a specific period of time, the agency ends at the end of the time period.

Depending on the contract of agency, there may be a question of when the parties may terminate it. If the agency agreement does not have a time feature, it is terminable at the will of either party. If the contract has a time feature or is for a specific function, the parties may agree to terminate it prior to the contemplated finale.

This is a common feature in contracts for sports agents. The agent has time and money invested in the agency agreement and wants to recoup his investment. Often the contracts will have clauses stating they may be terminated if one side gives the other side certain notice, or pays out a certain amount of money. The principal may always revoke the agency agreement, even if the contract states that it is irrevocable, however there may be a penalty for the termination. The same is not true for the agent. They may quit acting as an agent if there has been wrongful action of the principal, or if the agency is at will, but other than that, the agent will incur liability if he fails to continue acting as an agent.

There is no specific action required for revocation. Any action that indicates an intent to revoke the agency is sufficient. Thus, if I make another person my agent to run my business, I may file a revocation with the courts, contact my suppliers and customers and notify them that there is a revocation, tell the agent of the revocation directly, give someone else the authority or simply go to the store and run it myself. Any of those actions will result in a revocation.

Regardless of how the agency is terminated, the agency agreement doesn't actually end until the agent learns of the revocation. This may be done directly or indirectly. If the agent learns from a third party that his principal has signed with another agent, that is sufficient to end the relationship. While there is not requirement to notify third parties of the revocation, if they are unaware of the termination, they may unknowingly continue to deal with the ex-agent under the theory of apparent authority and thus still bind the principal. Usually the better practice is to place a notice in the paper, or file it with the court stating the agency action is revoked. Once filed with the courts, the third party cannot claim they had no knowledge, and there can be no apparent authority.

When a person has made another his agent, that agency ends upon the death of either the principal or agent. While it makes sense that it ends upon the death of the agent, some people don't understand that it applies to the death of the principal as well.

Powers of Attorneys expire upon the death of the person who made them. Similarly, agency agreements generally end when either party dies, becomes insane or files for bankruptcy. If the purpose of the agency becomes impossible, there is a termination, and if the parties are from different countries, war between their respective countries can be a termination until peace is restored. To do business for an enemy of the United States might be considered treasonous.

What if the principal is in an accident and goes into a coma? Is there still an agency relationship? It depends. If the agency was created by a standard Power of Attorney, then it would expire when the principal became incapacitated. However, there is a document called a Durable Power of Attorney which authorizes the agent to continue working even though the principal is incapacitated.

Today, agency is big business, especially with sports, entertainment and literature. Exclusivity is a big issue. An agent does not want to represent a principal if someone else is representing her as well. This creates confusion and can lead to a splitting of incomes and duplication of efforts. Remember Jerry Maguire? When he left his firm the big issue was whether his clients would sign an exclusive agreement with him or his old firm.

What are the duties of the agent and principal? There is a duty of loyalty between them. The agent must be loyal to the principal. He cannot make any secret benefit from the agency; he cannot take advantage of his position to make a profit. He must disclose ownership interests in property that may be involved in the agency relationship. For example, in real estate contracts, the real estate brokers must disclose if they own or intend to purchase a property. The agent cannot represent both parties unless he discloses it and the parties agree to it.

The agent has a duty of obedience and performance to his principal. If he is instructed to do something he must do it exactly as instructed. This is an absolute duty. Even if the agent is acting in the way he thinks is best, that will not be a defense for failing to follow instructions.

The agent owes a duty to make an accounting for the principal. If the agent errs and commingles his money with the principal's, the principal gets it all. As an example, if the agent commingles funds and then buys various stocks with it, he cannot later say which stocks were bought with whose money. The agent cannot simply give the principal a percentage of the stock because the stocks will not stay equal. If the agent's stock goes up and the principal's goes down, then the agent has made a profit at the principal's expense.

Finally, the agent has a duty to provide the principal with information. Even after the agency relationship is over, the agent still has a responsibility to the principal. He has the duty to perform his prior obligations and wind down the agency relationship.

The principal's duties are less onerous. He must perform the contract, he must pay the agent his commission, reimburse for expenses and indemnify the agent for his losses.

EMPLOYMENT

EMPLOYEE/INDEPENDENT CONTRACTOR

Now that we have touched on principal and agent, let's look at employment. As we mentioned earlier, an employee is one who works at the direction and control of an employer. This is opposed to the theory of an independent contractor who works at his or her own direction. The difference between the two is important, primarily for liability and tax purposes.

An employer has certain responsibilities regarding employees and has to pay taxes to the government for unemployment compensation. Not so with an independent contractor. All the employer has to do for independent contractors is send them an IRS Form 1099, showing how much they were paid which is used when the independent contractor prepares his tax return. The independent contractor is liable for his own taxes and social security filing.

Also, while employers are responsible for the actions of their employees, contractors are generally liable for their own actions. If an employee causes an accident, the employer is generally liable; if an independent contractor causes an accident, the contractor is liable.

However, just because there are some benefits doesn't mean you can simply decide to treat your employees as independent contractors. There are restrictions. An independent contractor is hired to do a job, but is left to his own devises as to how the job gets done. If the employer controls the manner in which the work is done (such as hours, location, tools, etc.), the independent contractor may be deemed an employee and the employer will then be liable for back taxes, fees and penalties. The Internal Revenue Service has developed what is referred to as the 20-question test for determining whether a person is an employee or independent contractor. While this is not an absolute test, if less than eleven of the factors indicate an independent contractor, the IRS will likely look at the person as an employee.

For the following questions, a "yes" answer indicates the worker is an employee.

- Does the principal provide instructions to the worker about when, where, and how he or she is to perform the work?
- Does the principal provide training to the worker?
- Are the services provided by the worker integrated into the principal's business operations?
- Must the services be rendered personally by the worker?
- Does the principal hire, supervise and pay assistants to the worker?
- Is there a continuing relationship between the

principal and the worker?

- Does the principal set the work hours and schedule?
- Does the worker devote substantially full time to the business of the principal?
- Is the work performed on the principal's premises?
- Is the worker required to perform the services in an order or sequence set by the principal?
- Is the worker required to submit oral or written reports to the principal?
- Is the worker paid by the hour, week, or month?
- Does the principal have the right to discharge the worker at will?
- Can the worker terminate his or her relationship with the principal any time he or she wishes without incurring liability to the principal?
- Does the principal pay the business or traveling expenses of the worker?

For the following questions, a "yes" answer indicates the worker is an independent contractor.

- Does the worker furnish significant tools, materials and equipment?
- Does the worker have a significant investment in facilities?

- Can the worker realize a profit or loss as a result of his or her services?

- Does the worker provide services for more than one firm at a time?

- Does the worker make his or her services available to the general public?

If it is determined that the employer has been treating the person as an independent contractor, rather than an employee, the IRS may fine the employer for a portion of the independent contractor's salary, plus part of the worker's share of FICA and Medicare, plus part of the workers withholding taxes, plus FUTA tax, plus additional penalties (both civil and criminal) and interest. In addition to all of the above, the worker may sue the employer for the employer's portion of withholding tax. Because the IRS losses 1.5 billion dollars a year in misclassified employees, there is a strong incentive for them to correct this.

RISKS IN EMPLOYMENT LAW

Because employment law affects almost everyone in one way or another, I want to spend the next several pages discussing it. First, some generalizations. Years ago there was no issue with hiring and firing. Employers hired who they wanted and fired who they wanted. If the employer didn't want to hire women, he didn't have to. Same with minorities, the elderly or handicapped people. Eventually, the workers had enough and they rose against the employers. After years of litigation and legislation, the law has changed. Congress and the courts have been passing laws and deciding cases that have restricted the rights of the employer in whom they can hire and who they can fire.

The law has also changed in regards to what an employer can ask of an employee. Before the laws changed, an employer could make sexual comments to their workers without fear of reprisal. An employer could tell an off-color joke without worrying about being sued for discrimination. Today, not only can't the employer tell these jokes, but he has to take efforts to ensure that the employees don't tell them either. How did we get to this point, where mere words are grounds for litigation, where a compliment over a woman's (or man's) appearance could lead to a lawsuit?

Today is the most dangerous time to be an employer when it comes to controlling personnel. We live in a litigious society. Many cases, especially employment law cases, are handled on a contingent fee basis; that is, the legal fees are paid as part of the recovery. If the employee doesn't win, there are no legal fees. If the lawyer wins a big judgment, he gets a big paycheck. This leads many people to take a People's Court mentality: don't take personal responsibility for your actions - sue someone. If an employee is incompetent but thinks he was fired for racially/sexually/religious/age motivated reasons, he can sue. He might win, in which case he may get a lot of money for being incompetent. If he loses, he may be ordered to pay the other side's costs. However, if he has no money he may be what we call "judgment proof".

I'm not saying that all employment lawsuits are frivolous. Many are, but many have merit. Employees are learning what their rights are. Many laws require posting of rights in the workplace. Reality TV gives us The People's Court, Judge Judy, Judge Joe Brown, Judge Mathis, Judge Alex, Divorce Court, America's Court With Judge Ross, We The people With Gloria Allred, and Justice for All with Christina Perez. Court TV (now TruTV) gives us a front row seat in the legal process and lets the layperson see what the law is. Today, the major news stories are often about lawsuits: Trayvon Martin, Jodi Arias, Bernie Madoff, foreclosures. Society is becoming more interested in what happens in the courtroom and as such more people are becoming more familiar with their rights.

Because the risks to employers have become so great, they have had to adapt. Many do this by creating an office of human resources or a personnel director. This person is responsible for hiring and firing. Often they also address any problems the employees have about the business or their fellow workers. They are also responsible for keeping the employer informed of the changes in the laws. Finally, they are responsible for finding ways around the laws. As an example, let's say you are the personnel director for Hooters, and a man applies for a job as a waiter. The law says you can't discriminate against applicants on the basis of sex. However, Hooters doesn't want men in the orange shorts and tight T-shirts. How do you get around this law? Keep this in mind; when we get to those sections we'll discuss it.

HISTORY OF EMPLOYMENT LAWS

There were four major employment laws passed in the 1930s - the Davis-Bacon Act (setting minimum wages for laborers and mechanics working under government contracts), the Norris-LaGuardia Act (allowing for the association of workers for collective bargaining purposes), the National Labor Relations Act (creating unionization rights of employees and setting procedures for collective bargaining), and the Fair Labor Standards Act of 1938 (limiting the number of hours an employee could work before the employer MUST pay time and a half for overtime). These all deal with labor relations, essentially. If you recall your history, the '30s was a period of strife in the labor field. There were a lot of labor disputes, strikes and unionization. These laws were passed to support unionization and set controls for collective bargaining.

The next major wave of employment laws came in the

1960s. This was a period of civil unrest, and, as you might imagine, the laws passed during this period affect discriminatory behavior and civil rights. Primary in this area was the Civil Rights Act of 1964 (preventing discrimination in the areas of race, color; religion, sex and national origin), the Equal Pay Act of 1964 (prohibiting sex-based discrimination in wages), and the Age Discrimination in Employment Act of 1967 (protecting workers over 40 from discrimination based on their age).

The Nixon-Ford era of the 1970s brought us several major laws involving primarily safety, education and retirement, along with a Vietnam Veterans Readjustment Assistance Act. The Carter years of the late 1970's brought the Pregnancy Discrimination Act.

During the Regan years, of course, the major issue was the budget and thus we see the major law was COBRA - the Consolidated Omnibus Budget Reconciliation Act. Finally, the first Bush years, the '80s, the me generation brought laws that impacted the worker as an individual, as opposed to the laws of the '30s which protected workers as a group.

In the 1990's, the issues involved individual rights and financial freedom. An example is the Personal Responsibility and Work Opportunity Reconciliation Act of 1996, which requires employers to report certain information to the government with respect to newly-hired employees (so-called "New Hire Reporting.") The primary intent of the new hire reporting law is to help track down "deadbeat daddies" (and mommies) who skip out on their child support obligations.

My purpose here is showing that employment law

reflects the issues of the day. This is not just true about laws passed, but also about their interpretation. Understanding when laws were passed might help you understand why they were passed and what their true purpose is.

There are numerous laws that apply to the area of equal employment. We have the civil Rights Act of 1964, the Equal Pay Act, the Age Discrimination in Employment Act, the Americans with Disabilities Act, and more. Entire courses are taught on some of these, but we are going to give them only a cursory overview. We will start with the most famous, The Civil Rights Act of 1964.

THE
CIVIL RIGHTS ACT

We begin with the Civil Rights Act of 1964 (also known as Title VII). The Civil Rights Act of 1964 was created to eliminate discrimination based on race, color; religion, sex and national origin. What is missing is sexual preference, which is different from sex (we will discuss this later). The law applies to discriminatory treatment where the employer treats some employees less favorably because they belong to one of the enumerated classes (disparate treatment).

It also protects from discriminatory impact where a neutral practice has the result of impacting one of the protected groups (disparate impact). Under disparate treatment, the employer has a defense if he did not intend to discriminate. This defense is not available under the disparate impact theory.

The Civil Rights Act is enforced be the Equal Employment Opportunity Commission (EEOC). The procedures for complaints are not easy to follow. Once a complaint has been made, it is forwarded to an office of the EEOC. You must then wait 60 days. At the end of that period, you can file a charge against the employer. The EEOC investigates and tries to reach an agreement between the parties. If an agreement cannot be reached, they give you a "right to sue" letter. Only then may a lawsuit be filed charging discriminatory practices. But the lawsuit must be filed within 90 days. Damages include compensatory damages, including back pay and are not included in computation of gross income for tax purposes.

Before employers start panicking and employees start running to the courthouse, you should know that the Civil Rights Act does not apply to every business. To fall under the requirements of the Civil Rights Act a business must affect interstate commerce and employ 15 or more individuals for at least 20 weeks during the current or previous calendar year. The question about the number of employees is pretty easy to calculate-just count the number of employees at any given time. If the maximum exceeds 20, then you must look to the next step. That is the more troublesome question-when does a business affect interstate commerce?

Let's say there is a local souvenir business in Key West with 21 employees. All of their souvenirs are made by local artisans, sold within the store, and there is an absolute policy against employing minorities. What recourse would an African American or Hispanic applicant have against such a business? They would have to look to state law, because the Civil Rights Act would not apply. However, if a souvenir store next door shipped items to patrons outside of Florida, or if they shipped merchandise from artisans located outside of Florida, or if they advertise their goods in publications that go outside of Florida, they would be subject to the Civil Rights Act.

The Civil Rights Act only applies to certain classes of people-it is not all-inclusive. The first class is **sex**. This means gender, not orientation. As much as some people wish it would, the Civil Rights Act does not protect homosexuals. This is one of the major issues in the Gay Rights movement. The Act applies not only when there is blatant discrimination based upon a person's gender (known as disparate treatment), but also when there is discriminatory practices that tend to have a sexual effect, such as height and weight restrictions, which tends to separate men from women (known as disparate impact). An employer may use his lack of intent as a defense to disparate impact only, not to disparate treatment. This Act also applies to different treatment based upon traits that apply only to one sex. For example, an employer may not treat a female employee different because she is pregnant. Several years ago there was a lawsuit filed by a group of waitresses who had become pregnant. They worked in a large restaurant and were required to walk up to seven miles each day while crossing the floor between the kitchen and their tables. When they became pregnant, the boss was concerned that the excessive walking might cause miscarriages, and to protect the waitresses- and himself- he reassigned them to jobs as hostesses until the pregnancy ended. The waitresses sued for discrimination under the Civil Rights Act, claiming hostesses made less money than the waitresses did. The waitresses won the suit.

Sex also includes sexual harassment - employers cannot permit a work environment that is sexually hostile. This applies to both men and women. If a female boss grabs a male employee's butt, she would be just as guilty as a male boss who gropes a female employee.

There are two types of sexual harassment. The first is when the boss uses his or her power over a subordinate to attain sexual favors. The second is when the boss allows a hostile environment, such as where employees tell off-color jokes or who repeatedly ask another employee on a date after being told no repeatedly. The boss must take actions to prevent this type of activity, or end it if it has already started. How do they do this? By educating their employees. Many employers require employees to attend sensitivity courses to prevent a hostile environment. This type of course can also act as a defense for the employer to show they have taken actions to prevent this behavior.

Race and Color: Many people think this act was designed to aid minorities. In reality, it protects all employees regardless of race, including white employees. It simply says "race" and therefore anyone who has been discriminated against based on his or her race is protected. For a minority-owned business to refuse to hire white employees is just as wrong as a white employer refusing to hire a minority employee. The act therefore allows for reverse discrimination suites when employers attempt to reserve openings for minorities to fill "quotas."

Many people above the age of 40 recall a case called Bakke vs. Univ. of California at Davis (I'm trying to be nice, as the case was decided in 1978). Bakke was a 32-year-old white man with a war record and an engineering degree, who applied to medical school. He was told he was too old, as he would be in his 40s before he graduated. He still applied. He was rejected, but he learned that minority students with lower GPAs and MCAT scores were admitted. The school had reserved 16 out of 100 places for "disadvantaged" members of racial minorities. He sued, challenging the use of quotas. The university argued that its programs did not require quotas; it was trying to establish a goal of minority representation in the School of Medicine. A divided U.S. Supreme Court was torn between upholding the medical school's minority admissions programs (including its quota plan), and striking down the plan and ordering Bakke's admission. The debate ended when Justice Lewis Powell formed a compromise. The Supreme Court upheld minority admissions programs, but stated that the school's use of quotas was unlawful and ordered Allan Bakke's admission to the UC Davis medical school.

The Civil Rights Act prohibits more than just refusing to hire someone based on his or her race. It also applies to differential treatment of employees based on race or color. An employer must treat all employees the same, regardless of race. While we are all familiar with the Civil Rights cases where the government was precluded from having separate facilities based on race, this also applies to private employers. In the 1971 case, U.S. v. Jacksonville Terminal Co., the federal court held that separate does not make equal in the employment field as well. Segregation of any kind by an employer is a violation of Title VII.

National Origin: Employers also cannot discriminate based upon what country a person is from. This is different from race. Bahamians may be black or white; Africans may be black or white. Years ago, the Irish and Italians were heavily discriminated against, even though they are predominately white nationalities. While you cannot discriminate based upon national origin, what many do not realize is that it is permissible to discriminate based on a prospective employee's status as a foreigner. An employee may refuse to hire all foreigners, but they cannot discriminate against citizens between other countries. What this means is that an employer may say they will only hire U.S. citizens, but it is unlawful to hire Canadians, while refusing to hire Mexican citizens. Once employers agree to hire any other nationality, they must be willing to hire all nationalities.

Religion is another protected class under the Civil Rights Act. Employers must attempt to respect and permit their employees' religious beliefs and practices and attempt to accommodate those practices.

If the employer cannot reasonably accommodate the employees' religious beliefs, the employer may then require the employee to violate his religious practices without violating the Act. If an employee's religion requires that he not work on Sunday (or Saturday), the employer must try to accommodate him. If the employer cannot find another person to work the shift, the employee may be required to work that day, despite his religious belief, and the employer will not have violated the Act.

The religious beliefs of the employee must be valid. If the employee creates a religion such as the "Church of Bob" to keep from working on Friday and Saturday nights, the employer need not make an attempt to accommodate the belief. This is a dangerous area, however, as the employer may not know which religions are legitimate and which are not or what religious practices are bona fide tenets of the religious faith.

The employer must often find ways to protect an

employee's religious beliefs without offending the beliefs or feelings of others. Several years ago, an employee claimed her religion required her to wear an anti-abortion button. The button contained a picture of a fetus, which was offensive to other employees. The court fashioned a compromise between the religious beliefs and the rights of her co-workers. They found that indeed the belief required that she wear the button, but not that the button be visible. Therefore, the employee could wear the button on her undergarments or on the inside of her clothing. By doing this, she wouldn't be violating her religious beliefs nor would she be offending her co-workers.

Another issue that arises is preaching. Some religions require their followers to recruit or convert others. This is often offensive to co-workers. The employer is allowed to have a blanket rule that employees may not talk about non-work issues. However if employees are allowed to discuss other lifestyle issues, such as sports, they must also allow discussion of religion. Whether an employer can stop extensive preaching is unclear. The courts have not given a decisive answer. The key questions to ask are the frequency of the preaching, the severity, whether it was physically threatening, intimidating or humiliating and whether it unreasonably interfered with work performance.

Certain religious discrimination is exempt from the Act. Religious schools may limit teaching applicants to teachers that belong to their particular religion. Also, churches may hire strictly from their belief group for church related jobs.

Let me provide a few case examples to show how the

Civil Rights Act applies to the area of religious discrimination.

Case facts: Mohen is a member of the Sikh religion. The practice of Sikhism forbids the cutting or shaving of facial hair. In accordance with his religious beliefs, Mohen wore a long beard. He applied for a position as a breakfast cook at a restaurant but was told that the restaurant's policy was to forbid cooks to have facial hair for sanitary and good grooming reasons. He was told that to gain employment, he would have to shave off his beard. Mohen contended that the restaurant had an obligation to make a reasonable accommodation to his religious beliefs and to let him keep his beard. Is Mohen right?

Answer: While the Civil Rights Act requires employers to make a reasonable accommodation for their employees religious beliefs whenever possible, the employer may violate the employees religious beliefs (and may require the employee to violate their beliefs) if accommodation would create an unnecessary business hardship. Sanitary reasons and a consistently applied grooming policy for all employees demonstrates that the restaurant could not accommodate Mohen's religious beliefs without an unnecessary business hardship, including the loss of customers who don't like facial hair on their eggs or who are turned off by seeing a cook with facial hair (However, would the use of a facial hair net act as an accommodation?).

Case facts: A born again Christian worked as a supervisor to a county office with 50 employees under his watch. He occasionally asked his secretary to type his Bible study notes for him and several employees would say prayers in his office before work. The supervisor even used biblical passages related to slothfulness to improve productivity. He was reprimanded and told to cease all religious activities on county time. He was also told to remove all items with religious connotations from his office. Several months later, he was reprimanded for a lack of judgment relating to financial constraints on the county budget. As this was not his first reprimand, he was fired. The supervisor claimed that the firing was due to his religious beliefs, not any inappropriate activity. Does he get rehired?

Answer: Yes. The employer is allowed to take certain actions against religious practices, such as prohibiting the supervisor from requiring his secretary type his Bible notes, or refusing to open the building early for prayer meetings. However, allowing him to pray with coworkers or make references to his Christian belief did not impose an undue hardship on the employer. The employer would have to show that the supervisor would have been fired absent his religious activities. As the prior misconduct involved the religious activities, they could not do this and therefore he must be rehired.

Case facts: Many religions require their followers to "spread the word". This can be an unpleasant experience for some coworkers (as an example, a Christian trying to convert a Jewish or Muslim employee may not be looked upon favorably). Can an employer state that employees are not allowed to discuss religion while working?

Answer: If the employer allows employees to discuss lifestyle issues such as sports, he must also allow discussions about religion. However, it is appropriate for an employer to tell his employees that they are not to discuss any non-work related topic while on the clock. Complaining employees should be told to put in writing all complaints and then the employer should do a complete investigation before taking any actions.

Exceptions (BFOQ's)

There are exceptions to the Civil Rights Act. If there is a claim of discrimination the employer can prevail if they can show that the discriminatory practice is a Bona Fide Occupational Qualification (BFOQ). This means that the protected trait (sex, race, national origin or religion) is necessary to do the job. If the practice (or trait) is a true BFOQ it will be allowed.

How can a discriminatory behavior be an occupational qualification? Let me give a real life example. A few years ago, a group of men filed suit against the Hooters restaurant chain alleging that Hooters practiced discrimination by not hiring the men to be waiters. While the restaurant would hire the men as kitchen staff, they only hired women for the wait staff. The men argued that waiters have the potential to make higher incomes than the kitchen staff. They argued that this was discriminatory as you do not have to be a woman to serve food and beverages.

The restaurant claimed that sex was a true BFOQ. They argued that customers didn't really go to the restaurant for the food (no big surprise there); they went there for the ambiance, mainly to see women in shorts and tight tops. The restaurant argued that if they were required to bring in male waiters, it would destroy the main theme of their business.

This was similar to an argument raised years earlier when the airline industry was sued for not hiring men as stewards. The airlines had argued that women had a calming influence over the passengers. The court, however, stated that the "calming influence" was not the central part of the stewardess job; serving drinks and giving safety instructions were. This could be done just as easily by men as by women. Thus, sex was not a BFOQ. The airlines lost.

Unfortunately before the court could rule on the Hooters case, the parties reached a settlement so the answer will never be known.

A BFOQ will serve as a defense to a claim of discrimination unless the court finds there is a less restrictive alternative. As an example, if a business hires men because they are taller and can reach items on high shelves, there may be an alternative of using ladders or stepstools. If however the alternative would be unduly costly or burdensome (like renovating entire portions of a building), the BFOQ may be upheld. We will be looking more at the issue of less restrictive alternatives when we discuss the Americans With Disabilities Act (ADA).

IS THERE
DISCRIMINATION?

How do you tell if there is in fact discrimination? It isn't easy. But there are some tools that can assist with the determination.

To determine if an employment practice has a disparate impact on one of the protected groups, the employer can calculate the percentage of minority applicants rejected over the percentage of non-minority applicants rejected. To make this calculation, look at the last 100 applicants for employment. Calculate the number of minority applicants that were rejected and the number of non-minority applicants that were rejected. Subtract these numbers from 100 to get the rate of selection. Then, divide the rate of selection of minorities by the rate of selection of non-minorities. If the result is less than 80% there is evidence of discrimination. Note that this is not proof, just evidence. Other factors may have taken part in the hiring decision that would explain the discrepancy.

Another tool the employer has is a comparison of his employee minority makeup versus the local population makeup. If minorities make up 25% of the local population and the employer hires 23% minorities, there would be evidence that the practices are not discriminatory. Again, this is just evidence, not proof. Whenever an employer uses one of these tools they should also look for other factors that might influence the result. For instance, an employer who hires based primarily on employee referrals will likely see the same minority composition maintained, while an employer who posts want ads in the newspaper may see a more representative mix.

CASE EXAMPLES

Case facts: There is a business with several divisions, some more desirable than others. The company has a rule prohibiting interdepartmental transfers. Historically, the company hired racially - only white employees got the better jobs while minorities got the less desirable. The employer realizes the hire practice is discriminatory and starts hiring without regard to race. Is there still discrimination?

Answer: Yes. While we commend the employer for changing the policies because of the prohibition on interdepartmental transfers, the previously hired minorities cannot advance to the more desirable positions.

Case facts: An applicant applies for a job and is rejected based on race. Subsequently, the employer stops advertising for the position and doesn't hire anyone. Can the applicant say that he was discriminated if the job goes unfilled?

Answer: Yes. If he can show that the employer stopped taking applications because of his, it is the same as if the employer hired another person.

Case facts: An employee files a claim against an employer for what he believes is a discriminatory action. It is later determined that the action is lawful. If the employer fires the employee, can the employee file charges against the employer for unlawful retaliation?

Answer: A strict reading of the anti-retaliation statute indicates it only applies if there were unlawful actions by the employer. However the courts are more kind and they have held that as long as the employee has a reasonable belief that what was being opposed constituted discrimination under Title VII, the claim of retaliation does not hinge on a showing that the employer actually was in violation.

Case facts: An applicant applied for a job as a city clerk, which requires dealing with the public. While the applicant scored high on the aptitude test, the city felt he was lacking in oral communication skills due to his heavy Filipino accent. He claims discrimination based on national origin.

Answer: National origin and accent are inextricably bound. To hold otherwise would allow any employer to avoid Title VII simply by using communication skills as a determinant. However, where the ability to speak clearly is an important job qualifications, the employer may use accent as a ground for denial.

Case facts: An employer required his employees to have a high school diploma and pass a standardized intelligence test in order to transfer to more desirable jobs. There was no discriminatory intent; he merely wished to upgrade the quality of his work force. The black employees challenged the rule stating that it had a discriminatory effect.

Answer: The lower and appellate courts held that there was no discriminatory intent and therefore no discrimination. However, the case then went to the

Supreme Court who held that Title VII not only proscribes overt discrimination, but also practices that are fair by form but discriminatory in effect. The touchstone is business necessity. Here there was no business necessity for these job applicants to have a high school diploma. The court pointed out that history is full of successful people who were not high school graduates.

Case facts: A photography studio turned down a black photographer who applied for a job because he had been convicted of forgery six years earlier. He had received a suspended sentence and five years probation. The applicant claimed the refusal to hire on the basis of his criminal record was essentially discrimination based on race as more minorities are convicted of crimes than non-minorities. He had completed his sentence and was qualified for the job. The employer stated that the employees routinely handled over $10,000 per year, which justified their policy of not hiring applicants whose honesty was questioned.

Answer: The court applied the business necessity rule and concluded that the conviction was related to the handling of money. However, due to the length of time since the conviction and his successful completion of his probation, it indicated that he would be a trustworthy employee. Generally, blacks are convicted much more frequently than whites and therefore a blanket rule against arrests or convictions would have a discriminatory effect. Therefore the employer must apply the business necessity rule to show the conviction is relevant to the employee's ability to do the job. To be a business necessity, the business purpose must be sufficiently compelling to override any racial impact, must effectively carry out the business purpose, and there must be no alternative which would better accomplish the business purpose.

HANDICAP DISCRIMINATION

Although we are discussing employment discrimination issues, it should be noted that these laws do not only affect employment, they may also apply to other circumstances. One example of this is college entrance standards. In the case Southeastern Community College v Davis, the U.S. Supreme Court had to determine if a college must admit a nursing student who had a serious hearing disability. The Court held that if the student met all the standards in spite of her handicap (not except for it) she should be admitted. The Court agreed with the trial court that Davis' handicap prevented her from safely performing in both her training and her desired profession. They held that in such circumstances the college does not have an obligation to lower or substantially modify their standards to accommodate a handicapped student (It is presumed that if she had a handicap that would allow her to train and practice safely, the holding would be different).

The Americans With Disabilities Act is probably the largest and most poorly written of any of the employment laws. This is an omnibus act that covers not just employment, but also public access, education, and much more. This will not be an in-depth look at the Americans with Disabilities Act. We simply don't have that kind of space in this paper. My copy of the ADA runs about 60 pages. And that doesn't include the hundreds of cases and guidelines that modify and clarify the Act. What we're doing here is a basic overview.

The Americans with Disabilities Act is probably the most comprehensive, and possibly the most controversial, law ever written on discrimination of the disabled. Let me start with a little history. The Americans With Disability Act was enacted in 1990. It was not the first attempt at civil rights legislation; the Civil Rights Act, also called Title VII, was enacted in 1964 to prevent discrimination based on Race, National origin, Religion, Sex and Color. The Architectural Barriers Act of 1968 required all federal buildings or federally assisted facilities to be fully accessible to the physically disabled. And the Rehabilitation Act of 1973 already prohibited discrimination against disabled people by recipients of federal funds. But the ADA expanded these Acts.

Now, let's look at the mechanics of the ADA. The purpose of the law is to guarantee disabled persons access to employment, public accommodation, transportation, public services and telecommunications; to prevent discrimination and to promote the integration of people with disabilities into our communities. The Act tries to ensure that all qualified individuals with disabilities enjoy the same opportunities as those without disabilities. We are going to focus on the ADA's impact on employment.

To understand the law, you must understand the terms and definitions used in it. There are five terms that need to be fully understood to comprehend the ADA: employers, disability, major life activity, mental impairment. As you will find, they are not necessarily what you believe them to be.

First employers. The law only applies to those employers who employ 15 or more employees for each working day in each of 20 or more calendar weeks in the current or preceding calendar year. The law does not apply to small business. If the employer has 14 or fewer employers, the law does not apply to them. Likewise, if the business hires over 15 employees, but only for short periods of time, so that the total period is less than 20 weeks in two years (for example, a Christmas gift wrapping business may need large numbers of employees for only about 4 weeks a year), they will not have to comply with the Act. To get around this, some employers try to classify their employees as independent contractors. While there is no clear delineation to separate an independent contractor from an employee, the determination comes down to control. If the employer exercises control over how the worker does a job, what hours they put in, or one of several other factors, the worker will be considered an employee regardless of how the employer classifies him.

Second disability. The term disability means a physical or mental impairment that substantially limits one or more of the major life activities of such individual; or a record of such an impairment; or being regarded as having such an impairment. This means that if a person does not have a disability, but is perceived to have one, they are still covered by the Act. This also means that if an employee has a problem that is controlled by medication they are protected by the Act. For example, employees who suffer from epilepsy, or depression which are controlled by medication are covered. However, employers are not required to make accommodations for disabilities they are not aware of. If the employee suffers from an illness that is not disclosed or readily observable, such as depression perhaps, there is no obligation to assist the employee. It is generally held that it is up to the employee to disclose their disability and to request accommodation. Still, the employer should be on the alert for signs that an employee may suffer from mental illness. Signs to look for include hostility to colleagues, chronic tardiness, and poor judgment. Regardless of disability, the person must be qualified to do the job. If the job requires an education, an uneducated person will not be covered by the Act regardless of their physical or mental condition.

Third is major life activity. A major life activity means things such as walking, sitting, seeing, hearing, performing manual tasks, caring for oneself, learning and working. Working, while a major life activity, is the last item thought about. Just because a person is unable to perform one job, does not make him disabled to perform others. As an example, a Supreme Court decision held that carpel tunnel syndrome, while hindering a person from doing a particular job, did not make them disabled. They could still perform other jobs. The Court explained the idea of having an impairment that affects a major life activity, stating that there must be an impairment that "prevents or severely restricts the individual from doing activities that are of central importance to most people's daily lives, such as walking, seeing and hearing." Although the Guidelines include working as a major life activity, the Court refused to consider whether working is a major life activity. This decision was a major restriction on the scope of the ADA. This case also continued the Supreme Court's trend in restricting the situation where the ADA applies.

The fourth term is mental impairment. The Act defines a mental impairment as any mental or psychological disorder, such as major depression, bipolar disorder, anxiety disorder, schizophrenia, and personality disorders. What is not considered a disability? The Act specifically excludes sexual behavior disorders and gender identity issues as well as compulsive gambling, kleptomania, pyromania and active drug use, although recovering drug addicts are covered, as are recovering alcoholics. There is a question as to when a drug addict is recovering and when there is active use. If a person starts attending Narcotics Anonymous meetings and has just received their white chip for one day sober, are they recovering? Probably not sufficiently for ADA protection. Two weeks? Two months? There is no set time period. Each case is determined on its own merits.

The Americans with Disabilities Act makes it unlawful for employers to discriminate against disabled applicants and employees in recruitment, hiring, firing, training, job assignments, promotions, pay, benefits, layoffs, leave or other employment related activities. This doesn't mean that there can be no difference between treatment of disabled and non-disabled employees. For example, it is acceptable for the employer to offer an insurance policy that does not cover mental disability. In fact, the law requires differentiation in treatment as it requires employers to make accommodations for disabled employees. We're going to talk about accommodation later, but I want to touch on a point here. Some people ask why we must make accommodations. Let me give an example. A man applies for a job at Winn Dixie as a butcher, but due to a medical condition, be it back, leg or arm trouble, he can't carry heavy weights. While he can cut meat, without accommodation,, since he can't carry the large sides of beef himself, he couldn't do the job. However, if Winn Dixie provides him a cart to wheel the beef on, or an assistant to help in moving the sides of beef, he could fill the position appropriately. Likewise, a person in a wheelchair might apply for a job as a receptionist, however the wheelchair doesn't fit behind the receptionist desk. If the employer got a different desk the disabled employee could do the job. These are qualified applicants. These are people who want to work. We don't want to penalize them for something they have no control over.

The Act does not specify which mental illness are covered or how to make the determination of mental disability, but the Guidelines to the Act adopt the determinations of the Diagnostic and Statistical Manual of Mental Disorders, put out by the American Psychiatric Association. The Act also does not state who must make a determination of mental illness or disability. The determination may be by psychologist, psychiatrist and even social workers in some circumstances. One of the areas to be careful in is depression. While chronic depression is covered, temporary depression, such as occurs with a boyfriend/girlfriend break up are not covered. As mentioned before, mental disability is still considered a disability even if it is controlled with medication. But what if the medication enhances the employment problems. Let me give you an example. An employee suffered from depression and was made sleepy at work from the medication he was prescribed to treat the condition. Also, because of his condition, he needed a work area away from public access and he needed substantial supervision to complete his tasks. He was terminated because he was routinely sleeping on the job, because he was unable to maintain contact with the public, and his need for constant supervision. He claimed a disability under the ADA, stating he was fully qualified to perform the essential function of the job and the employer had an obligation to make reasonable accommodations. Anyone want to guess how the Court ruled? While not giving a clear answer, the Court ruled that the employee was entitled to a trial to prove he could perform the essential functions of the job. While the catnaps were unprofessional, if the employee could prove he was qualified, the employer might be required to place the employee in a separate area with a cot. Just because the medication causes additional problems, the employee is still covered under the law, if he can accomplish the essential functions of the job.

Under the Americans with Disability Act, an employer need only hire someone if they can perform the essential functions of a job, with or without accommodations. The term essential function means the primary job duties that any qualified individual must be able to perform. Essential means that the function is a requirement of the job or requires some specialization. If an employee can perform the essential aspects of the job, even with the disability, they cannot be discriminated because of the disability. The employer is allowed to refuse to hire a disabled person if they feel, based on the information available, that hiring the disabled person would pose a risk to themselves or their fellow employees. As examples, the Supreme Court has allowed United Airlines to refuse to hire nearsighted women as pilots and has allowed Albertson's supermarket to refuse to hire a driver who was nearly blind in one eye. In refusing to hire an employee because of a disability, the employer can only use direct, factual information. As an example, many years ago, an employer fired an employee who had AIDS. His concern was that it posed a risk to the other employees, even though the county medical examiner and his own in-house physician, as well as the employee's physician told him there was no risk to the other employees. The employer cannot simply use stereotypical beliefs to do this. If the current medical thinking shows there is no risk, the employer cannot ignore that medical advice.

If the essential function of the job can be performed only with some accommodation, the question comes up whether the accommodation is reasonable. This is determined on a case-by-case basis. As an example, the following have been found to be reasonable accommodations: having a reader help a blind applicant, constructing ramps or elevators, lowering counters or drinking fountains, designing alternative forms of employee training, providing telephone devices for deaf persons. Accommodating a disabled employee may require restructuring job duties, or modifying work schedules. What is considered a reasonable accommodation in one case may not be in another. It depends on the situation of the business, the size of the business, the number of employees, the level of accommodation required, and many other factors. The employer will not be required to take action that involves an undue hardship such as changing the essential elements of the job or spending unreasonable sums of money. What might be considered reasonable for IBM's main factory may not be reasonable for a mom and pop grocery store.

It benefits the employer to accommodate employees with mental disability. Mental disorders are a major source of absenteeism, low productivity, accidents, turnovers, job dissatisfaction, and interpersonal conflict. Depression is associated with higher levels of disability than most chronic physical disorders. By working with the employees, the employer can increase company productivity and harmony. Further, there are financial savings to accommodating an employee. The average cost to accommodate an employee is only $955, while the cost to litigate an ADA lawsuit is $15,000.

What do you do if you or someone you know has been discriminated against in violation of the Americans with Disabilities Act? The ADA is enforced by two agencies- the Equal Employment Opportunity Commission (EEOC) and the Department of Justice (DOJ). For most purposes, the EEOC will be the agency you will report violations to. A complaint of discrimination must be filed within 180 days of the discriminatory treatment. The EEOC then is authorized to attempt to mediate and negotiate a settlement between the employee and the employer. If they fail to resolve the dispute, the EEOC has the option to either file a lawsuit on behalf of the employee in federal court, or issuing a "right to sue" letter to the employee which allows the employee to file a lawsuit on their own behalf. However, the time period for an employee to file an action after receiving the right to sue letter is VERY short- only 90 days.

The DOJ may also file suit in federal court. If successful, the Court may order compensatory damages and back pay to remedy the discrimination. They can also receive civil penalties of up to $50,000 for the first violation and $100,000 for subsequent violations.

What if your state law conflicts with the ADA? The Federal law pre-empts the state law. An example of this involves a bus driver in Kentucky who was in an accident and lost a leg. The driver received prosthesis and was able to drive again, however a State law stated that all bus drivers must have all their natural limbs. Under State law the judge would determine that the State could exclude the driver from the job. However, if the bus driver filed under the ADA the State could be ordered to reinstate him and give back pay and damages. Under our Federal constitution, when Federal law conflicts with state law, the Federal law will prevail.

I mentioned at the beginning that this is a controversial law. This has become more apparent recently. Many believe the law infringes on standard employment beliefs. Under normal employment law, unless there is a contract otherwise, an employer may terminate an employee for any reason or for no reason. The ADA prevents this. Many employers feel this is an infringement on their rights. Even the Supreme Court has weighed in against the ADA. Justice Sandra Day O'Conner stated that the Supreme Court must hear a high level of disability cases because the Act was so poorly written. She stated that Congress was in such a hurry to pass a disability law that they left too many holes and ambiguities in the Act, which means the Court must clarify and interpret it. Congress on the other hand disagreed stating that the Court was usurping Congress's power.

AGE DISCRIMINATION

After reviewing the Civil Rights Act and the ADA, it is time to turn our attention to another law: The Age Discrimination in Employment Act. This law protects employees over the age of 40 from being discriminated against based on their age. Specifically, it prevents employers from firing older employees to be replaced by younger (and cheaper) employees. The Act also forbids compulsory retirement policies. The ADEA forbids an employer from using age as a determining factor at all. If age plays any part in the employer's decision, no matter how small, a violation of the Act is presumed. The ADEA only affects those businesses with 20 or more employees.

Often, older employees have been with the company for extended periods and over the course of time have received pay raises that make them more costly than newer, younger employees. Also, as the employee reaches retirement age, certain benefits may start that the employer would rather not fund. Congress addressed this problem with the passage of the ADEA. Damages for a violation include doubling the actual compensatory losses and includes back pay and benefits. Employees can also get punitive damages under certain conditions, but there is a cap at $300,000.00.

In determining whether there has been a violation, the court will ask whether age was a determining factor in the sense that "but for the employer's motive to discriminate against him because of his age, he would not have been discharged". In other words, would the employee have been fired if he was younger? To make this determination, the Court may look at the company's hiring practices, the employee's performance evaluations, and the age of the employee hired to replace the fired worker.

This is not to say that an employer cannot fire an older worker. You can always fire an employee, no matter how old if their performance is unsatisfactory. Nor is it to say that a company cannot force an employee to retire at a certain age. However, to be subject to a compulsory retirement plan, the employee must be an executive in a policy-making position for two years before the termination or have a pension over $44,000.00. To use this executive exemption, the Court will not look at the employee's salary so much as the duties the employee performs.

Older employees may also be replaced with younger workers if labor costs have to be reduced. This is not simply for the employers convenience, but only if it is a true necessity for the business survival.

Employees may waive their ADEA rights. This is often done when companies ask their employees to take early retirement to reduce their labor costs. A waiver, to be valid, must meet specific legal requirements. If these are not complied with, the waiver will fail, even if the employee was paid for the waiver (the employee will also be allowed to keep the money paid for the waiver).

One of the requirements for an ADEA claim is that the terminated worker has been replaced by a younger worker. If the employee is replaced by technology, such as a robot or computer program, there is no ADEA claim.

What happens if the employee is terminated in violation of the ADEA but later the employer learns the employee was engaged in wrongdoing at the time? If the company is smart, it will re-fire the employee immediately upon learning of the wrongdoing. Otherwise, the damages for the wrongful termination may continue. The US Supreme Court has held that the purpose of the ADEA was not only to compensate victims of age discrimination, but also to deter employers from engaging in wrongful termination. On the other hand, the court recognized that the employer has legitimate interests that must be protected, and it must be permitted to discharge employees in cases of serious misconduct. As such, in the above example, the Court would award ADEA damages from the time of the first firing until the time of the second firing. If the employer has not re-fired the employee, it may be too late when the Court makes its ruling and a subsequent firing may look like retaliation.

THE EQUAL PAY ACT

Although there have been great strides through the years to increase the number of women in the workforce, to improve their salaries, and to allow them to work in areas previously restricted to men, progress is often slow.

Women as a whole make far less than men in similar positions. In 2010, for full time year round employees, women's median earnings were 81% of men's. For full-time wage and salary workers, women's earnings were 74.4% of men's. When race is considered, this disparity still exists, though not to the same extent. Black women make 94% of black men and Hispanic women earn 91% of Hispanic men. In other words, while black men as a whole make less than white men; black women make less than black men (under the same study, they found that Hispanic men made less than black men and conversely, Hispanic women made less than Hispanic men). There are numerous theories for this disparity, and there is insufficient room here to discuss them.

In 1963, to address the concern about this difference in salaries, Congress passed an amendment to the Fair Labor Standards Act called the Equal Pay Act. The EPA simply states that no employer shall discriminate in the payment of wages within a facility on the basis of sex for equal work. Unfortunately, this is easier said than done. A major question arises as to what is equal work.

In Montana, at the Yellowstone County Jail, this issue arose comparing the salaries of female jailers (called matrons) to the mail jailers (called jailers). The duties of the matrons resembled the duties of the jailers. Both had responsibility for booking prisoners, showering and dressing them, and placing them in appropriate sections of the jail depending on the sex of the offender. Because 95% of the prisoners were male and only 5% were women, the matron had more bookkeeping duties than the jailers. Yet, the jailers were paid $125 more per month than the matrons. The County argued that the discrepancy reflected the hazardous nature of the jailers work with male prisoners and the state's interest in protecting women because of the difference in strength between males and females. The Court, however, found that the working conditions were substantially equal for matrons and jailers and ruled that the wage difference was based on sex. The view of the county was exactly the type of anachronistic belief Congress intended to eliminate through the Equal Pay Act.

Through court decisions, there are essentially five guiding principles to help us determine the equal work standard:

1. The equal work standard only requires that the jobs be substantially equal; not identical.

2. When there is a wage difference between men and women, the burden is on the employer to show there is a reason other than sex.

3. Where some, but not all, of the members of one sex perform extra duties, those extra duties do not justify giving all members of that sex extra pay.

4. Women must be offered the opportunity to do the same extra jobs as men.

5. Job titles and job descriptions are immaterial in showing the work is unequal. It is the actual work performed that matters.

One escape that the EPA gives the employer is the catch-all exception. It states that a pay differential may be given for any reason other than sex. Examples are job assignments to lower-related jobs while retaining the previous salary, completion of a bona-fide training program, and part-time work.

If the Court does find a violation of the EPA, the employer's only remedy is to raise women's salary. Lowering the salary of the men is not an option.

SEXUAL HARASSMENT

A highly problematic area of employment is sexual harassment. There are two types of sexual harassment: "quid pro quo" which is the exchange of sexual favors for job advancement, and "hostile environment" which is where management allows an offensive or oppressive work place.

While quid pro quo cases are fairly easy to determine, hostile environment cases are not. What is offensive to some may not be to others. These must be determined on a case-by-case basis. Because every workplace is different, every situation is different. Although the courts will generally use a "reasonable man" standard, it is actually more appropriate to use a "reasonable woman" standard. In other words, would a reasonable woman be offended by the work environment? If the conduct is not pervasive enough to create an abusive work environment, there is no cause of action.

Also, even if the conduct is such that it would qualify, but the employees are not offended, there is no cause of action. As an example, let's say that a male employee makes sexually suggestive comments to a female employee on a regular basis. If this is unwanted and management makes no attempt to stop it, she may have grounds to sue the company. However, if the comments do not offend her (perhaps she even makes equally suggestive comments back to the man), then there are no grounds for a suit.

Management of a business has a responsibility to take actions to prevent sexual harassment from occurring. Sometime this is as simple as publicizing a sexual harassment policy. More often than not, more is required than this. The real problem is that often management will not know that harassment has occurred. In quid pro quo cases, where a supervisor is involved, knowledge of the harassment is imputed to the employer-whether they have actual knowledge or not. The reason for this is that many times the employee will feel that, because a supervisor is involved, reporting the action to the employer will be useless.

In these cases, mere maintenance of a fair treatment policy and a grievance procedure do not provide an automatic defense for the employer. In hostile environment situations, the employer has more protection in that a grievance procedure that is properly followed will give the employer more of a defense.

In hostile environment cases, the courts generally require actual knowledge by the employer and a failure to act. For the best protection, the employer needs to investigate fully all complaints of sexual harassment, regardless of how the employer individually feels about the actions. Just because the actions do not offend the employer, does not mean they won't offend the employees. A proper investigation includes interviewing both parties, interviewing other workers, having more than one person weigh the evidence and taking action or deciding not to take action depending on the circumstances.

To stand up, a sexual harassment policy:

1. Should include a statement prohibiting both quid pro quo and hostile environment situations and should state that the employer will investigate and correct any valid complaint.

2. Should require the employee to report any unwelcome event, and state that a failure to report the event will indicate a welcome relationship.

3. Should define hostile environment as containing sexual advances, innuendoes or vulgar statements that the employee objects to. The unwelcome relationship exists as soon as the employee says they object.

4. Should state that once the employer knows or should know of the event, the employer will investigate as soon as possible.

5. Should warn employees that once it is established that the policy has been violated, swift and severe action will be taken. If substantial facts cannot be established, the policy should call for the relationship to be monitored for a period of time.

6. Should state that there will be no retaliation for filing a complaint.

As an aside, it should be noted that employers may also be held responsible for harassment by their customers. If a customer makes unwanted advances to the employees, it is the responsibility of the employer to again investigate and take action against the customer, which may include barring the customer from the premises.

INVESTIGATION OF SEXUAL HARASSMENT

Whenever there is an allegation of sexual harassment, the employer needs to make a full and complete investigation of the facts. This leads to the question, "Can an investigation of sexual harassment be sexual harassment?"

In a case that explored this issue, government employees had accused a supervisor of promoting an employee based on a sexual relationship. Among the charges was that the employee was little more than the supervisors' "in-house sex slave", who provided sexual favors to the supervisor in exchange for more rapid promotions and other preferential treatment. Because this agency was an investigative office, the agency retained investigators from the defense department to carry out the investigation into the charges.

The investigators interviewed the supervisor, the underling and other employees in a hostile manner, and gave indications to the persons they were interviewing that they personally believed the parties were guilty of the charge. The manner in which the investigation was carried out spawned more rumors, widely circulated through the agency, including stories of incest and other sexual deviance, as well as a rumor that the supervisor was the true father of the underling's child. The supervisor and underling then filed charges of sexual harassment against the Department of Defense investigators for making these statements.

The Court determined that employers have a duty to investigate charges of sexual misconduct and must be given a long leash to conduct their investigation. If the employer fails to investigate a charge of sexual misconduct, they may be liable under Title VII. But, if the employer wants to demonstrate how seriously he takes such charges, and the investigation oversteps the proper bounds, causing humiliation to the targets of the investigation, should the employer then also be guilty of sexual harassment?

Police and other persons engaged in the investigation of misconduct, whether criminal or civil, sometimes stay across the line between vigorous and abusive investigation. The Courts were not willing to go to this level of responsibility; however, a prudent employer will perform any investigation with a level of professionalism to protect the reputations of all concerned until the employer is convinced otherwise.

Another area of concern in sexual discrimination is pregnancy and motherhood decisions. While pregnancy has several protections, motherhood does not. Often, especially with single mothers, absence becomes a major issue with their employer. Although employers often grant sick leave to their employees, this is for the employee's illness, not their children's. The employer may require documentation to prove the employee was ill. So what happens if the illness is to the employee's child? Sick leave is a benefit from the employer, not a right of the employee. There is no law that requires an employer to grant any sick leave to their employees (aside from the Family Medical Leave Act, but that is a different column). As such, the employer does not have to allow the employee any time off when a child is ill.

This is difficult, especially where there is a single parent. An employee who misses work because of a sick child risks being fired for the absence, unless approved by the employer first. Similarly, if an employer requires a parent to work late hours, to work the weekend, or to work overtime, the employee cannot refuse simply because there is a child to care for.

While motherhood is in the public interest, the courts have not recognized any public policy that would require the employer from demanding that their employees work long hours nor for the employees to refuse to work long hours due to their children's needs.

PREGNANCY AND FMLA

In the last column, I mentioned pregnancy rights and discrimination. It is unlawful for an employer to discriminate on the basis of pregnancy. The Pregnancy Discrimination Act articulates a per se rule that renders any distinction amount employees on the basis of pregnancy a sufficient bias for a prima facie case under Title VII. After the Plaintiff establishes a prima facie case, the burden shifts to the employer to come forth with a business necessity for its actions. Concern over a business necessity defense must be grounded on delivery of the services the business provides. There have been many challenges to this Act and most have failed. In one case, a hospital terminated an X-Ray technician upon learning about her pregnancy. The hospital claimed that Sylvia discharge was based on business necessity. They were concerned for the safety of the fetus given the X-Ray exposure that occurs during employment as an X-Ray technician. Moreover, the hospital claimed that the potential for future liability existed if an employee's fetus was damaged by radiation encountered at the workplace. The court held that a business necessity defense must be grounded on delivery of the services the business provides. Concern about possible future liability was not sufficient.

In a more recent case, a restaurant owner transferred

a pregnant waitress to a hostess position during her pregnancy, the waitress argued that the hostess position paid less than waitressing. The restaurant owner responded that the waitresses walked on average about 10 miles a day in the restaurant and he was concerned about the health of the fetus with such strenuous exercise. He was also concerned that the waitress might slip and fall, causing harm to herself and to the fetus. By transferring the waitress to a hostess position, he was attempting to accommodate the employee while protecting the baby. Once the baby was delivered, he would transfer the employee back to waitress status. The court deemed this too to be discriminatory behavior. Any discrimination based upon the condition of pregnancy is disfavored. While it is good to be concerned with the health of the child, the ultimate responsibility for that lies with the mother.

To accommodate mothers who have recently had children, Congress passed the Family and Medical Leave Act. Originally only to allow mothers time away from work to care for the newborn children, the Act now covers any medical condition of the employee or their immediate family. The FMLA allows employees who have worked 1250 hours in the last 12 months to take up to 12 weeks of unpaid leave. Except in cases of emergency, the employee must give prior written request for FMLA leave for the birth or adoption of a child, and for the care of child, spouse, or parent who has a serious health condition. FMLA only covers those employers with 50 or more employees within a 75-mile radius.

FMLA regulations define a serious health conditions one that result in three or more days of "incapacity" together with either at least two treatment visits with health care provider or one visit followed by a "regimen of continuing treatment". The Court has expanded FMLA to also include a series of medical illnesses, which individually would not qualify, but in the aggregate would. The Court summarized its conclusion with these memorable words, "after all, it is not the disease that receives leave from work; it is the person."

AFFIRMATIVE ACTION

Is Affirmative Action still necessary? Studies seem to indicate it is. There is, unfortunately, abundant proof that the U.S. is not yet a colorblind society. Attitudinal studies show that stereotypes are pervasive. In one study, 53% of the white survey respondents rated blacks less intelligent than whites, and 62% thought blacks were "less hard working." Government public education spending is clearly linked to race. Schools serving mostly minority, inner city children receive about one half the money per student than schools in surrounding white suburbs receive. In 1990, the average black male worker earned $731 for every $1,000 earned by a white male worker. Latino men earned $810 for every $1,000 earned by similarly educated white men. Although white males make up only 43% of the workforce, they occupy 97% of the top executive positions at America's 1,500 largest corporations.

The largest group of Americans to benefit from affirmative action thus far are women. Before 1964, women were excluded from many higher paying occupations and professions based on stereotype, custom and law. There were no women police officers, truck drivers or pilots, and women lawyers and doctors were rare. But despite progress, many barriers to full equality remain. Men make up 99% of all auto mechanics and carpenters; 98% of all firefighters; 97% of all pilots and 95% of all welders. Overall, American women earn only 72% of what men make for comparable work. Women hold only 3-5% of senior positions in the private sector.

Opponents claim affirmative action forces employers to "give preference" to less qualified minorities. Equating affirmative action with quotas, they argue that color-blind laws are fairer than those that take race into account. But affirmative action is not a quota system, nor does it give preferential treatment to unqualified minorities and women. Indeed, there is absolutely no law that requires an employer to hire a less qualified worker over a more qualified worker.

Employers and universities have always engaged in forms of "preferential treatment." It was only when race and gender became a factor in the effort to end discrimination that preferences became a problem. Yet there are many examples of long-accepted preferential treatment. University preference of veterans over non-veterans or of children of alumnae over other youth is one example; employers hiring the sons and daughters of their economic and social equals (the "old boys club") is another.

Requiring that qualified minorities and women be actively recruited and, whenever appropriate, hired is the only way that previously excluded minorities and women can gain a toehold in companies, occupations and schools that were previously reserved for white men. It's fairness itself.

Does Affirmative Action result in Reverse

Discrimination? Perhaps, although in fact only 1.7% of all race-based charges filed with the Equal Employment Opportunity Commission have been filed by white males.

Unfortunately, many people do not truly understand what an affirmative action plan is. To qualify, there must be a showing that a remedial measure is needed. If there is no history of discrimination or inequality in the workforce, an employer does not need an affirmative action plan. The only exception is private sector jobs that receive government funds, which must have an affirmative action plan. Next, the plan must be voluntary, must not unnecessarily infringe on the interests of white employees, and must be temporary. Once the racial or sexual imbalance is ended, the plan is ended.

PRIVACY RIGHTS

In today's more electronic world, the issue of privacy rights of employees arises more and more frequently. Privacy rights include how to supervise workers, use of electronic mail, and searches of private areas. While many employees don't like to be under such scrutiny, most of the laws in this area lean towards the employer. Privacy rights are based upon employee expectations. Employers can destroy employee expectations of privacy simply by establishing office rules. If these rules tell employees that their lockers, desks, file cabinets and so forth are subject to inspection by the company at any time, there can be no employee privacy expectations in those areas.

The common law right of privacy encompasses four distinct causes of action, only three of which are generally relevant as workplace torts. The four are: misappropriation of the plaintiff's name or likeness without his consent; intrusion by the defendant into an area in which plaintiff's reasonable expectations of privacy are violated; public disclosure of private facts about the plaintiff; and portrayal of the plaintiff in a false light in the public eye (Misappropriation of name and likeness, while a business issue, is generally not considered a workplace tort. We will discuss this with intellectual property rights later).

Intrusion rights must be considered whenever employees' desks or work areas are searched, or personal records such as credit card accounts or bank records are obtained in an investigation. In an intrusion claim arising from a workplace investigation, an employee may claim that the employer violated his legitimate expectation of privacy. The question of whether such an expectation should exist is generally an issue of fact.

As an example, if a company provided lockers and locks for the employees, it is likely that the employer would have the right to search the lockers at any time. However, if the company requires the employee to provide their own locks, then they develop an expectation that the locker will be free from intrusion and interference.

This issue arises in types of supervision as well. Many employers in today's world have learned that video can provide cheaper supervision than actual managers. This is especially true when the employer fears theft by the employees. The theory is that a video camera can watch numerous employees simultaneously, while a manager can generally only watch one or two workers. The company can install cameras to watch supervise the workers, and then hire a single employee to monitor the cameras. While many employees feel this is an infringement on their privacy (every move the employee makes is recorded), so long as certain guidelines are met, video surveillance is allowed. The Courts look at cameras as just another manager. If a manager could stand in the room and watch the employees, so can a camera. This is not to say there are no restrictions. The cameras must capture video only-not sound. Many states (including Florida) have wiretapping laws. These laws prevent the recording of a person's voice without their consent. The laws, however, do not prevent the visual recording of a person without their consent. So long as the cameras do not record sounds, they will not be in violation of the wiretapping laws.

Another restriction is where the cameras may be placed. Again, the cameras may be placed anywhere that a manager may lawfully observe workers. Therefore, the cameras may not monitor places where the employee expects privacy, such as restrooms.

To be safe, an employer should notify the employees that the cameras are going to be installed and where they will monitor. This is true, even if the cameras are going to be placed in plain view.

CONFIDENTIALITY OF EMPLOYEE RECORDS

Most employers know the Americans With Disabilities Act (ADA) require them to keep employee medical records in separate, confidential files. Many employers, however, are not completely certain how they should respond to third party requests for such confidential medical information.

What if an employee is the plaintiff in a personal injury action and the defendant's lawyer serves you a subpoena to turn over the medical records of the employee (this may be done to determine if there was a pre-existing condition, or if the injury may be work related rather than the result of an accident)? Or what if the employee's union representative wants access to the records so they can negotiate fully with management to protect employee rights or to ensure reasonable accommodation by the employer? Or what if the employee needs medical care on the property? Can you turn over their medical records to paramedics? The answer provided by the ADA is different for each situation.

Privacy of medical records is crucial. While some medical conditions may be obvious, like an employee who is a paraplegic, others may not be, such as an employee with HIV. Further, because many medical conditions, such as HIV, still carry a stigma with them, the disclosure of this information could result in poor treatment of the employee or even alienation by their co-workers.

Under the ADA, employers cannot disclose confidential medical information from their files to unions without the employee's consent. There are limited exceptions to this rule. While the union representative may argue that they need to be made aware of the employee's medical conditions so they can carry on effective collective bargaining, this is not sufficient grounds for violating the privacy of the employee. If the employee is not concerned about this, they can authorize disclosure.

Disclosure of medical records is permitted to first aid and safety personnel, government officials and even worker's compensation officers.

The more troubling situation arises with the Court subpoena. Common sense and traditional personnel practices would allow the employer to respond to a lawful court subpoena. Indeed, if the employer refuses to comply with that subpoena, they can be held in contempt of court. The answer provided in the ADA's confidentiality rules is that the employer would violate the ADA if it turned over the records in response to the subpoena. Congress did not make an exception and as a federal law, it pre-empts any state law. Congress made an exception for compliance with federal statutes or rules even where the other federal rule or statute conflicts with the ADA, but they chose not to make a similar exception for state laws. This means that while an employer can lawfully violate a federal law in order to comply with the ADA, they cannot defend against an ADA charge on the basis that the actions were required by state law.

Problems still remain for the employer. The State Court will certainly not be pleased that its subpoena was ignored by the employer and the employer may face a charge of contempt of court with possible penalties including fines and perhaps incarceration. At the same time, if the employer complies with the subpoena and provides the records they risk being sued by the employee for violating the ADA. This could also result in penalties such as fines against the employer. The employer would escape this dilemma only if the employee consented to the disclosure and released the employer from ADA liability.

PRIVACY AND EMAIL

When can you read your employee's personal e-mail? The answer is surprising. Various circumstances can arise in the work place which may allow employer access to employee e-mail. For instance, certain employer business records and documents may be stored on employee computer files. However, what if the employee is using the business e-mail system for personal correspondence? Employers may monitor e-mail to assure "that the system is not being used in a way that may be disruptive, offensive to others or harmful to morale." As an example, the employer may monitor e-mail to ensure that the employees are not transferring illegal or immoral material. In addition, employers may review e-mail in connection with the reasonable investigation of possible employee misconduct. If the company works with sensitive or confidential information, they may monitor e-mail to ensure that careless or disloyal employees are not disclosing such information to competitors.

Employees, however, are not without remedies which protect their communications from illegal monitoring by their employers. In 1986, the Electronic Communications Protection Act (CPA) was drafted to clarify the federal privacy laws based on the emerging telecommunication technologies. The CPA creates both civil and criminal liability for the intentional interception and disclosure of any wire, oral or electronic communication.

"Interception," as defined by the statute, is "the aural or other acquisition of the contents of any wire, electronic or oral communication through the use of any electronic, mechanical or other device." While this seems to give the employee a great deal of protection, there are three exceptions under which an employer may avoid liability under this statute: (1) the consent exception; (2) the business extension exception; (3) the provider exception.

Under the consent exception, an employer may monitor an electronic communication so long as one of the parties to the communication has consented to being monitored. There is no requirement that the other recipient consent or even know of the monitoring. The employer's interception of the e-mail's, however, must not exceed the scope of the employee's consent. In addition, an employee's knowledge of the employer's monitoring capability alone is insufficient to be considered implied consent. The employer must specifically inform the employees of the extent and circumstances under which e-mail communications will be monitored.

The business-extension exception allows monitoring of employee e-mail if the employer establishes a business-related reason for such monitoring. Under this very broad exception, the employer may monitor communications in the ordinary course of business, without being in violation of the CPA, so long as the employer can articulate a reasonable business purpose for the interception.

The final exception is called the "provider exception" which grants providers of an electronic communication service the right to monitor e-mail communications if the monitoring is needed to protect the provider.

To protect themselves from liability, employers should develop and adopt clear and concise policies and procedures regarding the use of company computers, specifically e-mail. These policies should state that the use of the computer system is limited to "company business" and that the employee has no reasonable expectation of privacy in the electronic messages and information transmitted, received and stored on and/or through the company's computer system. Each employee should be required to sign these policies. If this is done, the employer has a strong defense to a potential invasion of privacy claim by an employee if the employer later begins monitoring the employees' e-mail.

VARIOUS EMPLOYMENT LAWS

The Equal Pay Act is like a Civil Rights Act for salary. It is only gender based and the goal is to get women to a pay scale similar to men.

The Equal Pay Act is based on the theory of equal pay for equal work. Even if the jobs the employees are performing are different, if they require similar effort and similar skill, they should receive similar pay. There are four exceptions to the Equal Pay Act: seniority, merit, quantity/quality of work, and any factor except gender. Interestingly, the Act is not complied with by reducing the salary the men receive; the only solution to an Equal Pay violation is to increase the salary of the women.

The next law to look at is the Employees Retirement Income Security Act (ERISA). This law protects pension plans. It requires that employers protect their employee's interest in pension funds by requiring reporting and accounting of pension accounts. It requires vesting of pension rights after five or seven years. It also allows continuation of vesting, even after a short leave of absence. The Act requires the employers to sufficiently fund the retirement program and created an insurance program in case the employer goes out of business.

The next issue is Unemployment Compensation. Most of us are familiar with this. Unemployment compensation is available to any employee who is discharged due to no fault of their own. There are both federal and state unemployment plans. Usually, the employee must work for a period of time before they are covered and must be available for similar work after they are terminated. If the employee quits or is fired for cause, they are not entitled to get benefits (unless they can show that conditions at their job were so oppressive as to force them to quit). Unemployment benefits are funded through the payment of taxes.

Social security- Many of us are familiar with this program since we contribute to it every payday. Social security is funded by taxes to provide retirement benefits, disability, life insurance, and health insurance benefits. Social security is not just for retirees; many people of all ages receive social security benefits for a variety of reasons.

The Occupational Safety and Health Act of 1970 (OSHA) was passed to make sure employees had safe environments to work in. OSHA created rules to establish safety and health standards in the workplace and enforces compliance with those standards. OSHA requires every employer to provide a workplace free from hazards that are likely to cause physical injury or death. Under the Act, employers must keep records of occupational injuries and illnesses that results in death, loss of consciousness, one or more days off work, or medical treatment past first aid. OSHA is enforced by the Department of Labor.

Worker's Compensation (in some places referred to as Workman's Compensation) is basically an insurance program. It usually is only required of employers who have two or more employees (though the number of employees changes based on the industry). Generally, if the employer offers Worker's Compensation, and an employee suffers a work related injury, the employee's sole remedy is limited to Worker's Compensation benefits; the employee cannot sue the employer. Employers with less than the required number of employees may still carry Worker's Compensation, but it is not required. If an employer does not carry Worker's Compensation and an employee suffers a work related injury, the worker may be able to sue the employer and get far greater benefits than what Worker's Compensation would provide.

Next we have the various immigration laws. These laws require employers to only hire U.S. Citizens or legal aliens. They also require the employer to verify the status of their non-U.S. Employees. The burden of proof to prove the employee is legally able to work is on the employer when they hire the employee. However, as discussed previously, the employer cannot ask certain questions during the application process. They may only ask to see certain documents and ask if the applicant can legally work. Questioning a prospective employee more than that risks violating the Civil Rights Act.

The Fair Credit Reporting Act (FCRA) permits credit bureaus to release to employers the credit reports of prospective employees for employment purposes. Some employers use credit reports to screen applicants for sensitive positions, such as cashier or courier. Other employers use them to get a general indication of an applicant's honesty and personal integrity. When a decision to deny employment is based in part on a credit report, the employer must disclose this to the applicant, along with the name and address of the credit bureau used. The disclosure notice allows the applicant to obtain a free copy of the report to check it for accuracy. This disclosure is required even if the credit report was not the main reason employment was denied. The following examples illustrate situations where the notice must be given to job applicants.

■ A business receives 100 applications for a cashier position. It obtains credit reports on all of them and dismisses 50 from further consideration based on information contained in the credit report. The remaining 50 have good credit histories. All but 10 of them are ultimately rejected for other reasons. The first 50 applicants are entitled to the notice as their rejections were based solely on their credit reports.

■ A person with an unfavorable credit history is denied employment after review of their credit report. Although the credit history was considered a negative factor, the applicant is entitled to the notice because the credit report played a part - however minor - in the employer's decision.

■ An employer is looking for an employee to fill a particularly sensitive position. He rejects one applicant with a good credit repayment history because the report shows a debt load that may be too great for the proposed salary. Another applicant is rejected because a credit shows only one credit line, and the employer prefers to hire someone who has demonstrated financial responsibility. Both applicants are entitled to notices. If any information in the report influences an adverse decision - even though the information may not be otherwise thought of as "negative" - the disclosure must be given.

Employers who do not provide the disclosure when it is required may face several consequences. Under the FCRA, individuals can sue employers in federal court for actual damages suffered from an FCRA violation. A person who successfully sues under the FCRA is entitled to recover court costs and a reasonable attorney's fee. The law also permits suing for punitive damages if it is established that the employer willfully violated the law. In addition, the FTC (and other Federal agencies) may sue users of credit reports who do not comply with the FCRA. Most employers (except banks and a few other employers) are subject to the FTC's jurisdiction.

Employer polygraph testing is governed by the Employee Polygraph Protection Act of 1988, which broadly prohibits the use of polygraphs by employers. The Act makes it unlawful for any employer to require, request, suggest or cause any employee or prospective employee to take or submit to any lie detector test or to use or rely upon the results of any polygraph test for the purpose of discharging or disciplining any employee. The Act imposes restrictions on the nature of the testing, the person to whom the test results may be disclosed, and the uses to which the information derived from the test may be put. A limited exception to this prohibition is in cases of ongoing investigations involving economic loss or injury to the employer's business, such as by theft, embezzlement, misappropriation, or an act of unlawful industrial espionage or sabotage.

The various employment laws do not start when the employee is hired. They begin before the employee even applies for the job. It is impermissible to ask many questions in the hiring interview. Those questions include: How old are you? Where were you born? Are you married? Any children? Are you pregnant now? Do you have a military background? Have you ever been arrested? Are you a member of any organizations, like the Rotarians, the Jaycees, anything like that? Do you have any disabilities?

Each of these questions may elicit information that could violate one or more of the employment laws. The employer must be careful that improper information does not influence his decision to hire. Many times the information may be obtained, but only after the employer has made a conditional job offer.

EMPLOYMENT CONTRACTS

An employment relationship is a contractual one. It can be spoken or written, but in either case is usually expressly stated. Not always though. An employment agreement may be implied in certain situations.

An employment contract is usually negotiated between the employee and the employer. They discuss terms such as hours to be worked and wages to be paid. These are then usually incorporated into the employment contract. How many people (outside of Realtors and car salesmen) would accept a job if they didn't know how much it would pay?

Occasionally, when an employer has a large number of employees, they may do these types of negotiations in mass. One negotiation to cover a group of employees is called a Collective Bargaining Contract. It is a creation of the labor movement. When unions started gaining strength, they negotiated a single contract for all the employees performing a certain type of work. These collective bargaining agreements would set hours, wages, promotion and seniority, retirement and many other issues. After the collective bargaining agreement is negotiated, the employees must ratify or reject it. This is done by a vote of all employees in the union. If the contract is accepted, the workers go to work. However, if it is rejected, the negotiators must return to the table and start over again.

Usually employment contracts do not have a time component. In other words, they generally do not state that a person will be employed for a specified period of time. Employers do not want to be tied to keeping employees that may not work out. This is not to say an employment contract can't have a time line. If the contract states that a person will work for a specific period of time (such as a year), the employer generally cannot fire the employee during that period, without paying some compensation. They must wait until the contract runs out or they must buy-out the remaining term. This is seen with executive contracts occasionally. If a contract does not have a time clause, it is considered terminable at will. This means that the employer can fire the employee at any time with no notice. Usually, unless the contract states to the contrary, they don't even need a reason. On the other hand, the employees can also quit at any time.

There are some restrictions to the ability to fire at will. Usually an employer can fire with or without reason. If fired for no reason, the employee can usually apply for unemployment benefits. There are some instances where the employer is precluded from firing an employee. The Whistle Blower Act is one. If an employee reports the employer for violation of a statute or regulation, the employer cannot fire the employee for the reporting.

Occasionally when the employee actually tries to negotiate the contract, they can install a clause that states the employee can only be fired for cause. This is beneficial to the employee because it requires the employer to find a reason to fire the employee. Unfortunately, it is often not hard to do. Grounds may include: not performing duties satisfactorily, dishonesty, theft or fraud, insubordination, disloyalty, or use of drugs or alcohol while at work (or so near in time as to still be under the influence). Employers are often allowed to fire for economic reasons as well. These are known as layoffs or "reductions-in-force" and are usually based on the "last hired first fired" theory.

LABOR

HISTORY OF UNIONS

The first real attempt at a national labor movement was the Knights of Labor, started in 1869. This was a secret society with a membership at its highest of 700,000. It had two major goals: to change the existing labor-management relationship; and to attain moral betterment for employees and society. They believed that lawyers and money people were hurting society. They worked to achieve their goals by increasing political activity, encouraging employees to save their money to buy businesses, to actively avoid the use of strikes, and to educate the members of society. One of the main reasons the Knights of Labor failed is that their membership included almost everyone, not just workers. They failed to realize that people have different motivations and needs. By focusing on attacking the lawyers and money people, they forgot that the purpose of business is to make money and the goal of labor is to get higher pay and more benefits. These goals are mutually exclusive.

The Knights of Labor were strong believers in educating the workers. They required members to dress up and attend educational seminars in the evenings. For a guy who has already worked a 10-hour day, that's asking an awful lot. The Knights finally ended after a labor riot caused several people to be killed. Public sentiment turned against the union and it folded.

The next major attempt at a national labor union was the American Federation of Labor, formed in 1886. Rather than form one big union, the AFL wanted small unions to form a federation, or a co-operative. The AFL was not interested in educational seminars for their members, like the Knights of Labor. They simply wanted to create better work environments. They had two major objectives: get the workers more money, and enhance the capitalist system. This gave a focus on short-term goals. The AFL used three tactics to reach their goals: strikes, politics, and an increased status of collective bargaining. For the first time, they realized that different trades had different needs; automotive workers have differing needs than plumbers who have differing needs from electricians. They chose to form a federation because the concept of one big union wouldn't work due to the differing needs of the members. The AFL gained strength from a strike at the Carnegie Steel Mill. This was an extremely violent strike, which was ultimately won by management. But the AFL showed that they were willing to take care of their members during the strike. For the first time, the union provided funds to cover member expenses during the strike.

In 1905, a new unionizing effort was started: the Industrial Workers of the World (IWW). The IWW was a radical group seeking the overthrow of the existing capitalistic system. The IWW didn't last long. They lacked a permanent membership because most of the people they attracted were unemployed and often unemployable. Because they were a radical group, they alienated both the media and the government- not an easy thing to do.

The AFL survived partly because of timing. When World War I came, the government realized the need for a strong labor force and uninterrupted production and made a deal with the AFL. The government improved labor conditions and started enforcing labor laws. They gave the AFL seats on national commissions. The AFL was given a new level of respectability. However, after the war, the cost of living rose and the cost of labor didn't. This led to a lot of strikes.

In 1935 there was a split in the AFL and a new union group was created called the Congress of Industrial Organizations (CIO). They wanted to organize employees working in the mass production industries. The CIO had rapid growth for a number of reasons. First, the leaders sought out immigrants who had previously not been well represented. Second, they had realistic goals. Like the AFL they sought short-term gains not long term. Third was the use of sit down strikes. This was an effective tool until ruled illegal by the Supreme Court. Fourth was the passage of the Wagner Act which created the National Labor Relations Board (NLRB) and authorized collective bargaining. Finally was the realization by employees that unions could give them job security.

Since World War II, we've see increased concerns over the issue in collective bargaining. Issues such as employee benefits and cost of living increases have been included as part of the collective bargaining process. In 1955, the AFL and CIO merged, combining over 15 million workers.

WHAT THE UNION DOES FOR EMPLOYEES AND EMPLOYER

The National Labor Relations Act (NLRA) states that its purpose is to stimulate commerce and encourage collective bargaining. It guarantees certain employee rights, including the right to form and organize labor unions, the right to join or not join a union, the right to collective bargaining and the right to engage in protected concerted activities of mutual aid and protection. The Act details specific unfair labor practices of both the union and management. As examples, employers are forbidden from interfering, restraining or coercing employees from exercising their unionizing rights. This even includes creation of a company union or recommending to employees which union to join. Discrimination against employees for union practices is illegal, as is refusing to participate in collective bargaining in good faith.

As for the union, it cannot coerce employees from exercising their rights under the act. The union cannot take action to force an employer to discriminate against non-union members and it must also bargain in good faith. There are four specifically enumerated activities unions cannot do: They cannot require the employer to enter a "hot-cargo" agreement (an agreement that union members will not be required to handle goods produced by non-union companies or companies which are on strike); they cannot restrict the use, selling, handling or transportation of goods made under a labor dispute; they cannot force an employer to negotiate with one union if another union has already been certified to represent the employees; and they cannot cause the employer to assign work to a particular union rather than another.

The act is enforced by the National Labor Relations Board (NLRB). The function of the board is to supervise union elections and adjudicate unfair labor practices. If a complaint is filed for unfair labor practices, the procedure is as follows: First, a charge is filed. It is investigated by the regional director, who may refuse it, seek an injunction or file a complaint. The general counsel then reviews the decision of the regional director and may seek an injunction or withdraw the complaint. If the injunction is sought, the complaint goes to a hearing. At the hearing, the administrative judge may dismiss the case, issue a remedial order or remand the case back to the regional director. The court of appeals may review a dismissal or order which may also be reviewed by the Supreme Court.

The NLRB has its critics. Because most of the work is done on the regional level, the board is only as good as the various regions. The board also suffers in that it is unable to obtain re-instatement for employees and is often slow in discharging cases.

Now let's move to the Railway Labor Act (RLA), which

covers unionization of employees of railways and airlines, passed in 1926. It relies almost entirely on collective bargaining and established mandatory mediation of disputes before the National Mediation Board. In a dispute, if mediation is not successful, then the parties may go to arbitration, if both sides agree. If one side rejects arbitration, there is 30-day status quo period where the President of the United States may appoint an emergency board to resolve the dispute. The purpose of the RLA is to avoid interruption of commerce, forbid limitation of employee rights, to provide independence for the parties and have a prompt and orderly settlement of disputes.

The RLA was amended in 1934 barring the employer from influencing the elections, and forbidding the creation of company unions (a union formed by management for the employees and run by management) and yellow-dog contracts (an agreement between an employer and employee that the employee will not join a union nor assist in forming one). The RLA has proven very successful. More than 90 percent of grievances are resolved each year by neutral referees.

There are some significant differences between the RLA and the NLRA. The RLA holds elections by mail; the NLRA usually holds elections at the work place by secret ballot. A much higher percentage of employees are covered under the RLA than the NLRA. Under the RLA, the union cannot strike and the management cannot lockout employees until they have exhausted all other required procedures. Under the NLRA, the union can strike or management lockout employees after filing the appropriate notices. Under the RLA, grievances go to arbitration which is paid for by the government. Under the NLRA, arbitration is negotiated and is paid for by the individual parties.

PHASES OF LABOR RELATIONS

There are three phases in the labor relations process: First is the recognition of the legitimate rights and responsibilities of the union and the management representatives. This includes the right of employees to unionize and the responsibilities under the various laws. Second is the negotiation of the labor agreement, which includes the strategies employed during the negotiations. Third is the administration of the labor agreement; that is, making sure all the provisions of the agreement are followed. This includes the procedures for strikes and lock-outs when provisions are not followed. These phases are cumulative. Each relies on the previous phase to work. If you don't recognize a union's right to form, you won't negotiate an agreement. If you don't negotiate the agreement, there is nothing to administer.

Labor relations involve various participants: management officials, union officials, employees, government, and even third parties, such as mediators and negotiators. These players are grouped into two sections which reflect the workers and the management. The workers are often in a tough position here, especially if they like their employer. If the employer takes care of the workers, they may feel a loyalty to the employer as well as a loyalty to their union. This can cause a conflict, as their interest are not necessarily the same and a benefit to one may hurt the other. Management's primary responsibility is to the shareholders. If the management goes against the wishes of the union, the union may go on strike which could hurt the value of the shares.

There are various influences that affect labor relations. These include technology, the market, public opinion and the economy. Each of these plays a part in the negotiating a labor agreement. For example, if public opinion is against the unions, their position is weaker and the terms are less advantageous. This is why, when there is a strike, both sides try to flood the media with their positions to sway the public to back them. Another example is technology. If a business is trying to bring in robotics, the workers could see this as a threat to their jobs, even though it may strengthen the company as a whole. This will influence the negotiations.

The company may determine that for economic reasons it needs to take a non-union strategy. These include the following:

Union Suppression - This is an attempt to bust up an already existing union. It includes the use of illegal tactics, refusing to bargain with the union in violation of the NLRB, decertification of the union, filing for bankruptcy and encouraging strikes so that non-union replacement workers can be brought in.

Union Avoidance - The employer attempts to eliminate the need for a union through positive human resource techniques. Another method is to develop subsidiary companies - one with a union and one without (called double-breasting).

Union Substitution - This includes various tactics used to take over the purpose of the union such as forming employee committees for the discussion of grievances, paternalism - where the employer takes a fatherly position with his employees, worker participation in company decisions and company sponsored employee organizations.

If the company determines that the union is a necessary component, they have two positions they may take. The employer can stay neutral, or they can work with the union, forming a type of partnership where the two co-exists to their mutual benefit.

THE LEVELS OF UNIONS AND HOW THEY ARE ORGANIZED

There are four levels of unions: Local, national or international, intermediate and federations.

Local unions - these are branches of the national unions in most cases. They have day-to-day contact with the workers, which results in greater loyalty by the workers. Ask a union member what union he is with and he will usually respond, "Local 582" or something similar.

Within the local union, there are two subdivisions - craft and industrial. Craft unions are organized based on the skills of the members; industrial unions are organized based on the company they work for. As an example, a teachers' union may cover all educators within a geographical region, such as Monroe County. This would be a craft union. However, a union of all workers at Key West High School would be an industrial union as it covers all types of employees working at a single location.

This makes some differences in the unions. Agreements for craft unions can be shorter because they don't have to cover as many issues. Training issues also are different as members of a craft union already have their basic skills. Therefore, their training is more like continuing education. Since craft workers are doing the same job, they act like a closed shop. Participation in local union meetings is traditionally low, unless there is an issue which directly affects the employee's livelihood. Even though meetings have a low turnout, they are important. Decisions are made at this level and passed upward to the national level. This includes election of officers and ratification of contracts.

National unions - These are the unions with power, merely because of their size. A local union can go on strike and affect a shop; a national union can go on strike and affect an industry. Like our state and federal government, they operate under a constitution that spells out the rules. They usually hold annual conventions where they elect leadership and pass rules of the national organization. The convention is where the national leaders and the local leaders can get together.

There is more formal leadership structure on the national level with officers and an executive board to direct the affairs of the union. The national union offers various services to the locals. They negotiate with management, they arbitrate disputes, they administer the agreement, they coordinate strike movements, they provide advice, counsel, and occasionally legal services. The national unions also seek out partners to become bigger and stronger. Most of the labor leaders come from working-class families. While the majority have some college education, few are graduates.

Intermediate unions - these are the groups between the local and the national unions. They include the district and regional offices that act as intermediaries between the two groups. Also in the intermediate union categorizations are the independent unions that don't have any association with the nationals. There aren't many independent unions; they exist mainly in the service industry or health care industry.

Federations - A federation is a conglomerate of other unions. The biggest and most well-known is the AFL-CIO. It is composed of approximately 73 national and international unions with 14 million members. They let each of the affiliates conduct their own affairs, but they provide certain services to their members: They speak for labor throughout the world; they coordinate many activities such as education, voter drives and lobbying; they assist in conflict resolution; and they coordinate organizing efforts. The structure of the AFL-CIO reflects the size of the organization. The supreme governing body is the convention which meets every two years. The executive council is composed of the president, secretary/treasurer and 51 vice-presidents. There are standing committees for various subjects and a general board to act on matters referred to it by the executive board. There also are central bodies to advance their respective interest within the federation. The federation, like the union, is financed by member dues

HOW DO YOU GET A UNION STARTED?

There are three ways to form a union:

1) Voluntary recognition by the employer - if employee support for the union is clearly evident and the union is acceptable to the employer, no election is needed.

2) National Labor Relations Board directive - under certain circumstances, the NLRB may order the employer to recognize a union. To issue a directive, all of the following conditions must exist: a) a fair election would be impossible because of flagrant employer unfair labor practices.

b) the wording on authorization cards is clear and unambiguous.

c) employee signatures on cards were obtained without threats or coercion.

d) a majority of employees in the bargaining unit have signed authorization cards.

3) The third way to start a union is through secret ballot elections - this occurs in the majority of cases.

The process of bringing a union to a business starts when the employees or a union representative determines that there are problems and convinces the employees to sign authorization cards to allow the union to represent them in collective bargaining. At this point, the employer may do nothing or he may fight to keep the union out. When the union gets enough response (usually starting around 30 percent) it will request the employer to recognize the union. If he does, the union begins. If the employer does not agree, the union files a petition with the National Labor Relations Board along with evidence of employee interest. The NLRB then will discuss a consent election between the company and the union. If consent is not reached, the NLRB starts the process for a formal hearing to settle the matters. If there is substantial interest, the NLRB will direct an election. The NLRB determines which employees are eligible to vote. If the election is cleared, the employer must provide to the NLRB a list of all eligible employees. Then the NLRB holds the election. About 90 percent of the employees usually participate. The election is by secret ballot and the votes are tallied by the NLRB. About 25-30 percent of the time, the first attempt will fail. If it passes, there is a short window of time for the company to file complaints against the election. Then the contract negotiations begin.

Like a presidential election, there are campaigns before a union election. And like presidential campaigns, they can be clean or dirty. There are certain things that can't be done:

a) the employer cannot hold a captive audience speech within 24 hours of the election.

b) If the employer polls of the workers, the NLRB will look at the rest of the campaign, to determine if the questioning is coercive or threatening. If the questions have a tendency to interfere with the employees' free exercise of their rights, it is improper.

c) Distribution of literature by employees cannot disrupt the business, nor may it include any confidential company data.

d) If the business has a no-solicitation rule, it can only be enforced if the union organizer can still reach the employees by some reasonable method.

When things go wrong, the NLRB looks at the totality of the conduct before issuing sanctions. Once the union is in place what if the employees aren't happy with it? After 12 months have passed, they may petition to decertify the union if there is 30 percent support. If it is decertified, they cannot hold a new representation election for another 12 months. The employer cannot petition for decertification, but can question whether the union represents a majority and support a new representation election. Once the petition for decertification is filed, the employer can start a new campaign against the union.

The other type of decertification is the raid election. This is where a competing union steps up and the employees have to choose which union to join.

THE STEPS TO SUCCESSFUL COLLECTIVE BARGAINING

Collective bargaining is the cornerstone of a union. It is one of the primary areas where the union provides a major benefit to the employees. It is the process by which union and management resolve conflicts by exchanging commitments and entering into a contract to determine how issues will be handled. Generally, the parties to the negotiations are the employees and employers who will be subject to the labor agreement. Sometimes, the labor agreement will not cover all employees. When there is a trade union, it only negotiates for members of that trade. Often the union tries to negotiate the same basic contract among various businesses in the same industry. This is referred to as pattern bargaining. An example is when the auto workers' union tries to negotiate essentially the same contract with all automobile companies.

Centralized bargaining is where two or more unions who work in related areas negotiate their contracts together. This works especially well when you have several interdependent groups because all members of the bargaining units are on the same terms. The contracts have the same termination date, so the employer isn't continually worried about strikes and negotiations.

Before the negotiation begins, there are certain activities that take place. First is the selection of your bargaining team and determining its bargaining responsibilities. To lead the team, find someone who is cool and collected. Experience helps. Management will want someone who actually supervises the workers to provide better insight. The union will want a group that represents the various departments they are negotiating for.

The next step is to plan for the negotiation. What do you think the other side is going to ask for? Look at prior contracts, especially if the same groups have recently negotiated with others. Next, formulate your own proposals. Figure out what you want and how much you are willing to give. Also determine a range of acceptability. If management is willing to make concessions, but not as much as labor is asking, are the concessions an acceptable alternative? What is the lowest you want to go, and the highest you are able to go. Finally, cost it out. How much will the negotiated agreement actually cost the company. Only now are you ready to negotiate.

There are several bargaining situations that may occur. First is distributive bargaining. This is where one party's goals conflict with the other party's, for example, when the union wants a pay raise and management wants it to take a pay cut. This form of bargaining generally encourages the use of threats, bluffs and secrecy. Next is integrative bargaining. This is where the parties attempt to resolve a problem to their mutual interest. It encourages trust, a sharing of information, listening to the other side, and consideration to the concerns of the other side. Third is attitudinal structuring where each party attempts to change the other's attitude which influences collective bargaining and contract administration. This leads to actions such as role reversal to see the other side's concerns. It can also involve the use of scare tactics. Fourth, is intra-organizational bargaining by management and union negotiators to achieve consensus within their respective organizations. In other words, after the agreement is negotiated, the negotiators must still get the workers behind their position. This can be more difficult than negotiating the contract.

Now you need to decide what type of a negotiating style to take. In the top book regarding negotiations, "Getting To Yes," the authors list four approaches to negotiation:

1. Understand the other side's participants. Learn how the other side thinks. Figure out alternatives to allow the other side to save face if they make a concession.

2. Focus on concerns and interest rather than position. By focusing on concerns you may be able to modify positions.

3. Invent and broaden bargaining options for mutual gains. Brainstorm.

4. Use objective criteria based upon normal community standards.

Other things to look for in negotiating style: Language analysis - assess the statements of the other party to determine what isn't being said; body language- this can often give hints as to what isn't being said.

Issues can be packaged together for negotiation. This may speed the process because you don't need to negotiate each item individually. Finally, once you've made the sale, shut up. Don't try to oversell your position. Once the other side says yes, anything you say will only detract from that.

RATIFYING A LABOR AGREEMENT

Once the labor agreement has been negotiated, it has to be ratified by the members of the union. Unlike management, the negotiator for the union has no authority to bind the union. They must sell the negotiated contract to the union members, who vote on its acceptance or rejection. There are many reasons union members may ratify the contract even if it contains terms they are not happy with. They may vote to ratify because they are afraid that if they don't, it will lead to a strike, or layoffs. Or they may really want one provision of the contract and therefore will accept provisions they don't want to get the one they do. But they may reject the agreement too. The union may think that the contract is worse than what other unions are getting, there may be internal union politics that impact the agreement, the leaders may not have properly educated the members on the contract, the contract may have clauses that are less favorable to certain groups than to others, the employees may think they can get more than they really can, or they may vote it down simply as strategy to get a better deal.

If the representatives cannot convince the union to ratify the contract, the negotiations start again. If during the negotiations the parties cannot agree on an issue it is called an impasse. Here the parties have a few options. They can try to work it out between themselves (which may be tough because that's how they got to the impasse) or they can bring in a third party to resolve it through mediation or arbitration.

For mediation, the third party can be provided by the Federal Mediation and Conciliation Service, or through a state agency, or even a private mediator. The mediator has no binding authority and is there primarily in a persuasive manner. He makes recommendations to the parties based upon their presentation of the issues. The mediator can often view the situation in a way the parties cannot and therefore may be able to come up with a new solution, or may be able to convince one of the sides to back down on one point to win another.

If mediation falls, the parties can go to arbitration. Here you bring in a third party who has the authority to make a binding ruling. The arbitrator decides the way it will be. This only occurs in about 2 percent of private-sector labor disputes. One of the reasons for the low number is that arbitration takes the power away from the parties. Contract negotiators like to feel like they are in control. When a case goes to an arbitrator, only the arbitrator has control. Also, occasionally an arbitrator doesn't rule based on the merits. They are getting paid regardless, so instead of spending the time to determine what is right, they simply give a little to each side - splitting the decision down the middle. Historically, studies have shown that many arbitrators don't necessarily look at prior negotiation issues, but tend to focus their attention on wages. The problem is, many times the problems have little or nothing to do with wages.

To limit the arbitrator's power some, unions and management have developed "Final Offer Selection Arbitration." Here each party presents its best offer to the arbitrator and he merely decides which of the two offers to accept. There is also Mediation-Arbitration where the parties agree to mediate all disputes until a certain date. If no agreement has been reached by that date, then the arbitrator takes over and resolves the remaining issues.

DIFFERENCE BETWEEN A STRIKE AND A LOCKOUT

What happens if contract negotiations between a labor union and management fall through? What happens next?

Often it is a work stoppage. This can occur on either side. If the union causes it, we call it a strike; if management causes it we call it a lockout. Generally, when there is a strike, you will also see picketing and boycotting. There are a couple of reasons for this. First is to hurt the employers economically to pressure them to settle. By picketing in front of a business, it reduces the number of people entering the business and therefore hurts sales. Second is to get public opinion on your side. Surprisingly, many union negotiations are won or lost in the public arena.

There are various reasons for strikes. Wages is the main one. Most strikes are economic strikes. Second are plant administration issues. Sometimes the reasons for striking are interrelated: economic reasons, production issues, the market structure, plant location and work force characteristics all may play a part in the total picture.

Strikes may occur for strategic reasons as well. They may help to secure a contract by causing the workers to lose money for a period. Here it would seem that the union leaders are working against the workers, and you see where there can be internal problems. The strike may also be used just to show management what will happen if the contract doesn't pass.

Strikes can be short and peaceful or they can be long and violent. They generally cause a lot of stress, especially when they first start.   They often cause problems at home for the workers, and in fact, the striker's spouse if the most important influence on what the striker does during this time.

The first days of the strike are also the most exciting and enthusiastic. Before the strike actually begins, the union must make preparations. The union has to build the support of the workers. If the workers don't support the strike, it will fall. An example of this was the mass resignation of the major league umpires. The union did not have the support of all of the umpires. While many umpires submitted resignations, the majority did not and none of the minor league umpires joined. Major League Baseball knew they had stronger support than the umpires as they could simply replace the resigning umpires with minor league umpires.

The company must also prepare for a strike. It may need to ensure sufficient quantities of inventory and decide if it is going to hire replacement workers before the strike starts.

Next, union and management need to determine if the strike is legal. Generally, there is a right to strike for most people. This is based on court decisions and statutes. But there are limitations. Picketing at a strike is legal if it isn't so big that it effectively blocks the entrance to the business. A secondary strike which is non-strikers picketing, or picketing one business to stop doing business with the business in dispute is generally considered illegal. Also it is often illegal for certain groups to strike, such as those groups operating monopolies or government agencies.

It also is illegal for workers to refuse to handle strike products. These are called hot-cargo agreements and are only allowed in apparel and construction industries. An example of a hot-cargo agreement would be where garment workers go on strike and the truck drivers refuse to deliver the merchandise in support of the union. By law, the truckers must still deliver the items unless they too are on strike.

The employer can try to end a strike by hiring replacement workers. These can be permanent or temporary. For economic strikers (that is, where the reason for the strike is to get more money for the workers), employers often will replace striking workers. If the jobs are filled by new permanent employees, the strikers have no right to get their jobs back.

If the purpose if the strike is to improve working conditions, the strikers have an absolute right to return to their jobs immediately at the end of the strike, even if the job has been filled by permanent employees. However, in either case, if the strikers commit acts of misconduct while striking, the employer is not required to take them back.

LABOR GREIVANCES

A labor grievance is defined as any employees' concern over a perceived violation of the labor agreement which is submitted for eventual resolution. You notice I said perceived violation, not actual violation. A grievance is what the employee believes; not necessarily what is true. Most companies require employees to put their grievances in writing. This give advantages to the employer. First, it allows the complaints to be documented so there is a record the employer can point to. Also, it reduces the emotion of the issue so the employer can deal with it rationally.

Employees file grievances for many reasons: To protest a contractual violation; to draw attention to a problem within the plant; to make the grievant and union feel important; to get something for nothing.

Are grievances significant? Absolutely. They can cause a non-union company to become unionized. They can demonstrate the union's interests in its members. And it can serve two important organizational functions- conflict institutionalization and open upward communication.

Once an employee develops a concern, the grievance process begins. Each company has a different policy, but the standard procedure generally follows the following format:

The first step is usually to discuss the concern with the first line supervisor. This may be with or without the union steward present. Once the complaint has been discussed, the supervisor answers the grievance in writing. If this doesn't resolve the issue, then the grievance goes to the second step.

The second step is when the grievance goes before the union grievance committee person and the management labor relations person who discuss the supervisor's written response. Because these two have probably been involved in the company's grievance procedure on numerous previous cases, they are more aware of the company's policies. If this doesn't work, the grievance moves to the third step.

The third step involves the same basic group, but also adds an additional management person. This is to increase input since the grievance may at this point have plant wide impact. The union at this point takes a more aggressive stance and the management officials mainly sit back and listen rather than taking a more formal "let's resolve this" approach. This step is often a training ground for new grievance committee members and lets the union member see that his union is behind him. If the grievance is still not resolved, it moves to the fourth step, which is to bring in a third party mediator or arbitrator to finally resolve the matter.

If we go back to the first step, we see the two main participants are the union steward and the first line supervisor. These two can have a variety of relationships with each other in regards to how disputes are handled. First is the codified relationship. This is the relationship between the two as set out in the labor agreement. Here, the two treat each other as organizational equals. The union steward is encouraged to take the grievance to the first-line supervisor and the company is encouraged to give the first-line supervisor the authority to resolve the grievance.

Next is the power relationship, where each side tries to get the upper hand over the other. Here, the supervisor tries to find problems before they become grievances and the steward tries to get to the grievant before they talk to the supervisor.

Next we have the sympathetic relationship where each side is aware of and appreciates the other's position. They come in and try to get along with each other to resolve the grievance.

Finally, we have the flexible relationship where the parties try to resolve the disputes somewhere between the third and fourth steps by trading grievances. In other words, "If you let us keep doing X, we will stop doing Y."

The union has an obligation to treat all of its members fairly. This can be difficult as some grievances may be better resolved for some employees than for others. If the union settles a grievance and some employees don't feel the resolution is in their favor, they may file a complaint against the union. These complaints generally go to the NLRB. Other complaints are simply filed in the district courts. The courts and the NLRB have held that the union must consider the interests of all members and take its ultimate position in good faith and without hostility or arbitrary discrimination. If the union follows this guideline, its decision should be upheld.

WHY DISCUSS UNIONS?

Unionization is a major issue in the field of employment laws. Many of the issues I have discussed in regard to unions also arise in other areas of business as well. For example, the same methods to resolve negotiations in union grievances can also be used to resolve normal contract disputes, rather than going to court. Negotiation techniques are the same whether negotiating a sale or a collective bargaining agreement.

Another reason for focusing on unions is that unions exist even in small towns. For example, even though Florida is a right to work state, there are numerous unions in Florida. I'm from a small city - Key West, in Monroe County. In Key West, for example, we have the United Teachers of Monroe, American Postal Workers Union, the Police Benevolent Association, Key West Fire Fighters Local 1424, Monroe County Employees and Teamsters. In addition, there are unions at the Aqueduct Authority, City Electric, and UPS. Many of the airline employees are unionized and there is talk of unionizing the service industry. The total number of union members in Monroe County well exceeds 10,000 and may approach 20,000!

The third reason is the impact that unions have on business.

Why unionize in a small town? Traditionally, public

sector jobs have been unionized even in small towns. It is easier to organize such a well-defined group and some groups, such as teachers or postal workers, are organized from the state or federal level. The increased power of collective bargaining to get a fair share of the financial pie and other benefits, such as seniority rights and insurance benefits or paid sick and annual leave. Workers who are represented by unions consistently make more money and receive greater benefits for the same work that workers who are not. However, in some situations non-union workers get the benefits of the collective bargaining agreement. If the union is already present, there are perhaps a percentage of individuals who will take advantage of union representation without joining. But generally this percentage is not large. Most workers are happy to pay their fair share for good union representation and obvious benefits it brings.

Generally, if the union leadership acts in a professional manner, management will gladly work with them. This results in a difference in the bargaining process. Many unions in small towns have changed from collective bargaining to collaborative bargaining where the management and employees work together to bring the best services to the community. Information is shared to do what is best for the people of the community.

ARBITRATION IN LABOR AGREEMENTS

Arbitration of labor disputes was infrequently practiced until World War II. The unions and management frequently just relied on economics to resolve grievances. If there was a strike, whoever could hold out the longest won. The few times arbitration was used, the arbitrators had little authority and acted more like mediators trying to convince the two sides to reach an agreement.

This changed when World War II came. Uninterrupted wartime production was essential and therefore disputes had to be resolved more quickly. Arbitration was seen as a quick method of reaching resolution. Still, arbitrators had little power and could not issue a binding decision. This changed in 1957.

That year the United States Supreme Court decided that if an agreement had an arbitration clause and a party refused to arbitrate a dispute, they could be sued for violation of the labor agreement. Still, there was confusion, because both the arbitrator and the Courts could rule on a case. Who controlled? This question was answered in 1960 when the Supreme Court ruled on what became known as the Steelworker's Trilogy- three cases all involving this issue. The Court held that the arbitrators determined if a matter went before the arbitrators or the court, that the court would give deference to the decision of the arbitrators since the arbitrators have more shop knowledge than the court, and that the arbitrators had no obligation to explain themselves to the court. Over the next few years, the courts continued to strengthen the power of the arbitrators.

When the parties develop a dispute resolution policy that includes arbitration, they need to set up the procedures.

First is how many arbitrators will be needed. Usually this is one or three (avoid even numbers of arbitrators as this could result in a deadlock). The general rule for a three member arbitration panel is that each party picks one arbitrator and then the two arbitrators together select a third arbitrator.

Second is how long will an arbitrator preside over a contract. The arbitrator may be permanent- that is, he presides over the entire life of the contract, or he may be ad hoc where he just presides over one dispute.

Third, look at the characteristics of the arbitrators. The parties may want someone based on his or her reputation or location or they may want someone educated in a particular field. Interestingly, studies have shown little correlation between the arbitrator's background and how they rule.

Arbitration is similar to a trial. Once the arbitrators are chosen, the parties prepare prehearing briefs. These briefs spell out the position of the respective parties and lets the arbitrators know in advance what they are getting into. Some arbitrators insist instead on a stipulated statement. This is similar to a prehearing brief but is written by both sides together and sets out what issues they agree on and what issues are in dispute. At the start of the hearing the parties make an opening statement spelling out their positions and then go through with a presentation of their exhibits and witnesses to present their case. Of course, like a trial, the witnesses can be cross-examined by the opposing side. At the conclusion of the hearing, the parties either make their closing arguments or file a post hearing brief stating how the evidence supported their position.

There are some differences between arbitration and trials. First is the use of shop rules. The parties are not asking the arbitrators to base his or her decision on the law, but on the practices and rules of the individual business. Because of this, the arbitrators can't rely on a fixed set of principles. They must look at each labor agreement separately and review all past practices of the business.

Second are the rules of evidence. Courts have strict rules on when evidence will be allowed; arbitrators don't have to follow those rules. While this may open the way for fraud, it also allows the case to move faster and allows evidence that may be inadmissible in court.

Now it's time for the arbitrators to make their decision. In making the decision, the arbitrator is going to consider which party has the burden of proof, the credibility of witnesses, the intent of the parties when they signed the labor agreement, past practices, and previous arbitration awards. The decision will be in writing, and will cover a statement of facts surrounding the grievance, the pertinent provisions of the labor agreement, a summary of the positions of the parties, the validity of each position, and the award.

EMPLOYEE DISCIPLINE

During the 18th and 19th centuries, employers had complete discretion in disciplining their work crew. Discipline was harsh. As we came to the 1930's, changes were taking place. The Wagner Act took away discriminatory discipline and through the use of labor arbitration many policies regarding employee discipline have been modified.

Today, employees have certain protections. For instance, in general, most employees are considered to be employed at will. They can be fired at any time for any reason, or for no reason. However, the employee may file a wrongful discharge claim if the discharge is a violation of law, if there is an implied contract, or if discipline is in contravention to public policy.

There is an almost endless variety of possible work behaviors that call for discipline. When challenged, management's discipline decisions have been reduced or eliminated in a majority of cases that are heard by arbitrators. This can be expensive for management as it often requires them to give back pay to the wrongfully disciplined employee. Also, once the employee is reinstated, they often perform substandard work. Part of this may be because the employee has less confidence in the employer and that they feel protected having just won their case.

Discipline, if used appropriately has numerous purposes. It sets an example of appropriate behavior, transmits rules of the company, promotes efficient production, maintains respect for supervisors, and corrects improper behavior.

What are the elements of discipline that will pass muster with the arbitrator? There must be just cause. That means there must be clear and convincing evidence that an offense was committed by the employee; the discipline by management was appropriate for the offense; and the discipline is not arbitrary or discriminatory.

Management usually has the right to establish work rules for the business. These work rules must be clear, reasonable, consistently applied, and let the employees know what the consequences will be for failure to follow them. Yet situations arise that management has not thought of and therefore there are no set rules for them. How do you handle this? One way is to make some general policies that you can derive solutions from. While this is difficult it is not impossible, especially when you realize that the most important legal documents do just that. The Bill of Rights is very short and sets forth general rules. Similarly, think of the ten commandments. While not very detailed, these types of rules can give some guidance.

Many employers enforce a policy known as progressive discipline. This is where the punishment gets worse as the infractions increase. The first infraction may result in a verbal warning. Second may be a written reprimand. Third may be a suspension and fourth may result in termination. The benefit of a progressive discipline policy is that it give the employee more chances to save their job and lets them know that they need to watch their behavior. Even when progressive discipline is used, there are usually exceptions that allow for immediate termination for the most grievous violations.

The actual discipline must be reasonable to the offense. If there are mitigating circumstances, the arbitrator may use them to reduce the level of punishment. This can occur if management contributed to the problem, if the circumstances are so unusual it is unlikely that the problem will occur again, or if the employee was having personal problems that need to be worked out first and are not likely to recur.

Employees also have certain due process rights in disciplinary actions. What is due process? Due process means that there is a certain order that should be followed in all cases. It means that the employee's rights will be respected and he or she will be treated as any other employee. The employee is entitled to be told in writing what the specific grievance is. They have a right to know in advance what the rules are. If there are time limits in their contract, management must follow them. If the employer violates the employee's due process rights, the arbitrator has three choices. He may say that the disciplinary action is nullified; he can say that the action will be overturned only if the employee shows prejudice, or the arbitrator can give some other penalty but not nullify the action. Usually, the employee will not be reinstated just because due process is not followed exactly.

HANDLING LABOR DISPUTES NOT COVERED BY THE COLLECTIVE AGREEMENT

What happens when something comes up that is not addressed in the labor agreement?

Often management will say that since the issue wasn't addressed in the collective bargaining agreement, it is reserved to management's discretion. This is similar to the argument between states' rights and federal rights. When our country was being founded, there was a major disagreement over who should have more control - the federal government or the state governments. The disagreement was so great that it almost destroyed the country before we started. A compromise was finally reached that the Constitution would set out the rules for the federal system and anything not specifically mentioned in the Constitution would be reserved for the states government to control. An example is education. Because education is not mentioned as a federal right, it is controlled by various state boards of education rather than a national board. In business, we call this the reserved rights doctrine: What isn't specifically mentioned in the labor agreement is reserved for management to determine.

Another clause that can put restraints on management is a union security clause. The clause assists the unions by giving them certain rights and abilities so they can attract members. There are several terms in the area of union security that business owners should be familiar with:

■ Closed shop - A clause in the labor agreement that requires all workers in a business to be union members (This is not allowed in Florida).

■ Union shop - A non-union person may be hired, but must join the union after a short probationary period to keep employment. (Also not allowed in Florida).

■ Agency shop - The employee does not have to be a union member, but must pay a sum equal to union dues. This helps defray the costs of running the union and allows contribution for benefits.

■ Quasi-union shop - A provision found in labor agreements primarily in right-to-work states that says an employee must join the union as a condition of employment - usually stated in bold letters - and then contains a disclaimer in the footnotes or fine print that strikes that provision. Basically, it is an attempt to trick new employees into joining a union.

■ Open shop - A company that hires regardless of union membership or involvement. This applies to businesses in right-to-work states.

■ Contingency union shop - An open shop contract with a clause that says, if the states right-to-work law is repealed, the shop will convert to a union shop.

■   Union hiring hall - The union provides a list of applicants for management to choose from before outsiders get hired.

Florida is a right-to-work state. The employer and/or union cannot require an employee to be a union member in order to get a job. Supporters of right-to-work laws think employees have the right to choose whether to join the union. The Federal Constitution gives us the right to congregate, but that includes the right not the congregate as well.

Another area of dispute is the democracy view. Right-to-work supporters say that, if union membership is voluntary, the members will be more supportive. If you are forced to be a member, it could be more difficult to believe the union is supporting you. Opponents of the right-to-work laws think this is just a ploy to hurt unions. Employees can still get jobs; they just have to sign up. They look at the shop as a community. Just as all citizens must abide by the laws of Florida, the employees have to follow the rules of the shop as union members.

Currently, around 21 states have right-to-work laws and generally, the income in right-to-work states is lower than union states.

HIRING/FIRING PRACTICES

EMPLOYEE REFERENCES

There is a standard hiring practice among many employers to request information from an applicant's previous employers before hiring. This practice creates a great deal of risk for the prior employer.

Many employers try to soothe the pain of firing an employee by telling them they will receive a good job reference in the future. Such a blanket statement is bad policy. First, it opens the door to liability if the employer fails to give the employee a good reference because the court could find that the employee gave up rights based on this promise and therefore the employer is in breach of this agreement. Second, if the "good reference" is false, it creates even more liability if the information is something the future employer needs to know.

Often many companies have a policy to only release the most basic information, such as limiting job references to dates of employment, job title and salary. The concern is that to give more detailed information may create the risk of defamation suits from the employee. Some commentators have questioned whether there is a rational basis for this practice.

Just as there is a risk if the employer gives too much information, there is an equal risk if the employer doesn't give enough information. Former employers have faced lawsuits and liability for giving incomplete references that, as a result, are misleading. In one case, a former employer settled a lawsuit for an undisclosed amount after he allegedly sent an incomplete referral letter that neglected to mention that the former employee had been fired for bringing a gun to work. The employee was subsequently hired by an insurance company and went on a rampage, killing three and wounding two of his co-workers, before killing himself.

In another example, the California Supreme Court held that school district officials could be liable for negligent misrepresentation and fraud for a letter of recommendation in which they unreservedly recommended an employee who had been previously accused of sexual misconduct. The former employee was hired as the principal of a middle school. A case arose when a student at the middle school alleged that the principal molested her in his office. It was discovered that the employee had a history of disciplinary action for alleged sexual harassment and improper contacts with female students, yet he received a series of positive recommendations as he moved through a series of new jobs.

Even if the reason for discharge is given truthfully, the vagueness can open an employer to liability. In a suit between a doctor and a hospital, the doctor claimed that the hospital told a prospective employer that the doctor had been terminated "for cause" without any further explanation. The court felt that such a statement could have implied that the doctor was not competent. This could create liability for the hospital for defamation.

Finally, the employer must be careful that what he writes in the reference is based on fact and not opinion. A Texas appellate court affirmed a jury's award of $1.9 million to a former employee whose employer referred to the employee as a "zero" and a "classical sociopath" who was "lacking in compuncture [sic] or scruples."

To best protect themselves, an employer should provide complete and truthful information to a prospective employer. Any negative issues should be presented factually, and the prior employer should maintain documentation that will support the statements put forth.

AT-WILL EMPLOYMENT

Florida follows the "at-will" employment policy. What this means is that, unless there is a contract that specifies an employee is being hired for a specific period of time, they work subject to the employers will. In other words, an employee may be fired at any time for any reason, or for no reason. This policy works well for most employers. It allows the employer to cut back on staff if the payroll is too high; it allows an employer to rid themselves of a poor employee; and it allows an employer to modify working conditions, all without fear of reprisals. The policy isn't foolproof, though. There are exceptions and the definition of "at-will" employee is often blurred.

A case that shows this involves a major sports celebrity. When Mike Tyson was only sixteen, Cus D'Amato, Tyson's legal guardian and manager, allegedly promised Kevin Rooney that he would be Tyson's trainer "for as long as [Tyson] fought" and would be paid ten percent of Tyson's professional earnings if Rooney would train Tyson until he turned professional. This was never put into writing. Rooney trained Tyson for 28 months without compensation. Tyson then turned pro and became successful. Rooney received the agreed ten percent cut from Tyson's professional fights through 1988. During

Tyson's divorce, Rooney appeared on television and commented on the divorce. Tyson then fired Rooney. Rooney sued, claiming breach of his oral employment contract. The case went to a jury which ordered Tyson to pay Rooney $4,415,651 in damages. That was round one. Round two went to Tyson when federal district judge Thomas McAvoy vacated that jury verdict on the ground that Rooney was only an at-will employee who could be fired at any time for any reason. The issue that arose was based on the indefinite period of "as long as he fights". While this is a duration, it is too indefinite to make Rooney a term employee. However, there is other case law that would support Rooney's position. In another boxing case, Don King Productions, Inc. v. Douglas, the Court sided with the employee. That federal case held that a three-year promotional contract that would be automatically extended for the entire period the boxer was world champion and for two years thereafter was definite enough to escape the at-will employment presumption.

Another exception to the at-will employment status is the whistle-blower statute. A whistle-blower is an employee that reports illegal activities of the employer to the appropriate governmental agency. Under the statutes, an employer may not retaliate against a whistle-blower. This means that the employer may not suspend, demote, fire or otherwise penalize an employee for reporting illegal activity, despite their "at-will" status. Before everyone runs out and starts filing reports, it should be noted that private sector whistle-blower claims may be difficult to prove. The employee must demonstrate an actual violation of law or regulation. They must also demonstrate a substantial and direct threat to the public health and safety. Several whistle-blower claims involving health care employers and restaurants have survived summary judgment motions by employers and a few have even progressed as far as plaintiffs' verdicts and decisions. Nevertheless, the vast majority of such claims are dismissed.

Similar to the whistle-blower exception is the criminal request exception. An employer does not have the authority to request an employee to commit a criminal act. Although employment is at-will, public policy requires a narrow exception to this employment at will doctrine whereby an employer may not discharge an employee for refusal to perform an illegal act.

One of the more interesting cases about at-will employment involves a professional mime. The mime, named Kelbi (yes, it's her real name) performed as a mechanical wind-up doll with a large key on her back. She was hired by Circus Circus, in Las Vegas, as a strolling entertainer largely to amuse the casino patrons.

Although Kelbi had never been harassed by clients, Circus Circus had taken a number of precautions precisely to protect her against their overzealous customers. They gave her a "Stop, Do Not Touch" sign which she wore on her back. They told her to call casino security whenever customers gave her problems. She was allowed to enlist the help of others who could call casino security for her if they saw her in trouble, and others were advised to watch out for her. The casino even hired "a large man" dressed in a clown costume to accompany and protect Kelbi when she was performing. Finally, the casino videotaped its public areas, thereby enabling it either to spot threatening customers or, at least, to identify and deal with customers who acted inappropriately towards their employees.

Kelbi was approached by a male casino customer who announced to his friends that he would "prove one way or another if she's real or not." One of the casino employees warned him against touching Kelbi. Nonetheless, the customer moved towards her with his arms outstretched as though he planned to hug her. When he touched her shoulder, Kelbi, silently of course, punched the customer in the mouth. The entire exchange was captured on videotape by the casino. After reviewing the videotape, the management of the casino fired Kelbi.

This case made its way to the Ninth Circuit Court of Appeals on the issue of Title VII's retaliation section. That section has two separate elements that the employee must prove to prevail. The first part of an employee's prima facie case is that the employee is engaging in a "protected activity." The Ninth Circuit first decided only this issue when it concluded Kelbi's punch in the mouth was indeed an appropriate self-defense maneuver responding to the customer's aggressive, threatening actions. The Court stated that employees are allowed to take "reasonable steps to defend against physical harm". There is, however, a second element as well for Title VII retaliation claims. The employee must also be "opposing" an unlawful employment practice under that law.

Kelbi was seeking to hold her employer, Circus Circus, liable for this single customer's aggressive and threatening conduct. In order to do that, she had to show that the customer's harassment could be somehow imputed to her employer. An employer is not liable for third party harassment under EEOC guidelines unless the employer knows or should have known of the third party's conduct and, following that actual or constructive knowledge, fails to take immediate and appropriate corrective action.

When the case came before the Ninth Circuit on a second appeal, they found that Circus Circus had taken "reasonable steps to ensure Kelbi's safety from customer harassment." The casino had not merely made cursory efforts to protect Kelbi, they had made extensive efforts to protect her.

Kelbi further lost because she could point only to this single punch-in-the-mouth incident for a lack of safety measures. There was no evidence that other customers had harassed her or that other Circus Circus employees and/or her employer had allowed this type of behavior from customers on prior occasions. If there was a history of prior unremedied harassment of employees by third parties, it might show the employer had either ratified or acquiesced in that harassment.

So, while Kelbi has been told by the Ninth Circuit that she had the right to punch this annoying customer in the mouth, the employer has now been told by the same court that it had the right to fire her for that punch.

TERMNATNG AN AT-WILL EMPLOYMENT

A personnel director is in a precarious position. They must advise the company of the status of the law and at the same time, advise the employee as to their rights under the law. Sometimes, these can be conflicting positions. On top of all that, personnel directors are expected to comply personally with all company policies. They must set a proper example for other employees and they must not condone inappropriate conduct that comes to their attention. Because of their fish-bowl position, personnel directors, in short, are held to a higher standard of conduct. But, because of their position, it is often difficult for a company to fire them.

Lori was the personnel director for a company who was fired after she made efforts to bring possible FLSA violations to her employer's attention. That, of course, is the essence of a personnel director's job. Lori was originally hired as a receptionist and became personnel director ten months later. She became concerned that certain employees were not being properly paid overtime under the FLSA. She shared her concerns first with the company's attorney and then with the company president. Eight days after this report, the company began to investigate Lori's job performance. This was the first investigation in the company's history. Eight days later, Lori was fired.

Two principal reasons were cited. One involved an unusual "sex contract" Lori had witnessed and notarized. The contract was between a female sales clerk and male vice president, where the vice president agreed to give the sales clerk merchandise if she did not receive a Christmas bonus that year. In return, the sales clerk promised to provide the vice president "with a very special and provocatively intimate evening; time, place and duration to be negotiated" if Christmas bonuses were paid.

Lori admitted notarizing this contract. She claimed she neither read it nor was aware of its contents, and admitted she made a mistake in notarizing this "sex contract." This "sex contract" would have provided a sufficient reason to fire Lori, except for one problem. The company president testified that he saw the contract months before he fired her. The jury concluded this "sex contract" rationale was only a pretext.

However, the company also cited Lori for improperly disclosing confidential information to employees. It claimed she told certain employees they were the possible subjects of a criminal investigation and had also prematurely tipped off a manager that he was facing a demotion. The jury also rejected this reason and concluded Lori had indeed been fired in retaliation against her protected FLSA complaint. On appeal, however, the Court stated that Lori was simply performing her everyday duties as personnel director when she raised the company's possible FLSA overtime violations with the company attorney and with the company president. The Court found her actions "were completely consistent with her duties as personnel director to evaluate wage and hour issues and to assist the company in complying with its obligations under the FLSA." Because the whistleblower statute only applies when a person is participating in a "protected activity" (such as reporting the company to the Wage and Hour Division) the Court held that she was not engaged in protected activity under the FLSA when she undertook to advise her employer that its overtime policies may violate the FLSA. That was not a protected activity because it was part of her personnel director's job. The Court found she presented those FLSA matters "in her capacity as personnel director" and not in her capacity as an individual employee. As such, she had an obligation to inform her boss of their liability. Since there was no protection under the whistleblower statute, Lori was an at will employee who could be fired at any time.

LIMITATIONS IN EMPLOYMENT CONTRACTS

Written employment contracts, which were originally reserved for highly paid athletes such as Michael Jordan, have become fairly commonplace for many corporate executives and other employees. Employers are learning that these contracts can be customized to provide benefits that were previously unthought of. These contracts can be drafted to provide businesses with methods in which they can protect themselves from litigation, even over a breach of contract itself.

As an example, what if the employer could shorten the time period in which an employee could file suit against the employer? Few employers take advantage of the opportunity to add limitation periods to their employment contracts that is shorter than those allowed by state statute. However, employers should consider the opportunity to cut off many such suits by means of restrictive contract language. Most states allow the parties to a contract to bargain for a shorter limitations period. The usual requirements are that the shorter period chosen must be reasonable and must not conflict with public policy. The task for the employer is to choose a limitation period short enough to cut off employee lawsuits but long enough to be considered reasonable. This is by no means impossible and it can have great advantages.

In Florida, the statute of limitations period allows for a suit on a verbal contract to be brought within four years and a suit on a written contract to be brought within five years. An employment contract with its own internal one or two-year limitation period gives the employer a definite advantage. Adding a shorter limitation period to an employment contract stops potential employee lawsuits in two ways.

First, if the employee takes the contract to a lawyer to discuss a possible lawsuit against his/her former employer, that attorney may be discouraged from taking the case if the special limitation period has expired or is too soon for the attorney to safely draft the appropriate documents. The attorney should realize that sanctions may be filed against him personally for filing a frivolous lawsuit.

Second, special limitation periods also help employers dismiss cases that are brought too late. If the employee does file a suit, the employer can ask for dismissal at the early stages based upon the contract clause. This saves greatly in legal fees and costs.

How short a limitation period do you need? A six-month contract limitations period may work in some states. This was allowed by courts in Illinois, but was deemed too short in Michigan. The Michigan court was concerned that the shorter period would encourage more suits by pressuring employees to file prematurely before fully investigating and assessing their litigation prospects. Second, the courts were concerned about the special nature of employment contracts. The Michigan Supreme Court stated they would probably approve a limitation of two, three, four or five years.

While each state's laws will offer different contractual limitation precedents, it should not be difficult to determine what special limitations period would satisfy the reasonableness requirement in one or more states. You could look at other contract restrictions in employment contracts, such as non-competition clauses. These must also be reasonable in length and therefore the employer could use those same time periods for the special limitation period.

INTELLECTUAL PROPERTY

HISTORY OF TRADEMARKS COPYRIGHTS AND PATENTS

There are four basic types of Intellectual Property: copyrights, patents, trademarks, and trade secrets. We will start with a little history.

COPYRIGHTS: The purpose of copyright is to reward and stimulate creativity in the arts by granting exclusive powers over the created work. Copyrights have been with us since the Statute of Anne, enacted by the British Parliament in 1710. This was the first law that recognized an author's right to protection over his work for a limited time.

In drafting our Constitution, our founding fathers felt there was a need to promote the development of the arts by protecting artists and writers. To do this, they added a clause in the Constitution giving Congress the power to secure, for a limited time, the exclusive rights to writings and discoveries.

In 1790, Congress passed the first copyright law under the powers given them under Article 1, Section 8 of the United States Constitution. The law covered books, maps and charts, following the lead of the Statute of Anne.

In 1952, the United States assisted in developing the Universal Copyright Convention, which embodied the fundamentals of U.S. and European copyrights. The UCC was adopted by Europe with the Treaty of Geneva and later the Berne Treaty. There have been several revisions of the Copyright statute since then, the most prominent being in 1909, 1976 and 1989.

Today's copyright also covers prints, music, photographs, paintings, drawings, motion pictures, sound recordings, architecture and computer programs. The law also covers certain performances and displays. The Copyright Office was made a part of the Library of Congress in 1897.

The most recent major change in copyright law occurred when the United States adopted the Berne Treaty. This allowed the United States to recognize copyrights from other countries, and vice versa. It also modified the registration and display rules of copyrights.

TRADEMARKS: Businesses have long engaged in the practice of using symbols, name and designs for recognition purposes. Evidence of the use of symbols for trademarks has been found on ancient Chinese pottery and medieval swords.

The United States Congress passed the first Trademark law in 1870, and in 1883, a group of nations created the Paris Convention, to recognize foreign trademarks. In 1946, the United States passed the current federal trademark law, called The Lanham Act.

Trademarks are governed by the U.S. Patent and Trademark Office, a branch of the Department of Commerce. The reasons for trademark protection are many. Primary among them are to give incentives to creativity, to provide fairness to consumer by allowing them to know a product is coming from the same producer, and to provide a sense of morals to the market by disallowing theft of another's success.

On the other side, many people feel that trademarks create a barrier to entry into the marketplace by allowing larger, more well-known brand names to drive out lesser-known brands. The advertising also diverts funds that could be used to improve the products.

Finally, trademarks limit the words that other companies may use to advertise their products. Despite the viability of these arguments, which seem barely credible, the benefits of trademark protection greatly outweigh the negative.

PATENTS: The Department of Commerce also controls the registration of patents. The first patents in the United States were issued in 1641 and the first patent laws passed in 1790. This was modified in 1870, and again in 1952 to take the basic form it has today. The purpose of patent law is to encourage inventiveness by giving inventors a monopoly on their products for a period of 14-17 years.

COPYRIGHTS

The first type of intellectual property we are going to discuss is copyright. What is a copyright? A copyright is a protection given to authors, composers, architects, artists, and any other person who creates something of artistic value. A number of items may receive copyright protection.

These include books and stories, music, dramatic works, choreography, pictures, paintings and sculptures, motion pictures and other audiovisual works, sound recordings, and compilations. Items that cannot be copyrighted include titles, names and slogans, ideas, methods and procedures, common information, list of ingredients, blank forms, and government publications.

A copyright can be claimed only by people who have a right in the created work. Normally this would be the author, however, if the author is an employee hired to create the work, it is the employer who has the right to the copyright.

As an example, the cartoonist working for the Walt Disney Corporation cannot obtain a copyright for the cartoons he creates. That copyright would be held by the Walt Disney Corporation as the employer. This is what is known as a "work made for hire."

A copyright holder may also assign his copyright to a third party, and that person may then claim the copyright on the work. If, however, the item is sold without also selling the copyright, the new owner of the work does not have a copyright interest in it. Again, by way of illustration, the purchaser of a book cannot simply claim the copyright on that book, nor does the purchase of a CD give you copyrights in the songs on it or the purchase of a DVD give you the rights to the movie.

Previously, the length of a copyright was the life of the author plus fifty years. For corporate owned works the term was seventy-five years from publication, or 100 years from creation, whichever was shorter. However, years ago, Congress passed the Copyright Term Extension Act of 1998 (Sponsored by signer and Congressman Sonny Bono). This is also referred to as the Mickey Mouse Protection Act by some people. Why? Well, Mickey Mouse was created in 1928 in the movie "Steamboat Willie". Under the prior law, the copyright protection would have ended in 2003, putting Mickey in the public domain and ending Disney's exclusive rights. Under the Copyright Term Extension Act, the term of a trademark was extended to the life of the author plus seventy years. For corporate owned works or pseudonymous work, the term is now 95 years from publication, or 120 years from creation, whichever was shorter. This ensures that Mickey will be protected for an additional 20 years.

Pursuant to Federal Law, copyright gives certain protections and rights to the author for the work. The protections include the exclusive rights to reproduce the work; to prepare derivative works, such as translations, abridged versions, etc.; to distribute copies to the public for sale or rental; to perform the work publicly; and to display the work publicly. As an example of a copyright infringement: if you purchase a DVD of a movie, you are not allowed to burn copies of it to sell. This would be a violation of the right to copy and distribute. If the owner of a restaurant buys a CD, he cannot play it over the stereo at his restaurant. This would be a violation of the right to perform the work publicly. If you buy a painting, you cannot modify it and sell pictures of the modification. This would be a violation of the right to make adaptions. Copyrights can be legally infringed upon in certain situations, such as copying small excerpts, the use in parodies, and for use by educators.

A copyright does not need to be recorded or registered with the federal government in order to be in existence. A copyright begins immediately upon the creation of the writing, artwork, etc. Copyright is an automatic grant to the author of the work; however, it must be registered in order to effectuate a lawsuit for infringement. This is why many intellectual property lawyers refer to copyright registration as a "right-to-sue letter".

The benefits for registering your copyright include receiving monetary damages and payment of attorney fees for infringement suits, prima facie evidence of the validity of a copyright, evidence of permanent record for your claim to the work, compulsory royalty payments for recorded musical works, marketing opportunities, and correction of errors and omissions.

The copyright notice does not need to be placed on any item created after March1, 1989, however, it is a good practice to use the notice to inform others of the ownership rights. The proper form for the copyright notice is either the word "copyright," the abbreviation "co" or the symbol of a "©" along with the year of creation and the owner's name.

Copyrights can be sold, transferred, or assigned. This may be done in whole or in part. The transfer may be done by written contract, through a will, through a divorce, or even in a bankruptcy proceeding. However, after the sale of a legal copyright, the author can legally rescind the copyright after thirty-five years from the date of publication or forty-five years from the date of transfer, whichever occurs first so long as he sends the proper notice to the copyright owner. Copyrights will be recognized by certain other countries under various treaties, however, not all countries will respect or enforce your copyrights.

Copyright registration is handled electronically. The application can be found online at the Copyright Office's website. Once completed you submit a digital copy of the work being filed. Generally, you must submit an entire copy of the work, however there are some exceptions. The process takes roughly eight months. The application fee is currently $30 per application.

TRADE SECRETS

A trade secret is just what it sounds like: a secret. It is the weakest form of protection, lasting only as long as your business can keep it secret. Some companies are very good at keeping secrets. Once the secret is leaked, it loses its protective status. There are no government registrations or protections for it, except for certain statutory protections for trade secret theft. Indeed, if the government required any form of registration, it would destroy the secretive aspect.

So how do you protect a trade secret? It can be very difficult, and in some cases impossible. Let's start with a situation you cannot protect. What if you create a new type of product but it doesn't qualify for patent protection? As a new product, nobody knows what you have created. However, once you release the item for sale, it may be reverse engineered. That is, people can take it apart to see how you built it. Once done, they may legally start creating identical products and compete with you.

Luckily, some items cannot be reverse engineered. An example would be a computer program. Software is written in two aspects: source code and object code. While object code may be discovered by a programmer, the source code behind it cannot. Source code is available for copyright protection; however, many programmers choose not to copyright the code as it would release the source code, allowing other programmers to modify their program without the author getting his royalties.

For items that can be kept secret, there are ways to protect yourself. First, require all of your employees to sign non-compete and non-disclosure agreements. These agreements, if properly drafted and enforced, can prevent your employees from taking your secrets to your competition or from starting their own business to compete against you. If an employee attempts or actually does release your secrets to a competitor, you can go to court to obtain an injunction to prevent the competition from using the information. Next, only release your information to those employees with a need to know. As an example, popular rumor holds that Coca Cola keeps the recipe for their drink in two portions kept in two locations so that no one employee knows the entire recipe. Probably not true, but a good example of trade secret protection.

Some companies desire to keep their manufacturing process a secret. Plant design can tell a great deal about a company's product. For this reason, some companies restrict their plant design to in-house architects and designers and take other steps to prevent their competitors from discovering their methods. This can be more difficult than it sounds. In one case, a company (Company A) desired to learn their competitors (Company B) operation methods while their competitor was building a new plant. Company A hired an airplane to fly overhead and take pictures of the construction, which would disclose Company B's trade secrets. While this was not criminal and was not considered a trespass, Company B went to court to restrain the Company A from doing this. The Court stated that Company B should not be required to keep the construction site covered while under construction (they had already built a wall around the site to keep the methods secret) and that Company A had used improper means to learn the secret and found them guilty of trade secret theft.

There are various remedies for trade secret theft. Plaintiffs may recover both compensatory damages for their losses as well as punitive damages if they can show the Defendant acted in bad faith. In addition, successful plaintiffs may obtain an injunction, preventing the Defendant from using the secret (this may be true even if the Defendant obtained the secret innocently).

TRADEMARKS

A trademark is the right to use a word, name, symbol, design or combination of these to identify goods and distinguish them from goods made by others. The use of symbols or words to identify services such as restaurants are called "service marks" but follow the same rules as trademarks. Each trademark is only used in the specific category for which it is registered. That means that a clothing manufacturer may use the trademark "BILKO" even if there is a restaurant using the same name, and a car manufactured under that name. All three are different uses and fall under different categories. Currently, there are 45 different international categories for goods and services.

The basis for federal trademark protection is the Commerce Clause of the United States Constitution. Because federal law is not applicable unless the mark crosses state lines, federal trademark protection is only granted to those marks actually used in interstate or international commerce. For those marks used strictly in-state, the states offer state trademark protection as well. For those marks that are not registered with either the federal or state government, there is also a common law trademark, which though weaker than a registered mark, will provide for limited protection. Common law trademarks simply means that you are using the mark in business and can prevent another person from using the same mark in your regional market area. Protection applies only to those marks that have been used for a sufficient length of time to create name recognition. Because of the differences in state law, this column will discuss solely federal trademark law.

There are restrictions on what is covered by trademark law, but the list is liberal. Trademark protection has been granted to colors, composites, labels, letters, musical notes, slogans, names, numerals, packaging, and symbols. Examples of trademarks include: IBM, 7-UP, Wendy's, the green stripe on Burlington socks, the label of a Campbell's soup can, the shape of Coke bottles, the NBC musical notes, the "Noid" character for Domino's pizza, Burger King's hamburger sign, etc.

There are certain words and designs that cannot be given trademark protection. These include purely generic names, immoral, deceptive or scandalous names, flags or insignia of any country, the name portrait or signature of a living person without their consent, the name, portrait or signature of any deceased President of the United States during the lifetime of his widow, a mark which is primarily geographic, or a mark which is confusingly similar to an unabandoned or registered mark.

Trademark law gives the owner the right to stop any other person or company from using their mark, without having to prove that the other previously knew of the existence of the mark. The protections granted by federal trademark law includes: the right to sue in federal court; the right to recover profits, triple damages, court costs and attorney fees; and the right to stop the importation of foreign goods with similar marks. There are also criminal penalties for counterfeiters and trademark filing ability in foreign countries.

Certain activities are not affected by trademark protection. For example, registration of a trademark will not prevent a prior user from continuing their use of the trademark so long as they limit it to the same market where it has been used in the past. That is, they cannot expand their use of the trademark once it has been registered by another person. As mentioned above, a trademark also does not cover any items except those listed in the category stated in the application. If you register your trademark for clothes, you will have no protection if you start a jewelry line under the same mark, without filing another registration.

Trademarks can also be used by a competitor to compare items in advertising. Finally, the owner of an item may use the trademark of that item to sell it. As an example, it is not a trademark infringement to run a classified ad in the newspaper offering to sell a Honda Motorcycle.

The trademark application process is not a quick one. At a minimum, anticipate at least nine months from the initial filing of the application to final approval. Depending on the circumstances, this process can be extended even longer. The first step is completing the application. Trademark applications are available on-line through the Patent and Trademark Office. While the form seems fairly straightforward, thousands of trademark applications get rejected every year due to improper applications. Many details must be carefully completed. As an example, the goods that the trademark will be used on must be detailed.

It cannot simply say "clothing"; it must name all items of clothing that the mark will be used on.

Once the form is complete there is an additional page, called a "Drawing" that must be submitted. Again, the drawing page is available on-line, however, if you choose to create one yourself, you must follow exact rules issued by the Trademark Office.

With the application and drawing page, you must submit a sample of the mark actually being used. If the mark is for goods or merchandise, this would be the goods themselves, their packaging or a display at the point of sale. If the mark is for services, it may be placed on signs or in advertising. If the sample is large or bulky, photographs will suffice. Make sure that the sample shows the mark being used in exactly the same style as the application. Any differences will be viewed as a different mark and will be grounds for rejection. The filing fee for a trademark application is currently $335 per mark, per class (each class or category of goods or services the mark is used for).

Once the application, drawing page, sample and filing fee have been forwarded to the Trademark Office, the wait begins. Generally, the applicant authorizes the PTO to contact the applicant by email. If so, the PTO will contact the applicant when the application has been approved. Approximately three to four months from filing, the application will be assigned to an attorney in the Trademark Office for review. The trademark attorney reviews the application for legal sufficiency and performs a cursory search of the trademark office records to determine if the mark is already in use or is sufficiently similar to another mark which might create customer confusion.

Approximately a month after the attorney receives the application, they will do one of two things. The first option is to state the mark appears sufficient for approval. If this happens, the attorney will give a date when the mark will appear in the Official Gazette. This is a publication by the Trademark Office which displays all trademarks being considered for approval. The second option is what is called an Office Action, where the attorney rejects the trademark. There may be various reasons for rejection. There may be a similar mark already in use; the mark may contain geographic descriptions; the mark may be a generic term, etc. The Office Action will also contain the cases that the attorney is relying on for their decision. A few years ago, the Trademark Office modified their practices to become more user friendly. Now in the Office Action, the reviewing attorney will advise if and how the application can be modified to comply with the Office Action. The applicant will then have 6 months from the date of the Office Action to file a response. If the response is sufficient, the examining attorney may change their position and determine the mark is now suitable for publication, or they may file a final rejection.

If the mark is suitable for publication, the attorney will provide the date it will appear in the Official Gazette. This date will generally be at least a month after the date of the letter. Once the trademark is published in the Gazette, the public has thirty days to contest the use of the mark or request an extension of time to object. If there is an objection, you have three options: abandon the mark, attempt to settle with the opposing party, or challenge the opposition. The challenge process can take well over a year. If there are no objections, the mark will receive final approval after the thirty days and in another month a certificate will be issued, certifying the mark.

PATENTS

Patents are also regulated by the United States Patent and Trademark Office. While any lawyer may file an application for a copyright or trademark, only a certified patent lawyer may file a patent application for a client (Individuals can always file their own patent applications, however, the process is highly technical). To be a member of the Patent Bar, lawyers must have a scientific or engineering undergraduate degree and must pass a special bar exam.

Patents give inventors protection for their ideas. The ideas need to be written out in detail. There are three types of patents: utility patents (any new and useful process, machine, article of manufacture, or composition of matter, or any new and useful improvement thereof), design patents (a new, original, and ornamental design for an article of manufacture), plant patents (granted to anyone who invents or discovers and asexually reproduces any distinct and new variety of plant).

Before a patent is applied for, a patent search should be done to see if there is already a similar invention. There are various companies that can perform the search, or a registered patent attorney can do it as well. If there is already a similar patent, the process is over. If not, determine what type of patent you need and decide if you will apply yourself or hire an attorney. Like with trademarks, the application is filed electronically. If the patent is approved, the inventor gets an exclusive right to the invention for 20 years. It was estimated in 2000 that the cost to prosecute a patent application was between $10,000 and $30,000.

Patents can only be enforced in federal court. Damages are similar to those in federal trademark cases.

SALES

A SALE: AN EXCHANGE OF GOODS AND SERVICES

Now we are going to turn our attention to sales. A lot of this may seem repetitive because the laws we have discussed in the past cover some of this information as well, but read carefully-there are some major differences as well. –This section of the UCC does not deal with real estate, securities, or negotiable instruments. The sale of goods is defined as the transfer of goods in exchange for consideration, that is - money, property or service.

What are goods?

According to the Uniform Commercial Code, "Goods" are all things which are movable and identifiable at the time of the contract for sale "other than the money in which the price is to be paid, investment securities and things in action". It also does not include unborn young animals and growing crops.

Goods must be both existing and identified before they can be part of a sales contract. Goods which are not both existing and identified are called "future" goods. You cannot sell an item that does not yet exist, even if you plan on building it. Since something doesn't exist, there is no title and therefore no owner. However, you can make a contract for services to create the future goods, or make a future contract to sell goods.

What is a sale? Again, looking to the UCC, "A sale consists in the passing of title from the seller to the buyer for a price." It may actually be easier to say what a sale isn't. It isn't a bailment - that is where a person gives property to another but title doesn't change. It isn't a gift as there must be an exchange. It isn't an option, because it is a definite transfer, not a future right.

In general, basic contract law applies to the sale of both goods and services, with some exceptions. You can have a mixed agreement where the vendor agrees to provide both goods and services. Look at a janitorial contract. Not only do they provide cleaning services, they may also provide goods, such as soap in the dispensers.

Like with basic contact law, there must still be an offer and an acceptance. Here, however, we see the first changes from standard contract law. In sales, if an offer is made irrevocable for a stated period of time, the period that it can be irrevocable cannot exceed three months. If time is not mentioned then the offer will only stay open for a reasonable time.

An acceptance may be made in any manner that indicates the intent to accept, unless the contract requires a specific action. However, unlike general contract law, you may accept an offer and propose different terms at the same time. Under general contract law, this would be considered a counteroffer and would nullify the original offer. Under a sales contract, a contract would be formed on the terms of the original offer, but there is also a counteroffer that the vendor may accept or reject. It does not terminate the deal. If terms of the counteroffer conflict with the offer, there is still a contract, except the conflicting terms are ignored.

Also, unlike general contract law, the contract does not need to show what the consideration, or price, is going to be. It can merely state that the price will be determined later. This would be overly vague in a standard contract, but it is allowed in sales contracts. If the contract doesn't state a price, the price will be considered what is reasonable, or what is customary for the industry.

You can also have an open-ended contract as to the amount to be purchased. It is legitimate to say that a vendee will buy all the product produced by a vendor. Under standard contract law, this term would be overly vague.

A sales agreement may be modified without additional consideration (the price paid for the goods or service). In standard contract law, you must pay additional consideration to modify the terms of a contract.

Statutes may effect what sales may be done. Of course, as we have said since the beginning, you cannot contract for an illegal act. This applies to goods as well. But statutes may make certain sales illegal. For instance, forbidding the sale of alcohol before noon on Sundays is a standard law in most places. Also, sales of counterfeit goods bearing false trademarks are illegal.

FOCUS ON SALES AND THE UNIFORM COMMERCIAL CODE

Previously, we discussed the statute of frauds (which requires certain contracts to be in writing). Well, it pops up here again.

Florida Statute 672.201 states "Except as otherwise provided in this section a contract for the sale of goods for the price of $500 or more is not enforceable by way of action or defense unless there is some writing sufficient to indicate that a contract for sale has been made between the parties and signed by the party against whom enforcement is sought or by his authorized agent or broker."

It then goes on to give an exception: "A contract which does not satisfy the requirements of subsection (1) but which is valid in other respects is enforceable: (a) If the goods are to be specifically manufactured for the buyer and are not suitable for sale to others in the ordinary course of the seller's business and the seller, before notice of repudiation is received and under circumstances which reasonable indicate that the goods are for the buyer, has made either a substantial beginning of their manufacture or commitments for their procurement; or (b) If the party against whom enforcement is sought admits in his pleading, testimony or otherwise in court that a contract for sale was made, but the contract is not enforceable under this provision beyond the quantity of goods admitted; or (c) With respect to goods for which payment has been made and accepted or which have been received and accepted."

What this means is that, if you have a contract to sell goods for more than $500, it must be in writing, unless the goods are created specifically for the buyer, or if the buyer admits to the contract, or if payment has already been made.

Leases are also governed under the Uniform Commercial Code in Florida Statute 680. Most people think of leases for real estate; under the UCC the leases are for goods.

There are basically three types of leases for goods.

First is the consumer lease. This is a lease from a business to a customer, such as when a home furnishings company leases furniture or appliances. However, it only applies when the company is in the business of making such leases.

Second is the commercial lease. This is a lease of goods for business purposes. An example would be a restaurant that leases kitchen equipment, or a store that leases credit card equipment.

Finally is the financial lease. This is essentially a third party lease where the lessor (landlord in real estate parlance) does not select, manufacture, or supply the goods, but acquires the goods or the right to possession and use of the goods in connection with the lease. The requirements for a financial lease are slightly more detailed than a commercial or consumer lease, simply due to the third party aspect.

The statute of frauds attaches to leases also. A lease where the total payments will be more than $1,000 must be in writing. The lease must describe the goods, the lease term, and indicate the lease contract has been formed between the parties. While this last clause sounds unnecessary, a lease contract that does not state it is a lease may be construed as a contract for sale.

The Uniform Commercial Code also covers the areas of bulk sales. A bulk sales law basically prevents a party from selling all of the assets of a business and then keeping the money rather than paying their creditors. Bulk sales laws require vendors to send notices to all known creditors and run ads in the papers for all unknown creditors to advise them to file claims for their debts. If the vendor doesn't comply, the assets that have been sold may be seized by the creditor. Therefore, it is important to know if you are doing an asset purchase of a business, what the bulk sales laws for that state are.

'GOOD FAITH' IS A BIG PART OF A SALES CONTRACT

Contracts are meant to be fair. The parties to a sales contract have a duty to use good faith to not do anything that would impair the other party in complying with the contract. Merchants must comply with the commercial standards of fair dealing as defined by their trade (although some trades are less ethical than others).

Unless the contract states differently, a sale occurs concurrently. That is, when the goods are delivered, the buyer must pay. These events occur at the same time. In a situation where the two are not simultaneous, the contact is complete when the last event takes place. Whether the goods are delivered first or the payment is made first, the contract is not complete until both sides have completed their obligations.

We talked about anticipatory repudiation of a contract previously. To refresh your recollection, this is where a party to a contract cancels the contract because they believe in good faith that the other side is going to breach the agreement, even before the breach actually happens. An example is when the other side affirmatively states they are not going to perform their obligations, even though there is a contract. This also applies to sales contracts. However, with a sales contract, if you believe the other side is going to breach the contract, you may ask for a written assurance that the deal will be honored. If the written assurance is not sufficient, you may also require security to be put up to guarantee performance. If the assurance is not given within 30 days, you may treat the agreement as if the other party had already breached it.

There are three specific duties in a sales contract: the duty of the seller to deliver; the duty of the buyer to accept; and the duty of the buyer to pay. Each of these must be met or there is a breach.

The seller must turn over the goods to the buyer. He does not always need to make a physical delivery, but he must make the items available to the buyer. The details of delivery are determined by the terms of the contract. The agreement should say who must deliver, or who will pick up; the place of delivery, the manner of delivery, the time of delivery. (We will go into this topic in more detail later).

If these details are not written, you look to the standards for that industry. Unless otherwise stated in the agreement, the seller must provide all of the items at the same time. The buyer has no obligation to accept a partial shipment. If the goods do not match what is ordered, the buyer has the choice to accept or reject the goods. If the buyer rejects, the seller has the option of sending a second shipment that matches the agreement. This is different from standard contracts where a failure to perform is an automatic breach of the agreement. If the time for performance has passed, then the seller gets an additional reasonable time to conform. If the time hasn't passed, the seller needs to tell the buyer, before the expiration, that he will make a proper tender of conforming merchandise.

If seller has made a proper tender of conforming goods, the buyer has an obligation to accept the items. If the buyer does not accept the goods, there is a breach. As mentioned before, the buyer does not have to accept non-conforming goods. Therefore, the buyer has the right to inspect the goods before acceptance. There is an exception when the sale is COD. For COD sales, the buyer must pay first and examine later.

An acceptance is either express or implied. The buyer can say "I accept" or he may simply take possession and start using the merchandise. Or he may simply not return the items. All are forms of acceptance.

Once the goods are accepted, the buyer then has the duty to pay for the items. Usually the payment must be made at the time of acceptance. Payment may be made by any method acceptable by the seller. It can be cash, check, or promissory note. However, if the sales agreement doesn't state otherwise, the payment must be cash and the seller may refuse any other payment method.

SHIPPING HAS A LANGUAGE OF ITS OWN

When you buy something in a store, that is referred to as the point of sale or point of purchase. Rarely in business do business owners go to a store to buy the merchandise they are going to sell- they order it to be shipped.

In sales, shipping is a major issue and has a language all its own. In the process from manufacturing to final customer sale, there may be many shipping steps. The manufacturer will buy raw material to make the goods. These will be bought and shipped to the manufacturing plant. Once manufactured, the product may be shipped to a middleman who then ships it to the retail store, who may then ship it to the final customer. This is a common business practice.

But who is responsible if there is damage during shipping? Who is responsible for the costs of shipping?

Anytime a business needs something delivered, they need to enter into a shipping contract. The contract should spell out certain details, such as where the delivery is to be made, who has responsibility for it, at what point responsibility ends and at what point title transfers. Because this is such an important aspect of business, terms have been developed that specify in a shorthand method where these responsibilities lie.

First we have a CIF contract. CIF stands for "cost, insurance and freight." In these contracts, the buyer pays the seller for the cost of the goods, shipping and insurance against any damage. The seller is then obligated to provide insurance to protect the buyer from loss and deliver the goods to the shipping company for delivery to the buyer. The title to the goods transfers when they are placed with the shipper. The insurance protects the buyer until final delivery.

Next is the CF contract, which stands for "costs and freight." Here, there is no requirement for the seller to obtain insurance and the buyer takes the risk of loss. The buyer may buy insurance on his own. The seller is only liable until the goods are delivered to the shipping company. Again, the title passes when the goods are delivered to the shipper.

Next is the Free on Board contract. An FOB contract must state a location where liability shifts. The seller takes the risk of loss until the item reaches that location, and the buyer takes liability after that. An FOB contract may be "FOB (Place of shipment)," where the seller needs only deliver the goods to a shipper, or it may be "FOB (Place of delivery)," where the seller must deliver the goods to the final destination.

For example, if I order an item "FOB the Law Office of Albert Kelley," the seller must guarantee that I receive the item at my office. If I order an item "FOB Miami," I have to make arrangements to travel to Miami to pick it up, or I have to make separate arrangements to have it shipped from Miami to Key West. The seller's risk ends once the item makes it to Miami. The seller has the obligation to pay the costs to get the item to the FOB point.

The next contract is called Free Along Side. This is a true shipping contract as it only applies to vessels and ports. The seller must pay for the item to be delivered to a ship. Once delivered, the buyer takes the responsibility and risk. If the buyer wants more security that the item will reach a closer port, they may ask for an "Ex-ship contract," under which the seller's liability does not end until the item is delivered off the ship at its destination.

REMEDIES FOR SALE OF GOODS

Under the Uniform Commercial Code (UCC), a lawsuit on the sale of goods must be filed within four years from the date of the contract, or the date of delivery. The exception is a contract for future performance, which doesn't begin to run until the performance begins.

When there is a breach of contract by the buyer, the seller has numerous remedies. First, since the seller has an automatic lien on the goods in his possession, he can retain possession of the goods until the buyer pays for them. For the lien to be effective though, the seller must keep possession of the goods. Once possession has been transferred to the buyer, the lien disappears.

Second, the seller can resell the items to another party. If he cannot sell the items for the same price the buyer was to pay, the buyer remains liable for the difference. Before reselling, the seller must give notice to the buyer that he is reselling the goods, and allow the buyer the opportunity to pay for the goods.

Third, the seller can cancel the contract. This ends all obligations of the parties.

Fourth, the seller can sue the buyer for damages. This may allow the seller to recover his costs, depending on the terms of the agreement. The amount of damage depends on the circumstances. If the buyer accepts the goods without paying, then the damage is the full amount owed. If the buyer refuses acceptance of the goods, the damage is the difference between the fair market value of the goods and the amount on the contract, since the seller can still sell the items to recover part of his loss. However, if the items are specially built and the buyer refuses acceptance, the buyer may be responsible for the full amount, regardless of the fair market value, because the goods may not be easily resold.

What remedies does the buyer have if the seller breaches?

First, if the seller sends the wrong merchandise, the buyer may refuse to accept it. This is also true if the seller sends the right items but the wrong amount. The buyer does not have to accept anything except what he contracted for. The rejection needs to be made within a reasonable time after delivery of the items. The buyer must notify the seller of the rejection and then wait for the seller to give him instructions as to how to dispose of the goods.

Second, if the goods have some defect that is not immediately apparent, the buyer may revoke the acceptance upon discovery of the defect. The revocation must be made within a reasonable time though as a substantial delay may act as an irrevocable acceptance of the goods. After the acceptance has been revoked, the buyer may then cancel the contract or require the seller to deliver non-defective goods. As with a rejection, the buyer must merely notify the seller of the revocation. He does not have to physically return the items, until the seller gives instructions on how to return them.

Third, if the seller fails to deliver the items, the buyer may sue for damages. The damage is generally limited to the difference between the fair market value and the amount of the contract. If the buyer attempts to cover the goods (that is, buy them elsewhere), he may recover the excess of the price actually paid from the price contracted for.

Fourth, the buyer may cancel the agreement if the seller fails to deliver. This voids the contract and allows the buyer to get back any money paid towards the purchase.

An unusual occurrence arises when title passes, but possession does not. This is when an item is sold, but delivery is not made. The seller will be said to have converted the goods. The seller may be told to specifically perform the agreement and deliver the goods. If he doesn't, the seller owes the buyer the value of the item.

FALSE ADVERTISING

When advertising is done over the airwaves, either through radio or television, it is governed by the Federal Trade Commission. Print advertising and local advertising is usually governed by state statute. These laws protect consumers against false advertising. False advertising includes misrepresenting the goods being sold and intentionally misleading consumers. It also covers what is known as a "bait and switch".

In a "bait and switch" scheme, a store offers an extremely low price on an item, but has an insufficient amount of the items meet the expected demand. The store then offers to sell the customer a similar item at a higher price. Years ago, this was a standard practice by certain merchants. In a standard situation, a store offered a mink coat for around $10, just to get the customers to come in the store, however, they only had one coat available for sale at that price. Once the customers came to the store for the coat, the store could pressure them to buy something else. Like another coat for a much higher price. Since the customer was already in a buying mood, the sale was not difficult to make.

Many of the false advertising cases are filed under section 43(a) of the federal Lanham Act. That statute provides in part that: "Any person who, on or in connection with any goods or services ... uses in commerce any ... false or misleading description of fact, or false or misleading representation of fact, which ... in commercial advertising or promotion, misrepresents the nature, characteristics, qualities, or geographic origin of his or her or another person's goods, services, or commercial activities, shall be liable in a civil action by any person who believes that he or she is or is likely to be damaged by such act."

The question in false advertising isn't whether there was fraud, but rather was there deception. Even if there isn't an intent to defraud, if the ultimate result is a deception of consumers, there is a violation. This means that if a businessman makes claims about his product that he believes are true, and they turn out not to be, there may be a violation.

If a company is going to make a claim about a product, the FTC requires that the data used as the basis for the claim be maintained in a file for inspection. If the FTC investigates a claim of false advertising, all the material they inspect may be made public, except for trade secrets. This allows consumers to know the safety aspects of the products they are using.

If the advertiser makes a false claim, the FTC can require among other things that they make corrective advertising to contradict the improper statements. This is called retroactive advertising. This happened with Listerine in 1976. Listerine's ads claimed that Listerine prevented, cured or alleviated the common cold. Because there was no proof of this claim, the FTC required Listerine to issue $10 million in advertisements stating

"Listerine will not help prevent colds or sore throats or lessen their severity." Today's ads don't refer to colds, but only bad breath (Apparently they didn't learn their lesson in 2005 they had to pull ads that stated Listerine was as effective as flossing in preventing tooth and gum decay).

Not all false advertising is illegal. When the seller is boasting about his product, or slightly exaggerating its qualities, it is referred to as "puffing" and is generally allowed. This works best when the claim is "Our product is the best in its field," or a more specific example, "This medicine has the longest lasting ingredient available in an over the counter brand." Here they are not saying that they are the only medicine that lasts this long. It may be that other medicines last equally as long. Therefore, it is not false advertising.

RULES VARY WHERE LABELING, DISLOSURE PRICING CONCERNED

Just as there are laws regarding false advertising, there are rules as to labeling of products. These rules usually aren't that strong.

The exception is food labeling as far as nutritional information. But there are a lot of problems with labeling. Is extra-large truly larger than large? Who determines if there is a new improved flavor? Does low fat have to be lower than regular fat? There are few guidelines for these areas and therefore it may be difficult to bring an action for deceptive advertising.

There are certain groups that approve items for

consumers. Good Housekeeping is probably the most well-known. We've all heard about the "Good Housekeeping Seal of Approval." This is not a government agency and their recommendations are not a guarantee in the quality of goods. Any organization may issue seals of approval; it's up to the purchaser to have confidence in the approving organization. Advertising that you have a seal of approval is a guarantee that the goods have been so approved. If a company states they have received a seal of approval that has not actually been granted, it is considered false advertising.

The government has tried to reduce deceptive selling techniques by passing special laws regarding disclosure of certain issues. If contracts are written on two sides of a sheet of paper, the federal law requires a notice to be placed on each side letting the consumer know that there is a second side.

Occasionally, the law will require certain things to be made part of a contract. For instance, if there is a clause that the seller doesn't want the buyer to see, they might try to hide it in fine print. Certain clauses are required by law to be in larger or bold print so that the buyer will definitely see them. In financing a transaction, merchants must give you full disclosure of terms of the transaction. They must disclose interest rates, repayment terms, and annual percentage rate. These disclosures are part of the requirements of the Fair Credit and Charge Card Disclosure Rates. This law requires that the consumer know all the details that will affect the sale. What is the full price, what is the down payment, how many payments will be made, what will be the total paid in interest payments, and the percentage rate?

Also, for most credit purchases, the merchant must comply with the truth in lending act. This act applies whenever the payment schedule requires more than four payments. If dealing with a used car dealer, they must disclose if an odometer has been tuned back or rolled over.

Usually a sale is final when the transaction is made. However, when dealing with home solicited sales, there is generally a "three day rule of recession" that would allow you to void a sale within three days. A home solicitation means that the salesman actually comes to the house to make the sale - not just negotiate terms. This statute is designed primarily to protect consumers against door-to-door salesman. This three-day rule generally does not apply to any other types of sales.

Finally, the law doesn't allow price gouging if the demand exceeds the supply. This seems unusual. When we talk about free enterprise, we normally think that the price of the item should be whatever the market will bear. However, that can be unfair at times. When Hurricane Andrew came through Miami, people were without electricity for weeks. Those with electric generators could keep their refrigerators and air conditioners running. Suddenly the demand for generators skyrocketed. Some stores thought they would take advantage of the situation and doubled or tripled the price of the generators. This was illegal and many of the stores were cited for illegal practices. The same thing happened to food and water.

FINANCES
CREDIT CARDS

There is a special section of statutes designed to cover credit cards. These laws are in place to protect the consumer since credit cards create a large opportunity for consumer fraud, by the credit card issuer, by the merchant, and by other consumers. First, there are certain requirements for issuance of a card. The consumer must request a card and complete an application. The issuer cannot just send a card to a consumer without a request. If you receive a credit card that you didn't request call the company and ask for a copy of the application because there is a chance that it was forged. This happens much more frequently than you would expect. If the contract was forged, there is no liability for the charges incurred by the forger.

When you apply for a credit card, there are certain restrictions on processing the application. The issuer cannot discriminate against race, sex, color, national origin or age (except as to minors). They also cannot discriminate because you have filed complaints under the Consumer Credit Protection Act. If the application is denied you have a right to a written statement setting forth the reason for the denial.

Then there are laws that protect the user after the card is issued. Once you get a credit card and start making charges on it, payments are applied to the oldest charges first. Therefore, if someone uses your card and pays you for the item, their payment will actually be applied to prior charges. This is an important issue for asset protection. In the event a consumer fails to make payments, an issuer may obtain a lien on items not yet fully paid for. If the issuer applies payments to a portion of all items purchased, no item will ever be fully paid for, allowing the issuer to lien everything. This practice is not allowed under the UCC. The issuer must apply payments to the oldest items first, so that in event of a default, the consumer can retain those items.

What if the card is stolen? In the case of a stolen card, there may be liability, but if the issuer follows there notification rules, and the card holder acts promptly, the liability is limited to $50. The issuer may require the holder of a stolen card to pay $50 in charges once the card is reported stolen, only if when issuing the card they send the consumer notice of the liability, a preaddressed, stamped card for notification of loss, and provide a form so store owners can ascertain the identification of the consumer. This is why most credit cards have a signature strip on the back. If the issuer fails to comply with the above, they are not entitled to any funds once the card is stolen.

The consumer also must take action to limit their liability. Primarily, they must report the stolen card promptly so the company can cancel the card number. This $50 limit only applies if an unauthorized person uses the card. If the use is by an authorized person making an unauthorized purchase, the consumer is still liable. As an example, if a parent loans their (adult) child a credit card to purchase school supplies and the child then buys a new wardrobe, the parent is still responsible, even though the child was not authorized to buy clothes. Therefore, be careful before handing your credit card to your kids.

Once you get your bill, if you find a mistake, you have the right to notify the credit card company about the error. They then have an obligation to investigate and correct the mistake. Generally, a merchant reporting a charge must maintain a copy of the consumer's signature on file in order to defend a challenge of a false charge. These days, signatures are used less frequently, which I why cards now have an identification code on the back.

KNOW YOUR RIGHTS AGAINST DEBT COLLECTORS

In today's world, many people get caught up in credit and find themselves heavily in debt. Even here there are laws that protect the consumer. The Florida Statutes have provisions that prevent creditors from taking certain actions to collect debts. It is important to know your rights as some less reputable credit collection agencies are known for violating them. Creditors or collection agents working for the creditor may not do any of the following:

(1) Simulate a law enforcement officer or representative of any government agency;

(2) Use or threaten force or violence;

(3) Tell a debtor that he will disclose to another information affecting the debtor's reputation for credit worthiness without also informing the debtor that the existence of the dispute will also be disclosed as required by subsection (6);

(4) Communicate or threaten to communicate with a debtor's employer prior to obtaining final judgment against the debtor;

(5) Disclose to a person other than the debtor or his family information affecting the debtor's reputation;

(6) Disclose information concerning the existence of a debt known to be reasonably disputed by the debtor

without disclosing that fact;

(7) Willfully communicate with the debtor or any member of his family with such frequency as can reasonably be expected to harass to debtor or his family, or willfully engage in other conduct which can be reasonably be expected to abuse or harass the debtor or any member of his family;

(8) Use profane, obscene, vulgar, or willfully abusive language in communicating with the debtor or any member of his family;

(9) Claim, attempt, or threaten to enforce a debt when such person knows that the debt is not legitimate;

(10) Use a communication which simulates in any manner legal or judicial process or which gives the appearance of being authorized, issued or approved by a government, governmental agency, or attorney at law, when it is not;

(11) Communicate with a debtor under the guise of an attorney by using the stationary of an attorney or forms or instruments which only attorneys are authorized to prepare;

(12) Orally communicate with a debtor in such a manner as to give the false impression or appearance that such person is or is associated with an attorney;

(13) Advertise or threaten to advertise for sale any debt as a means to enforce payment;

(14) Publish or post or threaten to post before general public individual names or any list of names of debtors, commonly known as a deadbeat list;

(15) Refuse to provide adequate identification of himself or his employer or other entity that he represents

when requested to do so by a debtor;

(16) Mail any communication to a debtor in an envelope or postcard with words typed, written, or printed on the outside of the envelope or postcard calculated to embarrass the debtor. An example of this would be an envelope addressed to "Deadbeat, John Doe"; or

(17) Communicate with the debtor between the hours of 9 p.m. and 8 a.m. in the debtor's time zone without the prior consent of the debtor.

(18) Communicate with the debtor if they know the debtor is represented by legal counsel and the creditor knows or can readily ascertain the attorney's name and address.

(19) Cause the debtor to be charged for the collection efforts, such as collect phone calls

If a creditor violates this law, the debtor may sue the creditor and recover either their actual damages or $1,000, whichever is greater, along with legal fees and costs.

COMMERCIAL PAPER AND NEGOTIABLE INSTRUMENTS

When dealing with commercial paper, there are many terms that take on a special meaning. "Commercial paper" doesn't mean the ad section of your local newspaper, and "negotiable instrument" isn't a trumpet that gets traded. These are two phrases for a written, signed promise to pay a sum of money. Negotiable instruments are governed by Florida Statute 673.1041. The key issue to a negotiable instrument, or commercial paper, is that, if created properly, the written promise may be sold, traded, or given to a third party.

There are four basic forms of negotiable instruments: promissory notes, drafts, checks and certificates of deposit. In order to qualify as a negotiable instrument, the item must be made payable to the bearer or to order at the time it is issued, it must be payable on demand or at a definite time, it must not require any other undertaking or instruction to do any act in addition to the payment of money, and it must be for money, not services or other exchange. We will discuss these aspects in more detail later.

An instrument is a "note" if it is a promise to pay money and is a "draft" if it is an order for the payment of money. An "order" means a written instruction to a third party to pay money signed by the person giving the instruction. An authorization to pay is not an order unless the person authorized to pay is also instructed to pay. As an example, if you have ever written a check, that is an "Order" to your bank to pay money to someone else.

The term "check" is a specific type of draft, payable on demand and drawn on a bank. An instrument may be a check even though it is described on its face by another term, such as "money order." Other types of checks include "cashier's check" "teller's checks" "traveler's check".

The final type of negotiable instrument is the "certificate of deposit". This is an instrument containing an acknowledgment by a bank that a sum of money has been received by the bank and a promise by the bank to repay the sum of money. A certificate of deposit is basically a note from the bank.

There can be a number of people involved in any transaction involving negotiable instruments. First is the "maker". This is the person who writes or creates a promissory note. The "drawer" is the person who writes or creates a draft or check. Third is the "drawee". The drawee is the person to whom a check or draft is addressed and who has been ordered to pay the sum of money. In a check, the bank is the drawee. Next we have the "payee". This is the person named on the face of the instrument to receive payment. On your checks, for example, it states "Pay to the Order of John Smith". John Smith is the payee. Once the drawee has signified in writing their willingness to accept the draft and make the specified payment, they are called the "acceptor".

As with contracts, there are certain implied warranties made when transferring a negotiable instrument. There is an implied warranty that the transferor has the right to negotiate or enforce the instrument. There is a warranty that the signature is genuine. There is a warranty that the note has not been altered. There is a warranty that the note is not subject to any defense. And there is a warranty that the transferor does not know of any insolvency of the maker that would affect the enforceability of the note. The transferor, however, does not warrant that payment will be made. That is up to the transferee to enforce.

There are two types of parties who may enforce payment on a negotiable instrument. The first is a holder. This means the person the paper was originally issued to or any person who the commercial paper has been sold to. The second type of party who may enforce is an assignee. As an example, if I write a check to Bob Smith, he is the holder as long as he has the check. If he sells the check to Ann Jones, she becomes the holder. If he gives the check to her, she then becomes the assignee. The difference between a holder and an assignee is an assignee hasn't given any consideration for the note. Both types of parties have full rights to enforce the paper. They merely need to show the original paper to the Court, prove that the signature is original, and show that they have a right as a holder or assignee.

There is also a person known as a favored holder. This is a holder with certain rights over and above those of a mere holder. If the buyer is a favored holder, certain defenses will not be allowed against him if he attempts to enforce the note.

To be a favored holder, you must be either a holder in due course (also known as a bona fide purchaser) or a holder through a holder in due course. To be a holder in due course you must meet four requirements. First, you must give value for the paper. This doesn't mean money; it may be money or goods or service. You can also give value by using the note as security for a debt or by receiving it as payment for a prior or current debt. It generally doesn't matter what the value is, so long as there is value (however, if the value is too low, the Court may find that the transfer was made in bad faith and therefore there is no value). The value must be actual and must have been actually paid. A promise of future payment will not suffice.

Second, the buyer must act in good faith. Generally, good faith simply means that the person buying the paper is acting for proper purposes and is dealing honestly with the salesperson. If the buyer is acting in good faith, it doesn't matter if the seller is.

Third, the buyer must not know that the paper is overdue or has already been dishonored. While paper can still be transferred under these circumstances, if the buyer knows this, he is not a buyer in due course. Why would a person buy a note under these circumstances? Well, it allows a buyer to pay a much lower amount and then proceed to foreclose on the debt. If they prevail in Court they can then seize assets of the debtor necessary to pay off the paper.

Finally, the buyer can't know about any defenses or adverse claims against the paper. If there is notice of any potential defenses or claims prior to the purchase of the negotiable instrument, the buyer is not in due course. If, however, the buyer learns of defenses or claims after the purchase, they will remain a holder in due course. This status is based on the knowledge at the time of purchase.

A buyer can also be a holder through a holder in due course. This simply means they have purchased the paper from a holder in due course. A holder through a holder does not need to follow all of the requirements of a holder in due course. He may receive the paper without giving something of value, or he may know of defenses or claims. So long as the he is not a party to fraud or illegality that affects the paper, he will have all the protection that a holder in due course receives.

Once the holder of a note presents it for payment, if the primary party (either the maker or the acceptor) refuses to pay, it is said to be dishonored. After there has been dishonor, the presentor needs to give notice to secondary parties. For example, if Bob writes a check to Sam and Bob's bank refuses to pay, Sam must notify Bob. If this notice is not given, the secondary parties will not be liable for the note. The notice must identify the instrument and state that it has been dishonored. If the notice is being given to a bank, it must be given by midnight the next banking day after dishonor. If to a non-bank, notice must be given the third business day following the dishonor. Written notice is effective when sent, even if it is not received.

If there is a delay in giving notice, it may be excused for certain circumstances such as an equipment failure at the bank. Notice between branches of the same bank are treated as if it was between separate banks.

Liability may be discharged against just the secondary parties or all parties. However, you cannot discharge liability to the primary party without discharging liability to the secondary parties.

The primary party is discharged when payment is made to the proper person-AND the paper is turned over to that party. As I mentioned before, if the primary party doesn't get the note back, the note may still be negotiated to another person and the primary party will still be liable.

Liability may also be discharged if there is an accord and satisfaction, a novation (substituting one debtor for another), a bankruptcy, or by the passing of the appropriate statute of limitations. Liability can be discharged if the holder gives a writing to the primary party stating that the agreement is canceled or renounced. The cancellation may be as simple as writing the word "CANCELED" over the paper, by crossing out terms, or simply by giving the paper back to the primary party (Possession is a requisite to enforcement of a negotiable instrument).

If the note is secured, it may be discharged by the holder impairing the security. In other words, let's say I am holding a car as security on a note. If I sell or wreck the car, I have impaired the security and thus have discharged the note (This only applies if the holder of the note impairs the security. If the debtor impairs the security, the debt continues).

If you do not record the security, the note may be discharged. There is a government form called a UCC-1.

Anytime personal property is used to secure a promissory note, the parties must record the UCC-1. In Florida the UCC-1 used to be recorded with the clerk of the court and the Department of State, however, a few years ago the service was taken over by a private company. If the security is not recorded, you cannot enforce the debt against the security. This does not necessarily mean that the debt is discharged; only that the security is free and clear which may make collection impossible.

Finally, if the holder alters the note in a fraudulent and material way, they discharge the debtor. The holder is allowed to complete the note, such as adding the date, as this is not a fraudulent act. However, if the holder attempts to modify the amount even by only one cent, it will act as a discharge of the debt (though a subsequent holder in due course may still in all cases enforce the instrument according to its original tenor).

SURETY AND GUARANTEES

Most 18 year olds haven't had a chance to develop sufficient credit histories to allow them to make major purchases, such as cars or houses. Often times, even leasing property can be difficult because the landlord may not be sure if they can pay the rent for the property. Rather than telling these young people that they cannot buy a car or house until they have developed a credit history, the Seller (or Landlord) may request that the Buyer have someone sign a document assuring that all payments will be made. This document is known as a guarantee or a surety.

A guarantee is a secondary contract that binds the third party (in the above example, perhaps the Buyer's parents) to pay any debt or obligation of the Buyer, if the Buyer doesn't pay. The third party is known as a guarantor or surety, the Buyer is known as the debtor and the Seller becomes known as the obligee or creditor.

Sureties and guarantees serve similar purposes, but there is a slight difference between the two. A surety is liable for the debt immediately upon default by the debtor, without the Creditor having to first proceed against the debtor. However, under a guarantee, the creditor generally must seek payment from the debtor first and only after failing to collect can he turn to the guarantor. An exception to this is the absolute guarantee which acts the same as a surety.

Guarantees and Sureties are not used only for 18 year olds buying cars. They also are used often for any person with credit problems and more recently are often required when a corporation desires to enter into a lease for commercial property. Many landlords realize that if a company falls on hard times they can declare bankruptcy and discharge the lease debt; however, if the principle shareholder or director signs a personal guarantee they remain personally liable for the lease debt, even if the company fails.

Guarantees and sureties are contracts and therefore the same requirements to the formation of a contract are required. Because of the nature of the contract, a guarantee or surety must be in writing. Under Florida's Statute of Frauds, any agreement to pay the debt of another person must be in writing or it is not enforceable. Further, if the guarantee is entered into at the same time as the original sale or lease contract, separate consideration is usually not required for the guarantee, however if it is created after the original transaction, there must be an additional consideration.

Not every default will require a surety or guarantor to pay the debt. If the surety fears the debtor will fail on his payments putting the surety into an endangered position, the surety can notify the creditor to take action against the debtor. If the creditor can proceed against the debtor and fails to do so, the surety is then released from liability. If the surety pays the debt, he then takes the pace of the creditor and can proceed against the debtor for collection.

This is referred to as subrogation, where the surety steps into the place of the creditor. In addition, the surety is entitled to indemnification from the debtor and can proceed against him for reimbursement. If there are two or more sureties and one takes on payment of the debt, he may require the other sureties to contribute their portion of the debt to him.

Of danger to the surety is bankruptcy. If the debtor files for bankruptcy, the surety is not released from liability. This is the risk that guarantors and sureties undertake. The failure of the debtor to pay can affect the credit of the guarantor.

LETTERS OF CREDIT

In the business world, many people have heard the phrase "letters of credit" however, what these are is commonly misunderstood. A letter of credit is more than a loan; it is an arrangement where the issuer (a bank, for instance) agrees to pay drafts of the beneficiary of the letter, under instruction of the payor. As an example: John Smith desires to purchase merchandise for his store from Bob Jones. Smith can ask his bank to issue a letter of credit to Jones for up to a predetermined amount. Based upon this letter of credit, Jones has assurance that he will be paid for the merchandise from Smith's bank (For sake of oversimplification, I will continue to use this example through the article).

Letters of credit usually have conditions that must be met before the money is issued (the bank won't just give the money to Jones without some proof that the money is owed). The letter may simply state that the beneficiary (Jones) needs to provide a bill of lading showing delivery, or it may require more details such as proof of insurance, purchase requests, etc. The payor needs to take care in setting the conditions. If the conditions simply state that the bank will pay when the goods are delivered, the bank will be required to honor the letter of credit even if the goods do not meet the approval of the payor. Once the conditions are placed in the letter, the bank must honor the letter if the conditions are met.

The issuance and completion of a letter of credit actually involves several contracts. First, there is a contract between the issuer and the payor (the bank and Smith) where the issuer agrees to issue the letter under the payor's instruction. Second, there is a contract between the issuer and the beneficiary. This is the actual letter of credit, which is a contract, in that it obligates the issuer (bank) to make payment once the beneficiary (Jones) has met the terms of the letter. Finally, there is the underlying contract for sale of goods or services between the payor (Smith) and the beneficiary (Jones).

While the letter of credit is a contract, no consideration is required to establish or modify the letter. The letter of credit should state a time period that it will be valid, and cannot be revoked or modified by the issuer or the payor unless the beneficiary consents to the change or revocation.

A letter of credit must be in writing and signed by the issuer, and must state specifically that it is a "letter of credit". This is what is called a term of art which means that the words have a specific meaning in the law. If the letter fails to include these words, it may be considered a mere guarantee.

There are several risks with a letter of credit. The bank takes the risk that the documents presented by the beneficiary are those required. If the documents provided to the bank by the beneficiary are not those required under the conditions of the letter, and the bank makes payment, they cannot get reimbursed for their loss. The issuer, however, is not required to verify the details behind the papers submitted (in other words, if the paper says Jones will deliver 50 blue chairs and instead he delivers 50 red chairs, the bank is still obligated to pay him, even though the merchandise is incorrect). The payor will still be obligated to reimburse the bank. The bank also cannot get reimbursed if they honor the letter after the expiration date or if the payment is more than the amount in the letter.

BANKS AND LARGE FINANCIAL TRANSFERS

Now we get to banking and big business. So far we have talked about small transactions and small financial transfers. But what happens when we are dealing with major transactions. In other words, if an electronic transfer of $100 is made at 9:30 a.m., there really isn't much liability if it doesn't get processed until midnight. But what if the transfer is for a million dollars? At 5% interest, one day equals nearly $1,400.00. There are many companies that transfer millions of dollars each day. For these large transactions, there is a special portion of the UCC, (Article 4A) that governs the transaction, but only when the transfer is between highly sophisticated parties. It specifically does not apply to consumer transactions, and it does not apply when the transfer is not between banks. A highly sophisticated party is considered, essentially, any entity that routinely handles such transactions.

In these large transactions, the money doesn't actually change hands. The one bank doesn't really send the funds to the other bank. That would be too time consuming for the customers. Rather, what we have is a series of electronic transfer instructions. As an example, my business may instruct my bank to make a transfer of funds to Bob Smith's business. This is called the Payment Order. My bank then contacts Smith's bank and instruct them to transfer the funds to Smith's account. This is also called a Payment Order. However, there is no obligation by Smith's bank to accept this Order. A Payment Order does not have the same weight as a draft. If Smith's bank puts the funds into his account, then the Order has been accepted, and my bank must then pay Smith's bank from my account. The actual transaction takes place much later, but Smith gets credit for it now. Often, banks will use intermediary banks to assist with these transfers. In that case, the Payment Order would go from my bank to an intermediary bank and then to Smith's bank. The intermediary bank is generally a large institution that can immediately transfer these large sums.

Most of the work on a large funds transaction takes place on computers. Little is actually done in writing. What if there is an error along the way? Perhaps the account number was mistyped. Or perhaps the instructions are routed to the wrong bank. What happens then? If the money is routed to the wrong person, the wrong account, or if there is an overpayment or duplication, then the bank that made the mistake is liable for it. Thus, if the instructions from my bank were to pay Smith a million dollars but the intermediary bank makes a mistake causing an overpayment to Smith of two million dollars, they are not entitled to be reimbursed for the overage. They must send the extra million to Smith's bank, and can't ask my bank to reimburse them.

If the mistake leads to an underpayment, the bank making the mistake may simply send an additional instruction for the extra needed amount.

All of these transactions have various security measures to ensure they are correct and that the transaction proceeds properly. The banks have an obligation to ensure that their security measures are being complied with. If the bank fails to check their security provisions to ensure correctness they take the risk of loss for their failure. A breach of security will likely result in liability for errors. If the security procedure is followed, there is generally little liability to the bank and little risk of an error to the customers.

What if the bank fails to act on a proper Order? Generally, their only liability is usually limited to interest lost to the beneficiary.

SEIZING COLLATERAL

If the creditor, after seizing possession of collateral used to secure a debt, decides to sell it to pay off the debt, he may do so at either public or private sale. What this means is that the creditor can make a private deal with one person, or he can hold an auction and let the highest bid win. The debtor has a right to know what type of sale will be used, and if it is to be at a public auction, he has the right to know where and when. The sale must be done in a commercially reasonable manner. Just what that means is based on the creditor's interpretation for the most part. For instance, in a car repossession, the bank may choose to sell the car themselves for a decent price, or sell it to an auction house or used car dealer for a lesser amount, even though the amount they receive from the auction house may be far below the fair market value. For the bank, this is commercially reasonable as they are not in the business of selling cars and are only attempting to recoup their losses.

After the sale, the creditor needs to make an accounting of the proceeds from the sale and let the debtor know what the result was. The money received is first applied to pay the expenses of disposing of the collateral. In other words, if the creditor had to pay the Sheriff a couple of hundred dollars to seize the assets, then they get reimbursed for that amount off the top. Next, the proceeds go to pay the debt. If there is money left over, you pay other creditors who have debts owed on the same property. Finally, if there is still money left over, it goes to the debtor.

But what if there isn't enough money to pay the debt? The debtor remains liable for the deficiency. This happens often in car repossession cases. When banks must repossess cars, they generally sell them to special car clearance companies. It is common for the bank to lose money in the process. They then file suit against the debtor for the deficiency. In a real life example, a debtor bought a car for $7,625. When the car was repossessed, they still owed $4,110 on it. The bank sold the car for only $500, but there were also repossession and reconditioning expenses of $660.00. In addition, there were attorney fees and court costs. In the end, the debt had increased to a total of $5,225 which the debtor still owed, and they didn't even have the car! So the repossession actually increased the debt by nearly $1,100! The debtor will be required to pay this to the bank, or have a judgment against them.

Is there any relief for the debtor? It depends on the bank, however, most large creditors are willing to work with debtors. Before a debtor gets behind in payments, banks are often willing to restructure the payment system. Even after collection procedures are started, many banks are willing to allow the creditor to make a smaller lump sum payment or to extend a payment system that will allow the debtor to pay off the debt over time.

BANKRUPTCY

ankruptcy is a special procedure created by federal
law to assist people and companies that are going
through serious financial problems-when their debts are
greater than their income or assets. Because it is a federal
protection, a filing in one state affects all others. In other
words, a debtor who files bankruptcy proceedings in New
Jersey can affect collection suits from creditors in Florida.

There are three basic filings that we will discuss here.
They are named after the section of the bankruptcy code
that discusses them. First is a Chapter 13 filing. These are
filings for people with regular incomes and total debts of
less than a$1.44 million dollars, which is divided into
unsecured debts of less than $360,475 and secured debts
of less than $1,081,400. After filing, the debtor comes up
with a planned payment schedule for all of the debts (or
bills), setting up extended payments, even if the creditors
hasn't agreed to accept a payment schedule. There is a
hearing where the Court must approve the plan and the
creditors have the opportunity to object. Generally, if the
plan has been drafted in good faith, the Court will approve
it. Once approved, the creditors must comply with the
payment plan. If the debtor pays off the plan as scheduled,
the bankruptcy is discharged.

When the debts are a little worse, the debtor can file
for Chapter 11 protection. This is what we call
reorganization. When the debtor files for protection, the

debtor or his trustee puts together a plan to pay back the debts, sort of like a Chapter 13, but they also may review contracts and determines if they should be accepted, rejected or assigned. If the trustee determines that a contract is not in the debtor's interest, he may simply reject the contract and the creditor has little recourse for the now-legally-breached contract. The debtor and trustee also try to find alternative ways to pay off certain debts, such as giving stock options rather than payments. Again, if the plan is filed in good faith, the Court will usually approve or confirm it. The creditors cannot change the terms once confirmed. Both Chapter 13 and Chapter 11 allow the debtors to stay in business, end their debt and keep all of their assets.

If the debt structure is even worse, the debtor may file for Chapter 7 bankruptcy. This is what is called a liquidation bankruptcy. Here, the debtor files for protection and the Court appoints a trustee to take over the assets of the debtor. Chapter 7 bankruptcy may be filed either by the debtor, or by creditors. If there are more than 12 creditors, three of them, with joint claims of at least $14,425, must join together in filing a petition for involuntary bankruptcy. If there are less than 12 creditors, only one needs to file, but still needs to have a claim of at least $14,425.00.

If the bankruptcy is filed by creditors, the debtor may challenge the filing. If the debtor succeeds in challenging the bankruptcy petition, the court can award him damages, including attorney fees and costs. If he doesn't contest the filing, the court must find that the debtor is not paying his debts when due, or that there has been a custodian appointed within 120 days before the filing.

Once the bankruptcy petition is filed, the debtor must provide a schedule of income and expenses, a list of assets and liabilities, and a list of creditors. There will then be a meeting of the creditors where the debtor must appear and answer questions about their finances under oath. The filing of the bankruptcy petition acts as an automatic stay of any litigation or action to collect debts. Therefore if you have received a judgment against a debtor and the next day he files for bankruptcy, you will be precluded from enforcing the judgment. Indeed, I handled a case where we got a judgment at 11:00 a.m. and at 12:00 the debtor filed for bankruptcy. If he had filed just an hour earlier, the Court would have to reverse their decision because it would have been made after the bankruptcy filing. As luck would have it, since we beat the filing by an hour, the judgment stood, but we couldn't enforce it until the bankruptcy was thrown out.

Once the filing is done, the Court appoints a trustee over the assets. The trustee takes control over everything the debtor owns. The trustee has a great deal of power over the estate. The trustee is authorized to reject any contract of the debtor. He is authorized to reverse any transaction that occurred in the three months prior to the filing. So if you get a great deal on a car from a debtor and he files for bankruptcy the next month, you may have to return the car to the trustee and get your money back. The trustee then can resell the car for a better price. The trustee must marshal all the assets of the debtor and evaluate all the claims of the creditors. If the debtor has transferred assets to a friend to avoid it being claimed by the bankruptcy court, that can be looked at as fraud on the court. Any transfer that occurred within 1 year of the filing can be reversed and the item added back to the debtor's estate.

Generally, certain transactions cannot be reversed. These include a straight cash sale, a payment in the ordinary course of business, a consumer debt of less than $600, and child support or alimony payments.

The debtor must provide to the court a list of debtors who will then be notified about the filing. The creditors must then file a proof of claim with the Court, even if the claim is already known to the trustee. Once all the claims are in, the trustee must plan a payment schedule according to the priority of claims. The secured creditors get paid through their security. The unsecured creditors get paid according to their priority schedules. The priority is as follows:

First to all costs of administering the bankruptcy, including the trustee's fees and the lawyer's fees. See, us lawyers know that if we don't get paid first, we won't get paid at all, so we put ourselves in the top priority.

(2) Claims for wages and salaries, including vacation, severance, and sick leave pay;

(3) Taxes legally due and owing to the United States or any state or subdivision thereof;

(4) Debts due and owing the United States, including the National Credit Union Administration;

(5) General creditors, and secured creditors (to the extent that their respective claims exceed the value of the security for those claims);

(6) Shareholders to the extent of their respective uninsured shares and the National Credit Union Share

Insurance Fund to the extent of its payment of share insurance;

(7) In a case involving liquidation of a corporate credit union, holders of then-outstanding membership capital accounts and nonperpetual capital accounts or instruments to the extent not depleted in a calendar year prior to the date of liquidation;

(8) In a case involving liquidation of a low-income designated credit union, any outstanding secondary capital accounts; and

(9) In a case involving liquidation of a corporate credit union, holders of then-outstanding paid in capital or perpetual contributed capital instruments to the extent not depleted in a calendar year prior to the date of liquidation.

Each claim is paid in full for its priority. If you don't have enough to pay the full priority level than all creditors in that level must be treated equally on a pro rata basis, such as giving each creditor in that level 30%.

The debtor is allowed to keep certain things out of the bankruptcy estate. First and foremost is the debtors homestead. This means the actual residence of the debtor. And it can be limited. There are size restrictions for residences based on whether the debtor lives in a city or in the country. You may also protect your car up to a certain value, household furnishings up to a certain value. You may also keep free and clear child support and alimony payments, life insurance policies and personal injury awards.

Once the bankruptcy has been concluded, the debts of the debtor are discharged. From that point on, the creditors cannot seek payment from the bankrupt party. In fact if they do, there are several penalties that the debtor can seek against the creditor. Certain debts do not get discharged. Child support and alimony obligations cannot be wiped out in bankruptcy court, nor can taxes, loans to pay taxes or student loans received within 7 years of the bankruptcy. If a debt was not listed in the schedule of debts, it is not wiped out. Debts for fraudulent activity are not discharged nor to willful and malicious injury to property. DUI judgments are not dischargeable or certain consumer debts or cash advances.

SALE OF BUSINESS

One of the advantages of owning a business is the ability to sell it at a later date. If the business is run as a sole proprietorship, the business sale is simply a sale of assets that are held by the individual. These assets include the business name, phone numbers, inventory, client lists, trade secrets, business licenses, etc. A contract for sale and purchase of assets should be drawn up, spelling out specifically which assets are being transferred. If any assets are titled (such as a car or boat), the titles should be transferred and for the non-titled assets, a bill of sale should be completed which identifies the items as specifically as possible. Business licenses need to be changed through the appropriate City, County and State offices.

If the business is run as a partnership, the transfer is still done through a sale of assets; however the buyer must ensure that all partners consent to and sign the contract. A partner is not allowed to divest the partnership of assets with the consent of all other partners. A sale of assets not consented to by the other partners is voidable and the transaction can be reversed.

If the business is incorporated, there are two ways to transfer the business to a new owner. The corporation has the advantage of being owned by shareholders. Therefore, the corporation can sell its assets, like a partnership, or the individual shareholders can sell their stock. With either procedure, certain steps must be followed.

For a corporation to sell its assets there must first be a proposed contract for the sale. Next, the Board of Directors meet and evaluate the contract. If they determine the contract to be in the best interest of the corporation, they draft a resolution recommending ratification of the contract. The resolution is then presented to the shareholders of the corporation, who discuss it at their meeting. If the shareholders disagree with the resolution, the contract is denied; if they agree with the resolution, the contract is ratified and the sale can take place. The ratification is then delivered to the President or CEO of the company who signs the contract.

To make the process a little easier, many sales are effected simply by selling the stock of the company. This is a private transaction between the shareholder and the buyer and requires no meetings or discussions with outside persons. The transaction occurs relatively smoothly as there is no need to retitle the assets. Once the sale of stock has occurred, the corporation usually calls a special meeting of the shareholders and directors to elect new officers and directors. While the assets don't need to be retitled, in some situations government agencies need to be informed of the stock change. This is especially true when the business involves any type of alcohol or tobacco sale. The buyers should contact their state and local licensing departments to determine what forms and documents need to be filed after the sale.

The sale of stock is generally an easier transfer than the sale of assets, however, it also poses more risks. The purchase of stock also purchases the debts and liabilities of the company. If the company is about to be sued, the new shareholder will be dragged into the Court process. Many contracts contain an indemnification clause whereby the Seller will pay all expenses if a lawsuit is filed for an event that occurred before the sale. While this is a nice clause, it still must be enforced. If the Seller doesn't pay the expenses, the Buyer may be left with no recourse. For this reason, it is important to complete a due diligence search on the business to discover any potential liabilities that may arise in the future.

INTERNATIONAL TRADE

In today's global economy, international trade is almost required for many businesses. No longer is a small business limited to sales in a local neighborhood. With the growth of the internet, sales to foreign nationals is increasing. With this, of course, comes a whole set of legal issues. For example, whose law will apply to the sale? Whose currency will be used to pay? Where will litigation take place? All these and more must be taken into account when trading in foreign countries.

Much of international trade is governed by treaties. A treaty is an agreement entered into between different countries to spell out agreements between them and their citizens. The United States is a party to numerous treaties and other international agreements. Probably the most encompassing is GATT.

In 1994, the United States and 124 other countries entered into the General Agreement on Tariffs and Trade (GATT). This agreement was an update of an earlier agreement and has the purpose to encourage trade without discrimination and to protect trade through the use of tariffs. GATT features a "most favored nation" clause which sets out a requirement that each member nation treat all other member nations with an equal footing. This requirement is not required to non-members.

313

There are certain exceptions to the most favored nation status. When there are regional trading agreements, or when the participant is a developing nation, the rules can be modified. An example of a regional agreement is the North American Free Trade Agreement (NAFTA). This is an agreement between the United States, Canada and Mexico where products created in one of the three countries are protected from tariffs for a period of 15 years.

In order to participate in international trade, a company must decide how it will act in the foreign country; that is, what business style shall they use to sell their products. The simplest way is to make a direct export sale. In other words, a buyer in another country simply orders the item from the United States supplier. The business makes the sale in the United States, even though the recipient is elsewhere. There are some concerns the merchant must be aware of which we will discuss later.

If the U.S. company wants its products to have a presence in the foreign country, there are several alternatives. First, the company can hire an agent to represent them. By doing this, the company actually has a person in the other country that can make contracts for the company for a commission. This subject the company to taxation in the foreign country, as well as other potential liabilities as they are actually doing business in that country.

The company can also find a foreign distributor. Here, the distributor actually purchases the items from the U.S. company and bears any financial risk for them. In a similar manner, the U.S. company can license a foreign company to sell items bearing the U.S. companies trademarks, or using the U.S. company's technology.

The U.S. company can created a subsidiary company in the foreign country when they desire to have greater control over the sales and manufacturing. This also subjects the company to both U.S. and foreign taxation. Generally, however, the IRS will give companies credit for taxes paid to other governments.

Finally, a U.S. company can create a joint venture with a foreign company. This allows the foreign company to deal with their local laws while the U.S. company deals with U.S. laws. These joint ventures require written agreements to spell out the rights, responsibilities and liabilities of each company.

There are numerous governmental regulations that apply to international trade. More than we can list here. The government may regulate trade for a number of reasons, including national security, foreign policy, and to protect our citizens' rights.

Before a company can start exporting gods to another country, they must first ensure whether they must obtain a license before making the export. The license is based on the item being exported, not the company. Generally, no license is required unless the Department of Commerce has issued a specific regulation requiring a license for a particular type of item. To make a determination if a license is required, the company should review the Commerce Control List. Products included on the list are given control numbers (called Export Control Classification Numbers). Once the number is obtained, the business should consult the Commerce Country Chart to determine if the license is required. There is a reason for this: some items may be freely exported, some may be exported only to certain countries, some may be exported only for certain purposes. This is especially true for items that have a national safety component. As an example, items needed for nuclear reactors may be allowed for countries such as England and France, but may be disallowed for countries such as Iran and Iraq. Certain items may be allowed into Iran, but only if they are to be used for non-weapon purposes. It is up to the business to identify to the Department the use that will be made of the item, along with the location where the item is to be used, so our embassy may make an on-site inspection to ensure the item is not being used for the wrong reason.

Exports are also restricted for foreign policy reasons. The best example we see here in Florida regards trading with Cuba. Due to our policy not to support a communist regime, trading with Cuba is highly regulated and subjects violators to serious federal criminal sanctions.

Import/Export laws also help us protect our citizens from unfair competition. As an example, under the Lanham Act, once a company registers a trademark on the Principle Register of the Patent and Trademark Office, they are entitled to prevent any other product bearing that mark from being imported into the Country. Any company importing falsely trademarked goods is subject to civil and criminal remedies and may have to pay to the trademark holder triple damages, as well as surrender all counterfeit goods and the equipment used to make them. The laws also prevent other countries from selling goods in the United States for less than their fair market value (called "dumping").

U.S. businesses are also protected from foreign businesses through our anti-trust laws. While anti-trust is not recognized by all countries, any company doing business within the United States must comply with our anti-trust provisions. This even covers companies located outside the United States if the impact of their business has a foreseeable, direct and substantial impact on United States commerce.

The most frequently used tool to prevent imports and exports are tariffs. These are also known as duties or import taxes. The tariff is enforced by the United States Customs Service at the port of entry. Part of the purpose of the tariff is to increase the price of the imported good to make it commensurate with similar goods produced within the United States.

As a benefit to U.S. businesses, the federal government provides certain financial incentives to businesses that form foreign sales corporations to promote exporting of U.S. products to other countries. They also offer loans to foreign importers for the purchase of U.S. goods.

PROPERTY OWNERSHIP

What is property? Most people think of real estate when they think of property, but it applies to personal items and in some cases ideas as well. Basically, everything that can be owned is property. Personal property includes whole or partial rights in tangible property, claims and debts, and intangible property such as trademarks and copyrights.

People obtain property in many ways. The most common way to obtain property is to buy it. Purchases in this instance includes trading for other property (Money is considered property).

In addition to purchases, property may be acquired as a gift. Giving someone a Christmas or birthday present transfers ownership of property to him or her. There are several types of gifts. When a gift is made between two living people it is called an inter vivos gift. When the gift is made in anticipation of impending death it is referred to as a gift causa mortis and is only effective if the giftor actually dies before taking the gift back. Gifts can also be made to a minor through a guardian. Gifts can also be made conditioned on an event happening or not happening. There are two types of conditions: a condition precedent requires an action to occur before the gift is made (such as "this is yours if you graduate"); a condition subsequent the gift continues unless an event occurs (such as "the car is yours unless you drop out"). Finally, a person may make anatomical gifts through being an organ donor or donating their bodies to science (yes, your body can be considered property).

In order for a gift to be effective, two things must occur. First there must be an intent to make a gift. If the intent is to loan the item, there is no gift. Second, there must be actual delivery of the item. If a person intends to make a gift, but dies before the item is delivered, there is no gift-the property must be transferred through probate. Delivery does not have to be of the actual item-it may be symbolic or constructive. As an example, you may make a gift of a car by handing someone the keys to the vehicle. While you have not made delivery of the vehicle, you have delivered control of it.

Gifts are considered one-sided. With a contract, there must be consideration; each side sacrifices something-one gives money, the other service. With a gift, only one side, the giver, needs to act. However, because there is no consideration, a gift is not enforceable. If a person promises to make a gift, the recipient cannot sue to require performance.

Property can also be obtained by finding lost property. By finding lost property, the finder gains possession but not title to the property. In other words, if the owner can prove ownership, he is entitled to regain his property. This right to reclaim may be discharged by the passage of time or by where the property was lost.

Possessory rights also are transferred by theft, but title cannot pass through a theft. Registered vehicles, such as automobiles cannot be transferred unless their title is properly endorsed. In some cases, title may pass by occupation or possession of property. Examples of this include the capture of a wild animal. Homesteading of land was an additional example how title could pass by occupation, though rarely heard of today.

BAILMENTS

When a person gives property to another person to hold, store, or deliver to a third party, it is referred to as a bailment. To create a bailment, there must be an agreement and delivery and acceptance. The agreement may be express or implied and needs to have all of the elements of a contract. You may create a bailment of any personal property, but not real estate. The delivery may be actual or constructive. The key is that the bailee is aware that the property has been placed in their possession and they have accepted it. If you give property to another person without an agreement, there is no bailment and it may be considered a gift. If you leave the property with them, but without their knowledge (such as leaving an item in their home without telling them) no bailment is created.

A bailment is an important legal status. Duties and rights arise with bailments that don't exist without this status. First is ownership. In a bailment, ownership stays with the giver, also called the bailor. The recipient, or bailee, does not gain ownership, but merely possession. Because title does not pass to the bailee, they cannot lawfully sell the property. An attempt to sell does not pass title and the bailor can recover his property. There are exceptions to this. If the bailor indicates to others that the bailee can sell the property, they may create that right in the bailee. Also if the bailee is a dealer in the type of goods that have been bailed (such as a car dealer), and they sell the property to a buyer in due course, title does pass to the buyer.

Bailments where the bailee is paid are called contract bailments; where the bailee is not paid are called gratuitous bailments.

In some situations the bailment may be created by the situation rather than by express agreement. This situation arises when the bailee obtains property without the permission of the bailor. An example would be lost items that are found. The finder of lost items usually holds the item as a bailment and must return it to the proper owner if the owner can be discerned.

Bailees have certain responsibilities to the bailor. First, they must perform the terms of the contract. As an example, when a car is left at a shop for repairs, the shop holds the car as a bailment. Under the contract, they are required to make repairs on the car as part of that bailment.

Second, the bailee also is under a duty to care for the property. If the property is damaged due to the bailee's failure to use reasonable care, the bailee must pay for the damage. The bailee must also pay for the damage if it was caused by the bailee's unauthorized actions (such as an auto repairman making personal use of a car left for repairs). The bailee is only required to use reasonable care in light of the circumstances. This duty may be extended under the bailment contract.

Third, the bailee must maintain the property if he is being paid for the bailment. In this circumstance, and unless stated otherwise in the contract, the bailee must pay for the maintenance.

Fourth, the bailee must not use the bailment for their own personal use, unless authorized by the agreement. If the bailee takes over the property as his own, he can become liable for conversion and be required to pay the bailor the fair market value for the item at the time it was converted.

Fifth, the bailee is required to return the property, unless directed otherwise in the agreement. In most cases the actual item must be returned; in some, it merely needs to be an equivalent article. The bailee has a lien on the property while it is in his care. The lien allows the bailee to retain possession of the property until he has been paid for the bailment. If the property is returned to the bailor before payment is made, the lien is lost.

COMMON CARRIERS

Another type of bailment is the common carrier. A "common carrier" is a business who agrees to furnish transportation for goods for compensation, without discriminating against who they ship for. Examples are Federal Express and UPS. All members of the public may employ the common carrier to ship their goods. This is as opposed to a contract carrier who transports goods based upon individual contracts for service, or a private carrier where the transportation is performed by the shipper. The person sending the item (the shipper) is also referred to as the consignor; the person receiving the goods is the consignee.

Usually, when a common carrier accepts a shipment of goods, they will issue a bill of lading, when the shipment travels by land or water, and an air bill when the goods travel by air. This is an important document as it actually can transfer title to the property. If the bill of lading states the goods are to be delivered "to the bearer" or "to the order of" a named person, it becomes a negotiable bill of lading. In other words, the consignee may sell the goods being shipped merely by transferring the bill of lading to another party. When the shipment is staying within state boundaries, the bill of lading will be governed by the Uniform Commercial Code; when the shipment crosses state lines, it becomes governed by the Federal Bills of Lading Act. While the Uniform Commercial Code makes no restrictions on the form of the bill of lading, the Federal Act does. Under the Federal Act, negotiable bills of lading must be printed on yellow paper, and non-negotiable bills must be printed on white paper.

Common carriers may charge any reasonable rate necessary to continue their business and obtains a lien on all goods that they transport to ensure payment. If the carrier is not paid, they may retain possession of the goods until paid or until the lien is enforced and the goods are sold to make up the lost money. In return, the carrier is required to accept goods from any person who offers them for shipment, without discrimination, so long as the carrier has room to ship them. They must furnish storage facilities sufficient to store all items that are waiting shipment and furnish sufficient equipment to properly and safely ship the items. The carrier must follow the directions given by the shipper, must load and unload the goods and must deliver them to their stated destination. If the goods are shipped under a negotiable bill of lading, the shipper must not deliver the goods until they receive a properly indorsed bill of lading, showing the person claiming title. When the goods are shipped to the wrong location, the common carrier is liable for breach of contract and for conversion of the property.

During shipment, the carrier is liable for any damage or loss that occurs to the goods in their possession, unless they can clearly show that the damage or loss was due to an act of God, an enemy of the United States, a public authority (such as a law enforcement officer or health agency), an act of the shipper, or the inherent nature of the goods. The carrier is also liable if they do not ship the goods in a reasonable time without ordinary delay. If the delay in shipment results in a decrease in value, the carrier is responsible for the lost value.

In order to protect their financial status, many common carriers will limit their liability by contract. As an example, one common carrier has on their air bill "Our liability in connection with this shipment is limited to the lesser of your actual damages or $100, unless you declare a higher value, pay an additional charge and document your actual lose in a timely manner." By turning the property over to the carrier, you are accepting the limitations of liability printed on the bill of lading.

HOTELKEEPERS LIABILITY

The final type of bailment we will discuss is hoteliers. Hotelkeepers have a bailee responsibility for any property that has been specifically entrusted to the hotelkeepers care. A hotelkeeper is anyone operating a transient rental housing facility such as a hotel, motel, or guesthouse. For the purposes of this article, I will use the word hotel to refer to all transient housing. These rules do not apply to boarding houses, apartments, or other more permanent living quarters. Permanent residence is not created merely by length of time. A hotel guest may keep their status, even if they stay at the hotel for a period of months (This is as opposed to a tenant, lodger or boarder. A tenant is one who has temporary use and occupation of another's property; a lodger is one who rents a part of another person's house; and a boarder is one who receives regular meals, either with or without housing).

The duty of the hotelkeeper lies only to the hotel guests. These are the actual persons registered and staying at the hotel. Through registering, the guest develops a special relationship with the hotelkeeper. People who visit or stay at the hotel at the invitation of a guest are not considered guests of the hotel, and there is no duty as to them. In most cases, the duty to the guest ends when the guest checks out, however, the duty may continue for an additional period in certain circumstances. For example, when a guest checks out of a hotel but leaves their luggage with the bellcap so they may go sightseeing.

Liability of the hotelkeeper does not apply to everything the guest brings into the hotel; it is limited to those items left in the hotelkeeper's care. As indicated above, this includes items left in the bellcap's chambers, items left with the desk clerk, or, in the case of some hotels, items left with the hotel's catering department, among others. The key is that the item is specifically entrusted to the hotel, and the hotel has accepted the item and the responsibility for it. Under Florida law, items left in a hotel room are not protected unless, before the loss, the guest provides the hotelkeeper an inventory of all items in his room, with their value, and allows the hotelkeeper to inspect the inventory. Only then will the items in the room be covered, and then only up to $500.

In Florida, the hotel does not have an obligation to take any property for safekeeping; the duty to provide for the safety of belongings is with the guest. If the hotel does accept property, Florida Statutes limit the hotel's liability for loss to $1,000.00 so long as hotel gives the guest a receipt for the property (stating the value) which states, in type large enough to be clearly noticeable, that the hotel was not liable for any loss exceeding $1,000 and was only liable for that amount if the loss was the proximate result of fault or negligence of the hotelkeeper.

As with most bailees, the hotelkeeper obtains a lien on the baggage of the guest for the amount of the reasonable value of the accommodations. If the guest has not paid the fee for the stay at the hotel, the hotel may retain possession of any property brought into the hotel, whether or not it is specifically left with the hotelkeeper. If the guest fails to pay their bill, they may be ejected and the hotel may retain all property in the room. The lien remains until the guest pays the bill, until the hotel converts the baggage to their own, either through use or sale, or until the hotel returns the bags to the guest.

INSURANCE

Insurance policies can be put into essentially five groups: business liability insurance, marine insurance, fire and homeowners insurance, automobile insurance and life insurance. We will address each of these in order.

A comprehensive business liability insurance covers all damages that a business might incur through property damage or physical injury due to their actions or inactions. This can include anything from product liability cases (such as where an item the company makes is defective and results in injury or property damage through its use) to employment liability (such as wrongful termination). It can also cover issues such as sexual harassment, false advertising and trademark and patent infringement cases. Through this insurance, the insurer must not only pay the damages caused by the business, but also must defend them, i.e. provide attorneys to fight potential lawsuits.

In addition to all of the above, business can also obtain insurance for their directors and officers, to protect them from liability for the decisions that they make. This is referred to as D&O insurance. Malpractice insurance is another form of business liability insurance. Malpractice insurance protects professionals, such as doctors, accountants, and lawyers, in the event they make a mistake that results in a loss or injury to another.

Marine insurance protects against loss of property due to transportation. The word "marine" is only partially correct as marine insurance can also involve transport across land (termed "inland marine insurance"). Ocean marine insurance protects items that are shipped against "perils at sea" and covers the four major categories of hull, cargo, liability and freight. Hull insurance protects the vessel itself; cargo protects the owner of the items being shipped if they are lost at sea (it does not cover loss or damage that occurs prior to boarding the ship); liability covers the ship-owners liability if the ship causes damage to another; and freight insurance guarantees that the ship-owner will be paid for his services. Inland marine insurance protects all goods transported by land, air or rail. It also covers all items shipped over the inland waterways such as rivers and lakes.

Fire and homeowners insurance protects the homeowner from loss or damage of their home. Fire insurance is just what it sounds like: it pays the homeowner for any destruction or damage to their home as a result of fire. Homeowner's insurance provides additional protection to the homeowner for accidents and injuries that occur on the premises. It can also protect the homeowner from loss of property due to theft from the home.

Automobile insurance is required in most states. For example, in Florida, all drivers must have Property Damage Liability and Personal Injury Protection (PIP). Property Damage Liability covers damages or injuries to others caused by the driver's actions, and PIP covers injuries to the driver or other covered person. In addition, there are other automobile insurances you can obtain, such as uninsured motorists (covers damage to your property or person when struck by a driver without insurance or by a driver whose insurance company denies coverage), and collision coverage (covers damage to the driver's property). Usually, these policies cover the owner of the vehicle and all family members who reside in the same household.

Finally, we have life insurance. There are three forms of life insurance: term, whole life, and endowment. Term life is written for a specific period of time and terminates at the end of that period. For example, you may purchase term life for a year. If you die within the year, your beneficiaries receive the insurance benefits. However, if you do not die, the policy ends and no benefits are owed. Whole life provides protection for the person's entire life. They are covered from the time the policy is written to the day they die. This is usually a little more expensive than term life, in that it not only provides a benefit for the beneficiaries; it also has an investment portion that can be cashed in by the insured before they die. Endowment insurance is similar to term life in that it is only for a specified time; however, if the insured is still alive at the end of the term, the insured receives the benefit. Some policies also offer a disability clause which pays the insured if they become permanently disabled and are no longer able to work.

It is important to remember that insurance is a contract. As with all contracts, it is crucial to read it carefully before agreeing to its terms.

REAL ESTATE

Real estate is different than any other type of asset or personal property. It is one of the few things that is truly unique. No two pieces of land are the same – they may be similar, but you cannot simply replace one piece of land with another. (This is why the Courts may order a real estate sales contract to be specifically enforced, as no other piece of real estate can substitute for the piece contracted for.) Another difference between real estate and other assets is permanence. Other assets may come and go, but real estate is forever. Aside from erosion or a severe earthquake, land is not destroyed (although things on the land may be).

What is land? This sounds like a simple question but the answer is more than people think. Land is not just the surface of the earth; it also includes the air above the ground (subject to the right of aircraft to fly over). It includes everything below the ground (technically as far as the middle of the earth). It includes the minerals in the ground and the water on it.

When a building is placed on land, it becomes part of the land. That is, the building and the ground are treated as one. Further, if any personal property is affixed to the land or to any building on the land, that personal property also becomes part of the land. As an example, if a tenant to an apartment installs a ceiling fan inside the apartment, the tenant cannot take the ceiling fan with them when they leave. By attaching the fan to the ceiling, it becomes a "fixture" or part of the building and thus part of the land. As such, the ceiling fan now belongs to the landlord.

Portions of land may be sold or transferred without transferring other parts of the land. A property owner may sell mineral rights to his property without selling the land itself. This allows the property owner to build a house on the property, but allows the holder of the mineral rights to mine under the house for ore. A property owner can also sell profits. Here the word "Profits" means the right to remove things from the land of another. As an example, the property owner may allow a person to cut timber from their property or may allow a person to use water from a spring on the property.

A property owner may also transfer rights of passage over his property. These are usually referred to as easements. Occasionally, a person will buy a piece of land that cannot be accessed from any roadways. This is called landlocked. To gain access to their property, a neighboring land owner may grant the person an easement of ingress and egress, which means they have the right to travel over the land owner's property to reach their home.

Interest in land can be held in many ways and by many types of entities. When a person owns land outright, that is, when there are no others who can claim any rights to the land, it is referred to as "fee simple". In a fee simple, the owner has rights to the entire property and has the unconditional right to dispose of the property during their life or through their estate after death. When a person owns land in fee simple, they own it forever or until they sell it or transfer it by some other means. One of the few limitations is the rights of creditors to seize the property to satisfy judgments against the fee simple owner (except homestead property).

A fee simple can be qualified when additional terms are added. A "fee simple conditional" transfers the fee simple if a certain act is done or not done. If there is a breach in the condition, the transferor may reenter or retake the property. A fee simple conditional may also be used to limit the heirs that may take the property.

A "fee simple defeasible" allows the fee simple to be ended upon the occurrence or non-occurrence of a certain event. The fee may last forever, or may end if the qualifying event happens. As an example, land that is sold "so long as it is always used for residential purposes" creates a fee simple defeasible, because the transfer reverts if the holder uses the land for commercial reasons.

Another method of holding an interest in property is a "life estate". The holder of a life estate has the right to possess the land during their life, but does not have the right to sell the land. Upon death, the property transfers automatically to the fee holder, or remainderman. The holder of the life estate has nothing to leave their heirs. A life estate can be sold, however, it has little value as the term is unidentifiable and remains based on the life of the original holder. In other words, a person who holds a life estate in a house may sell their life estate to another person, however, the life estate will only last as long as the seller is alive. Immediately upon their death, the buyer must vacate the premises. Therefore, if the buyer takes possession on Monday and the seller dies in a car accident on Tuesday, the buyer's interest is over.

Related to the life estate and the fee simple defeasible is the future interest. A future interest means that, while you don't have a right of possession today, you will in the future. A prime example of this is the remainderman to a life estate. A remainderman has no interest in the property today, but will have when the life estate ends. Similarly, the seller of a fee simple defeasible has no interest in property, but will regain their interest if the qualifying event occurs. These are both considered future interests in the property.

CONDOMINIUMS

A common method for owning property today is a condominium. Most of us think of condominiums as glorified apartment buildings, where the person buys an apartment and has an undivided interest in the common area. Condominiums apply to business property as well. Like with a residential condominium, business condominiums allow businesses to purchase office space in a building, and to receive an undivided interest in the common areas. In most situations, the unit owner only purchases the space within the walls of their office. While they can make modifications to the walls (such as painting and hanging photographs), often major changes such as knocking holes in the walls are prohibited.

With the purchase of the unit, there is also ownership of common areas. Common areas (sometimes referred to as common elements) include all of the condominium property except the actual units. This includes the hallways, walkways, driveways and stairways, parking lot, elevators, exits, yard, plants, roof and exterior walls. The common areas also include easements for the passage of plumbing, wires, ducts and conduit. Maintenance of the interior of the condominium unit belongs to the unit owner; maintenance of the common areas belongs to the condominium association.

To form a condominium, all the owners of the various units (usually the developer before the units are sold) must file a Declaration of Condominium with the County Clerk's Office. The operation of the Condominium is handled by a Condominium Association. The Association is a corporation, either for profit or not-for-profit and must be run like a corporation. It must have by-laws and officers; it must hold annual meetings and must prepare financial records and must keep its records available for the members to see at reasonable business hours. There must be an annual budget, setting out the anticipated expenses for the Condominium. As with any other corporation, the officers and directors have a fiduciary duty to the unit owners and can be held personally liable in certain circumstances for failure to follow the condominium laws (as an example, an officer who fails to allow members to inspect corporate records may be held personally liable for all attorney fees and costs incurred to enforce inspection). The unit owners are the shareholders or members of the corporation.

The Association is responsible for things such as painting the buildings, landscaping, and repaving. While the unit owners are responsible for repairs that pertain to their unit only, the Association is responsible for repairs that affect the entire building. As an example, a broken toilet is a unit owner's responsibility; a broken sewer line is the Associations. To pay for maintenance and repairs, the Association is authorized to charge a regular maintenance fee and when necessary, to make a special assessment against the units for larger expenses. If the owner fails to pay an assessment or maintenance fee, the Association may place a lien on the unit for the amount owing.

Albert L. Kelley, Esq.

Before purchasing into a condominium, the buyer should request to inspect the Articles of Condominium, the Declaration of Condominium and the By-Laws. They should also review the current budget and if possible, the most recent minutes of the Association meetings so they know what issues are currently under consideration.

DEEDS

Real property is transferred by recording a deed with the County Clerk's office. There are various types of deeds and each has a different legal significance.

The most common type of deed is the Warranty Deed. A warranty deed not only transfers the title to the property, it also acts as a guarantee that the seller will defend the property against any claims against the title to the property. It warrants that there are no encumbrances on the property and no other persons have interest adverse to the purchaser's interest in the property. This is the strongest form of deed.

Another common transfer document is a quitclaim deed. Often people make the mistake of calling this a "quickclaim" deed due to its use to speed transactions. The true name, "quitclaim" comes from the purpose of the deed. The seller, by issuing the quitclaim deed, quits his claim on the property to the buyer. This deed transfers any rights, title or interest the seller has in the property, if any. There are no warranties or guarantees with a quitclaim deed. Indeed, the person giving the deed does not even need to own the property mentioned. The deed does not even assert that the title to the property is valid. Technically, I could grant a quitclaim deed to the Washington Monument to Bob Smith. The quitclaim deed would be valid, however, it would serve no purpose as I have no ownership interest in that property. Bob Smith could record the deed, but he would have no ownership right in the building because of it. Quitclaim deeds are often used to transfer property between joint owners or to transfer rights in property where the seller does not want or agree to defend against all possible claims.

Another form of deed is a Limited Warranty Deed or a Special Warranty Deed. These serve the same purpose as a warranty deed, but limit the warranties the seller is granting. In other words, the deed may warrant the title is clear as to everything but potential ingress and egress easements of neighboring properties.

Other forms of deeds include probate deeds, whereby the Court issues a deed through a probate proceeding after the property owner passes, and the foreclosure deed, whereby the deed is issued by the Clerk of Court after the property is sold at a foreclosure sale.

In Florida, deeds must be signed by the seller and must be notarized in order to be recorded. The deed also must be signed by two witnesses who actually watch the seller sign the deed (A notary does not have to watch the seller sign the deed, however, the seller must be standing before the notary when the deed is notarized). Because the notary is only notarizing the seller's signature, the notary can also act as one of the witnesses. The deed does not need to be recorded to be effective, however, if it is not recorded, third parties may rely on the public record for the purposes of encumbering the property. In other words, a mortgage issued to the previous owner will be deemed valid if the deed has not been recorded.

MORTGAGES

After the deed, the next most important real estate document is a mortgage. Now to be fair, mortgages do not need to involve real estate; personal property may be mortgaged as well. A mortgage on personal property is referred to as a chattel mortgage and has the same effect as a mortgage on real property. If the note isn't paid, the personal property can be seized to satisfy the note.

A real estate mortgage is the method by which banks, finance companies, and private lenders protect themselves financially. It is not a conveyance of legal title or possession, although it can lead to a change in title and possession. A mortgage is a document given by the buyer, called the mortgagor to the financier, called the mortgagee. I say it is a document because a mortgage MUST be in writing. A verbal mortgage is unenforceable. No particular language must be included in the mortgage. Under Florida law, any conveyance or bill of sale, or other instrument providing for the sale of property with the purpose or intent of securing the payment of money, shall be deemed a mortgage. A mortgage does not have to be recorded to be valid. However, if the mortgage is not recorded, it is unenforceable as to a bona fide purchaser without notice. In other words, if I give a mortgage to Bob Smith and he doesn't record it, and then I give a second mortgage to the bank who does record it, the bank's mortgage takes priority. The mortgage does not have to show the exact amount owed. It can be set to fluctuate to allow for future draws, but it must contain the maximum principal amount allowed.

Often the mortgage will call for smaller monthly payments with a large lump sum payment made at the end of the mortgage period. This is referred to as a balloon mortgage. A mortgage is deemed a balloon mortgage when the final payment is more than twice the amount of the regular monthly or periodic payment. In Florida, a balloon mortgage MUST contain the following legend at the top of the face page as well as above the signature line on the signature page:

> "THIS IS A BALLOON MORTGAGE AND THE FINAL PRINCIPAL PAYMENT OR THE PRINCIPAL BALANCE DUE UPON MATURITY IS $_____, TOGETHER WITH ACCRUED INTEREST, IF ANY, AND ALL ADVANCEMENTS MADE BY THE MORTGAGEE UNDER THE TERMS OF THIS MORTGAGE."

A failure to include this legend will act to automatically extend the maturity date of the mortgage until the normal payments would pay off the mortgage if timely made.

It is extremely important that mortgages be prepared properly. If there is an error in a mortgage which impairs another person's title to property, the prevailing party in an action to clear the title may be awarded all costs, including attorney fees as well as any damages the error caused. This could be extremely costly if the error results in the failure of a person's right to sell their property. For this reason, it is crucial to have real estate sales handled by a real estate professional.

Because a mortgage secures property, the mortgagor has certain obligations. The mortgagor must pay all taxes and assessments on the property. He does not have to insure the property, unless the mortgage requires it. The mortgagor may not take action that impairs the property or reduces its value. If the property is damaged by a third party, both the mortgagor and the mortgagee have an action against the third party.

If a mortgagor wants to transfer his interest in property without paying off the mortgage, he may do so by one of two methods. First, he may assign the mortgage, if the mortgagee allows. In this situation, the mortgagor will no longer be responsible for the mortgage. The mortgagor can also sell the property subject to the mortgage. In a "subject to" transfer, the mortgagor is still liable under the mortgage and the property continues to be secured.

When a bank makes a loan, they are required to comply with numerous laws and regulations:

TILA: Many homeowners are familiar with the term "Truth in Lending Act" (TILA). TILA requires the lender to provide two copies of a notice to each borrower on the note advising them of right to rescind the note and mortgage. Failure to provide this notice is an absolute defense, allowing the borrower to rescind the note and mortgage during the foreclosure proceeding.

HOEPA: This is actually a subsection of TILA and requires the lender to give a notice to the borrower at least three days before closing that advises the homeowner that they do not have to enter the loan and that they could lose their house and any money put into it. Both HOEPA and TILA can be asserted against any assignee of the note and mortgage.

RESPA: This is an anti-kickback statute that prevents the bank from giving anything of value for the provision of settlement services. This includes paying a mortgage broker a premium for getting the borrower a mortgage rate higher than what the homeowner qualified for or if the bank pays for services such as title searches or postage and then charges the homeowner more than they paid for the service.

In the event of a default by the mortgagor, the mortgagee may proceed to foreclosure. Some people believe that foreclosure is a request to get the property back. That is not the case. In most mortgages, there is a clause that says if the mortgagor defaults on payments, the mortgagee may accelerate the payments and demand payment of the entire balance. To enforce this, the mortgagee files a foreclosure action in Court, asking the Court to enter a judgment awarding them a sum of money for the balance due. The judgment does not turn possession over to the mortgagee. Rather, the Court orders that the property be sold at auction to pay the amount of the money judgment. When the judgment for foreclosure is issued, the Clerk must post a Notice of Sale in a newspaper of local circulation. The Notice must run once a week for two consecutive weeks and must describe the property and location of sale. The last publication must be at least five days before the sale.

The auction is held between 20 and 35 days after the judgment. While previously the sale occurred on the courthouse steps by the Clerk of the Court, today many foreclosure sales are handled online. Anyone may bid on foreclosed property, however, the mortgagee, as the holder of the judgment, is allowed to use his judgment as a credit against the purchase price. In other words, when others are bidding on the property, the mortgagee may bid up to the amount of their money judgment and not be required to pay any money for the purchase.

What happens at a foreclosure sale? The sale is handled by the Clerk of the Court. Anyone may place a bid on property up for foreclosure. The bids can start as low as one dollar. They continue taking bids until the high bid is reached. The winning bid must immediately deposit the full purchase price with the Clerk of the Court. However, the judgment holder is given a credit for the full amount of the judgment. In other words, at the auction, the judgment holder may bid up to the amount of their judgment without having to pay any money to the Clerk of the Court towards the property.

If the property sells for less than the judgment amount, the money received goes to the judgment holder. The amount received is deducted from the judgment and the balance of the judgment continues to be owed, however, the judgment holder must find a way to collect it. For this reason, the careful judgment holder should attend the auction and ensure that the bid reaches at least the judgment amount (Often the judgment holder will start bidding below the judgment amount. They do this so that they obtain the property being foreclosed and still retain a balance on the judgment to be collected later). If   the property sells for more than the judgment amount, the amount of the judgment is paid to the judgment holder and the excess is paid to the foreclosed party. There is an exception to this rule when there are other secured parties who have filed claims in the Court during the foreclosure process. If other secured creditors come forward, the excess funds may be paid to them after the judgment holder is paid.

Once the auction is over the winning bidder must post a deposit immediately with the clerk equal to 5% of the winning bid. They then have a specified amount of time (usually by the end of the day) to pay the remaining balance. Once paid, the money is held in trust by the Clerk. The Clerk issues a Certificate of Sale and forwards copies of it to all parties to the foreclosure action. During the 10 days immediately following the sale, the parties may object to the form or process of the sale. They may not object simply based on the right to hold the sale, as that right was granted by the Court. If an objection is not filed within the 10-day period, the Clerk issues a Certificate of Title which confirms the sale and passes the title of the property to the successful bidder. The Clerk then issues a Certificate of Disbursements and pays the appropriate funds to the judgment holder.

Before the Clerk files the Certificate of Sale, the debtor may still redeem the property by paying to the Clerk of Court the total amount stated in the judgment of foreclosure, or if the judgment has not yet been entered, by paying all of the amounts due under the security agreement, including interest, the reasonable costs to file the foreclosure action and the reasonable attorney fees and costs of the creditor. If the above amounts are not paid prior to the issuance of the Certificate of Sale (or other period specified in the Foreclosure Order), the property may not be redeemed and the property will pass to the successful bidder.

LEASES

For many businesses, the lease is one of the most important legal documents they will sign and has the greatest impact on the success or failure of the business. A lease is a contract between a property owner, referred to as the Landlord or the Lessor, and the business or person wanting to occupy the property, called the Tenant or Lessee. A properly drafted lease transfers occupancy of the property without also transferring ownership. However, a lease does more than say how long a tenant can stay in the property and how much rent must be paid. If drafted properly, it controls who makes repairs on a building, who pays the taxes and insurance. In short, it defines what rights the landlord and tenant have.

Why is this document so important? Most states are considered as pro-landlord. This does not mean that the courts ignore tenants, but the statutes provide greater rights to the landlord than to the tenant. These benefits can be modified in many cases through the terms of the lease. The power in a lease is also controlled by the local market. When there are numerous properties available, tenants have more success negotiating the terms of a lease. When vacancies are few, the landlord has more power to dictate the terms of the lease. A lease can assist the success of a business by providing for continuity, or it can destroy a growing business if the term is too short. It may be beneficial by providing the tenant with peace of mind from the responsibilities of property ownership, or it might drown the business in massive repair bills.

Real property leases are generally divided into residential, commercial and self-storage. The rules for each differ. Usually, commercial leases are more detailed as the statutes give less guidance for commercial leases. The legislature deems that businessmen are able to negotiate the terms sufficiently.

A lease can be written or verbal. If the lease is verbal or does not address certain terms, you look to the statutes to determine certain aspects of the lease. As an example, Chapter 83 of the Florida Statutes spells out some of the items that would normally be stated in a lease. In a residential lease, this may include mandatory repairs by the landlord, maintenance obligations of the tenant, how to terminate the lease and eviction procedures. In commercial leases, the statutes are generally silent about some of these items.

An unwritten lease is considered a lease at will. In other words, it can be terminated at any time by either the landlord or tenant. The term of the lease is based solely on when rent is paid. If the rent is paid on a weekly basis, the lease runs from week to week; if the rent is paid monthly, the lease runs from month to month. In Florida, the statutes also allow for quarterly leases and annual leases. These terms are important because they determine how quickly a landlord can end a tenancy. Under the statute, if a lease is weekly, the landlord needs only give the tenant one weeks' notice that the lease is ending. If monthly, the notice extends to 15 days from the date the next rent payment is due (Many landlords misunderstand this statute and believe the 15 day notice can be given at any time. The law is clear that the notice must be delivered at least 15 days from when the next rent payment is due). Technically, the tenant is bound by the same 15-day rule. The notice MUST be written or it is invalid. For a quarterly lease, the notice must be given at least 45 days before the end of the rental period. For an annual lease, the notice must be given at least three months before the end of the rental period.

What about repairs? While the statute details responsibilities for repairs in residential leases, it does not do that for commercial leases. Maintenance must be agreed to by the tenant and landlord as part of the lease. Many tenants mistakenly believe that they can withhold rent if the landlord does not repair the property. Only if there is an affirmative and express agreement that the landlord will maintain the premises can the tenant withhold rent for the landlord's failure to maintain the property, and then only if the lack of repairs have made the premises wholly untenantable. If the repairs are just an inconvenience, the tenant must still pay rent. To withhold rent, the tenant must give the landlord notice declaring the property wholly untenantable (this means that the property is unfit for occupancy) and demanding that specific repairs be completed. The tenant must give the landlord at least 20 days to effectuate the repairs. At that time, the tenant may start withholding rent, however, once the landlord repairs the premises, the tenant must turn over all rent withheld to the landlord.

EVICTIONS

The landlord-tenant statutes in Florida are strictly construed by the Courts. This means that they must be followed to the letter. Failure to comply with the statutes can result in a loss of rights by either the landlord or the tenant. Nowhere is this more obvious than in a breach of the lease.

When the tenant fails to pay rent on time, or if the tenant fails to complete any of the duties he is required to perform under the lease (such as maintaining the property), he is said to be in breach (or default) of the lease. While we discussed contractual breaches quite some time ago, a breach of a lease is handled in a different manner. Once the tenant is in breach, the landlord must provide to the tenant a written notice that they are in default and give them an appropriate time to cure the default. The time to cure depends on what the default is. When the tenant has failed to pay rent on time, the period to cure is three days from the time he receives the Notice. When the breach is any other obligation, the period to cure is 10 days (There are times when the landlord is not required to give the tenant an opportunity to cure a default. As these issues are case specific, I would recommend consulting with a lawyer for specific case situations).

For the purposes of this article we will use the following scenario: Tenant, Bob Smith, has a three year lease with Landlord John Jones at $1,000 per month, starting January 1, 2013. The tenant failed to make his monthly payment for March 1, 2013.

At any time after the tenant fails to make his monthly rent payment, the landlord may provide him with a three-day notice to pay rent or vacate. The notice may be handed to the tenant directly, or if the tenant is not at the property, the landlord may tape the notice to the door of the property. Although this Notice does not have to be in any specific form, it must contain certain information according to the statute. If the Notice does not comply with the legal requirements it will be considered invalid and the landlord will be required to give the tenant another notice before proceeding to eviction. Why is this a problem? During the three-day period, if the tenant tenders the rent to the landlord, the landlord is obligated to accept the rent. Many landlords simply want to get rid of tenants that do not pay on time. So long as the rent is paid before the three-day period expires, the landlord cannot evict the tenant for non-payment of rent. If on March 8, John Jones hands a 3-day notice to Bob Smith, Jones must wait until March 13 for the rent as the three-day period does not include weekends or holidays. By March 14, if Smith has still not paid rent, Jones can file an eviction action in Court.

An eviction lawsuit generally has two parts: possession of the property and payment of rent owed. Both of these can be alleged in the same Complaint, however, there is a different time period for the summonses that are issued. For a case just involving possession (or for the possession portion of a combined case), the Court issues a 5 days summons. This means that once the Tenant is served with the Complaint, he has 5 days (not including weekends or holidays) to file a response with the Court. For the rent portion, the Court will issue a 20-day summons. For a 20-day summons, the court DOES count weekends and holidays.

Once an eviction action is filed, the Complaint and Summons must be served on the Tenant. Service must be made either by the Sheriff or a licensed process server. If the action is only to evict the Tenant and the Landlord is not seeking any monetary damages, the Complaint may be either served on the Tenant directly, or if the Tenant is not at the property, by posting the Summons on the door of the property. If the Landlord is also seeking monetary damages, the Complaint must be served personally on the Tenant. For the eviction portion of the Complaint, the Tenant has five working days in which to file an answer with the Court. If the Tenant wishes to give any defense other than that the rent has already been paid, they must pay to the Court the amount of rent due under the lease. If there is a dispute as to how much rent is owed, they can ask the Court to determine the amount to be paid and upon the Court's determination, that amount must immediately be deposited with the Clerk of Court. If the Tenant fails to pay the money into the Court by the fifth day, the Landlord is entitled to obtain a default judgment against the Tenant. Along with the money, the Tenant must also file an Answer to the Complaint that sets forth the defenses the Tenant has for not leaving the property. Even if the Tenant pays the money into the Court's registry, if there is not also an answer filed, the Landlord is still entitled to a Default. In our example, if Jones filed for both back rent and eviction, he would serve two summonses on Smith, one is the five-day notice and one is the 20-day notice. These are served personally on March 15. Smith now has until March 22 to file an Answer and pay the rent due to the registry. If Smith fails to answer, Jones will obtain a default from the Clerk which can then be delivered to the Judge. The Judge would issue a default judgment and then the clerk will issue a writ of possession. The writ of possession is posted by the Sheriff and gives the Tenant 24 hours from posting to vacate the premises. 24 hours after the writ is posted, the Sheriff will return to make sure the tenant has vacated the property. If the Tenant does not leave the property by that time, the Sheriff may remove them from the property and give the property back to the Landlord.

If Smith does file an Answer in time, the Court schedules a hearing on the eviction matter. Eviction cases are given priority on the Court calendar and a hearing is scheduled as quickly as possible-often in just a week. The hearing is a trial. The Landlord puts forth why they filed the case against the Tenant. After the Landlord is finished, the Tenant tells the Court why they should be allowed to stay. At the end of the trial, the Judge makes a ruling.

If the ruling is for the Tenant (and truthfully, it rarely is), the Landlord must allow the Tenant to stay. The Court then determines who is entitled to the money in the Court's registry and issues an Order directing the Clerk to forward the money to the appropriate party. If the ruling is for the Landlord, the Judge again issues an Order and a Writ of Possession. Again, the Tenant has 24 hours from the posting of the Writ of Possession on the property door to vacate the property.

RENTAL DAMAGES

If a tenant is in default and the landlord must seek a court action to collect rent the landlord has several options. First, the landlord may sue the tenant each month as the rent comes due. So if the tenant owes $1000 per month, the landlord can file a small claims action each month for $1,000.00 until the landlord either rerents the property or until the term of the lease expires.

The landlord may also evict the tenant and retake possession for his or her own use. An example is if the landlord opens his own store in the vacant property. If this is the case, the landlord still has an action against the tenant, but his remedy is limited to the difference between the amount of rent owed and the fair rental value of the property. In other words, if the tenant is to pay $1,000 a month but the fair market value is only $700 a month, the landlord can only sue for $300 per month.

The landlord's next option is to retake possession of the property and rerents it to another person for the tenant's account. Here the landlord finds a new tenant and can only go after the original tenant for the difference between the actual rent received and the amount of rent the original tenant was supposed to pay. This happens often if the landlord has problems finding a new tenant and reduces the rent in order to obtain a tenant more quickly. If the lease calls for rent at a $1,000 a month and the landlord reduces the rent to $800 a month, they can still sue the original tenant for $200 a month.

Finally, the landlord may declare the entire lease is due and payable immediately. Here the landlord will accelerate the rent through the term of the lease and demand that the tenant pay all of the money immediately. If the lease calls for rent at $1,000 a month for three years and the tenant vacates after 5 months, the landlord may sue the tenant immediately for $31,000 (36 months x $1,000 a month = $36,000 - 5 months paid= $31,000). If the landlord chooses this option, they cannot then rerent the property unless they give a rebate to the original tenant. The landlord will not be allowed to double dip or receive rent from two people for the same property during the same term.

The process for filing this is similar to what we discussed last week. Because the landlord is seeking money damages they must obtain personal service on the tenant. Service by posting or publication in a newspaper will not be considered sufficient. Also, because the landlord is seeking money, the tenant must be given 20 days to file an answer to the lawsuit. As with the eviction action, if they do not answer, the landlord may obtain a clerk's default. However, here there is a difference from an eviction action. Once the Clerk's default has been obtained, the Landlord must file for a Default Judgment and request a hearing. The landlord must also file an affidavit that they have not received payment and that the tenant has not contacted them since the lawsuit was filed. If the tenant shows up for the hearing on the Default Judgment, they must show the court that there was some excusable reason why they did not answer and prove that they have some meritorious defense to the action. If they cannot show both of these the Judgment will be entered. If the tenant does answer the complaint on time, the case enters what we call the discovery phase where the parties can obtain information from each other. Many cases are settled at this point. After the discovery phase ends (20 days after a pleading is filed if no other pleading is filed in the meantime) either party may request a trial date. At the trial, the landlord proceeds first to present their case. After the Landlord is finished, the tenant can present their case. The judge then enters a ruling for one of the parties (the judge may take the matter under advisement and not issue a ruling immediately, but research the issues and rule later). Then comes the truly difficult part – trying to collect the money.

COLLECTION OF RENTAL DAMAGES

If the tenant had paid the rent money into the registry of the Court, collection is easy. The Judge will simply direct the Clerk of the Court to send the rent to the landlord. But if the tenant did not pay, the landlord must find a way to collect the money. This is often easier said than done.

Before attempting to collect money, it helps to know what the tenant owns. There are several ways to do this. The Court can order the tenant to prepare a financial statement that sets forth all of their property, money and assets. The landlord can also send the tenant a set of interrogatories-a list of questions that the tenant must answer under oath. If the tenant fails to complete the financial statement or fails to answer the interrogatories, the Judge may hold the tenant in contempt, subjecting the tenant to numerous penalties, including an order to pay the landlord's attorney fees and costs. The landlord can also require the tenant to appear to have their deposition taken. A deposition is an interview before a court reporter. The answers are sworn to and may be used in court. At the deposition, the landlord may ask the tenant to list every piece of property he owns, including real estate, cars, boats, stereos, televisions, jewelry (including wedding rings), paintings, coin collections, furniture, and even pets. All of this property, subject to few exclusions, may be seized to pay off the debt. The landlord can also order the tenant to produce bank statements, car titles, IRS filings, and other records indicating worth or property ownership.

If the tenant fails to appear for his deposition, the landlord may apply for a Writ of Bodily Attachment. This is a Court order to the local Sheriff to take the Tenant into custody to be brought before the Judge to explain why he failed to appear for the deposition. The Judge may then require the Tenant to post a bond to ensure that the Tenant complies with future discovery requests. Some judges will not issue these writs, viewing it as the same as debtors prison which has been abolished.

Once the landlord has learned what property the tenant owns, it is time to collect. If the tenant owns little, the landlord is probably out of luck. However, if the tenant has substantial property, the landlord may seek seizure of the property. If the tenant owns real estate, the landlord may record the judgment in the County where the property is located in order to obtain a lien on the property. The tenant will not be able to sell the property until the judgment is paid off. If all the tenant owns is personal property, the landlord may apply for a Writ of Attachment which authorizes the Sheriff to seize specific property of the tenants. The Writ must be accompanied by a fee and written instructions to the sheriff directing them where and how to seize the property. The fee varies based on the item to be seized. There are exemptions from seizure and the landlord needs to know what particular items they can or cannot seize.

When the Sheriff seizes property, a notice is published that the property will be sold at auction. Once sold, the money obtained is first applied to reimburse the Landlord for their expenses, including the Sheriff's fee. The balance is then applied towards the tenant's debt. If more money is raised then the tenant owes, the overage is to be sent back to the tenant. If the money is not enough to pay off the landlord, the landlord may then seize more property until the debt is paid off.

While I have tried to make this as simple as possible, in reality it is a difficult process. While it can be done without an attorney, the average layperson should expect to spend numerous hours learning the details of the process.

Another and often more successful option is to garnish the tenant's wages. If the Landlord learns where the tenant is employed, they can apply for a writ of garnishment. This writ is delivered to the employer, who then has 30 days to advise the Court whether the tenant works for them, how often he is paid and how much he is paid. The employer must then withhold a percentage of the employee's wages which will be applied against the landlord's judgment.

While this is a very effective method of collecting against a judgment, many tenants are exempt. Garnishment cannot be claimed from a single parent or from a head of household. You cannot garnish retirement income.

THIRD PARTIES ON PROPERTY

Who has responsibility for injuries that happen on property? This question has many answers for various situations. The answer changes based on the usage of the property, the control of the property, and the nature of the person who is injured.

Before we go into who is responsible, we need to define the types of people who may be on the property. Aside from the owner (landlord) there are four types of people who may be on a piece of property. First we have tenants. A tenant has a special standing due to their contractual rights to possession of the property. Next we have invitees. These are people that the property owner or the tenant has asked to come onto the property and have the highest level of protection. Third are the licensees. These are people who have not been invited onto the property, but are allowed to stay. An example would be a neighbor who comes over to borrow a cup of sugar. Finally, the fourth are trespassers. These people have no authority or right to be on the property. Never the less, trespassers have certain rights against property owners for injuries that occur on their property (Hey, I don't make the rules; I just report them).

Owners generally have no responsibility for injuries that occur to tenants by defective conditions that exists on the property that has been placed under the control of the tenant. Further, the landlord is not responsible to the tenant for injuries that occur on obvious conditions or hazards. For example, if there is a stairwell with no railing, there is an obvious dangerous condition. By signing the lease, the tenant takes responsibility for any injury that may occur by virtue of falling off the stairwell (Likewise, landlords are not responsible for criminal acts that result in harm to the tenant, unless the criminal act was reasonably foreseeable).

Once the property has been leased to a tenant, the liability of the property owner is essentially eliminated. The tenant steps into the property owners' shoes for the purposes of liability to third parties. This means that the tenant takes over the responsibility for defective conditions on the property and may be held liable for those injured on the property.

As mentioned before, invitees get the highest level of protection. Invitees in Florida may be social or business related. Whether a person is an invitee or not is determined by whether they were "invited" onto the property. This does not mean that a written invitation was sent to them, but rather that the person or business in control of the property held it out so that the guest reasonably believed that the property was open for the use by visitors and their particular reason for going onto the property was in accordance with the use of the building. In other words, a customer to a department store will be considered an invitee, however, a person who enters an office building to escape the rain or to look for a pay phone, will not be an invitee as their reason for going inside was not related to the offices themselves. By the way, a customer in a store does not actually have to buy something to be an invitee. They may simply be window-shopping. Social visitors are also considered invitees. They're status begins once the owner knows or reasonably ought to know they are on the property.

A guest's status may change once they are on the property if they use the property in a way it was not intended. An example is too often seen in hotels during spring break. When a hotel guest invites friends to their room and one of the friends climbs over the patio railing to climb to another room, the student is changing their status. The purpose of the railing is to prevent people from falling off the patio. To ignore this purpose and use it as a source of transportation violates the purpose of the railing and can change the student's status from invitee to an uninvited licensee or even a trespasser.

INVITEES

While it is clear that a store customer, or a social friend at a party is an invitee on the property, there are some grey areas in making the determination of an invitee as opposed to a licensee, which we will describe later. For example, if a house catches on fire and the owner is not home, how do we classify the firefighters who come to put the fire out. Or if a burglar breaks into the house, how do we classify the police officer who comes into the house to capture him? Under what was called the "fireman's rule" firefighters and police officers were treated as licensees when they entered the property to perform their duties. However, Florida, by statute, changed this rule so that after 1990, firefighters and police officers who are lawfully on the property are treated as invitees and are owed the same duty of care as an invitee. Even though the statute increases their protection, police officers must still be careful in the practice. If their presence on the property violates the search and seizure laws, they may be deemed trespassers for liability purposes.

Other persons who qualify as invitees include employees, independent contractors, and building inspectors.

The reason persons want to be categorized as an invitee is for protection against injury. If a guest is injured on the property, and they are deemed an invitee, the property owner owes them a greater duty and thus is more likely to be responsible for their injuries. Generally, a property owner must use reasonable care to keep their property in a reasonably safe condition. Because invitees, by their very nature, have been invited onto the property, the property owner must also warn all invitees of any latent or concealed perils that are known or should be known to the owner of which the invitee is unaware and which they cannot discover using reasonable care. This requires the property owner to routinely inspect his property and to take reasonable measures to eliminate known dangers, to exclude invitees from dangerous areas, or to provide warnings of the dangers. In Florida, a property owner cannot comply by simply posting warnings at every danger; they still have a duty to maintain the property in reasonably safe conditions. This means that dangerous conditions that are known or should be known must be corrected, if possible.

Property owners also may be held liable to invitees for actions of others under their control. If a business hires an independent contractor to do work on the premises, while keeping the business open to the public, the property owner may be responsible for injuries that occur if the contractor is using unsafe equipment or methods, or if the contractor creates an unsafe condition. The storeowner has an obligation to inspect the equipment used by the contractor, and to direct the contractor to operate in a safe manner so as not to create an unreasonable risk to their customers.

Invitees also have certain responsibilities. Although the property owner has a duty to the invitee, the invitee must also exercise reasonable care for their own safety and must observe conditions that are obvious. If an invitee fails to exercise due care, they share liability with the property owner, so that each will be responsible for a portion of the invitees injuries.

The duty to maintain premises is not absolute. A property owner is not required to keep the premises free from all dangers, just all foreseeable dangers. Further, the duty only applies to those portions of the premises where the invitee is intended to visit or use during the course of their visit, or which the invitee reasonably believes he is invited to use. As an example, if a customer to a store sits in a display chair which then breaks, there is a legitimate question as to whether the storeowner had sufficiently warned the customer that the chair was not for their use, but display purposes only. The property owner must also ensure that the entrances and exits to the property are maintained.

LICENSEES

Alicensee falls between a trespasser and an invitee. It is a person on the property owner's property who has not been invited, but whose presence is permitted or tolerated. This category includes contractors before they have a formal contract, persons who come onto the property for their own personal business-such as door-to-door salesmen, mail carriers, garbage men, people walking across the property when the business is closed, and invitees who proceed beyond the invited area. The category also includes discovered trespassers who have not been chased off the property, people who come to a business for a reason outside of the business' main purpose (as an example, a person who enters a store to ask if they could use the store's phone is a licensee, not an invitee).

In some places, the distinction between licensee and invitee does not exist. In Florida, however, a property owner has a lesser degree of responsibility to a licensee than they have to an invitee. The property owner must refrain from wanton (def.: showing an utter lack of moderation or justification) negligence or willful misconduct that would injure a person. The owner must avoid intentionally exposing the licensee to danger and must warn of any dangerous or defective conditions that are not open to ordinary observation. Unlike the duty owed to invitees, a property owner has no duty to licensees to keep the premises in a safe condition. They will, however, be responsible for injuries caused when the property owner had actual knowledge of a dangerous condition, realizes that it poses an unreasonable risk to a licensee, has reason to believe the licensee will not either discover the dangerous condition or realize the risk it presents, and yet allows the licensee to enter or remain on the property. While for invitees, an owner was responsible for those dangerous he should have known about, as for licensees, the duty only applies to those dangers the property owner actually knows about. As an example, if a stairwell is rotting in an unobserved area, and a person falls through, the property owner would be liable for the resulting injuries if the injured person was an invitee, but not if the person was a licensee. If a danger is not discoverable, even with frequent inspections, there is no liability for injury to a licensee.

The property owner must warn licensees of dangers that he knows about, but only if those dangers are hidden or are not such that a reasonable person would notice and avoid. If the danger is readily observable, there is no duty to warn and the licensee carries the responsibility to watch for it and take due precautions. A property owner also has no duty to warn if they do not reasonably believe any licensees will be on the property. Licensees may take on a portion of liability based upon their own actions. If the licensee acts in such a way to increase their risk, even with a violation of duty by the property owner, the licensee may be held partially responsible for their injuries.

TRESPASSERS

The final category of people on property is that of the trespasser. A trespasser is someone who enters the property of another without a license, invitation, or other right. He is intruding on the property for reasons of his own, for convenience, or for no other apparent reason. In some circumstances, a licensee may become a trespasser. This includes if they continue on the property after being told they are no longer welcome, or if they use their license to allow another unauthorized person onto the property. Trespassers include not just people on the property for no reason, but also those on the property for criminal purposes, such as burglars.

As hard as it may be to accept it, property owners have a duty to trespassers. That's right- a trespasser, including a criminal, may sue the property owner in some circumstances if they are injured on the property owner's land.

The only duty that a property owner has to unknown trespassers is to avoid willful and wanton injury. It is not necessary that a property owner actually know of a trespasser's presence before the occurrence of an injury for liability to set in. Once the trespasser is known, there is also a duty to warn them of any dangerous conditions that are not readily observable. The property owner who has knowledge of a danger that might create a risk to a trespasser is bound to take steps to protect the trespasser.

One of the classic law school examples of a property

owner's liability for injury to trespassers involved an elderly man who was having problems with burglars. After being robbed several times, he set up a trap for the burglars, consisting of a rifle pointing to the door that the burglars used for access. The trigger of the rifle was tied to the door so that opening the door would fire the rifle. A notice was posted, however when the thieves returned, one was shot. Although a warning had been posted, it was determined that the man's actions were clearly willful and wanton misconduct and he was found fully liable for the trespasser's injuries.

The property owner must consider the following for liability to trespassers: was there an existence of a dangerous condition, what was the seriousness of the danger, does the property owner have actual or constructive knowledge of trespassers, does the property owner know of the dangerous conditions, does the property owner know of the location of the trespassers, was there an injury, could the property owner have avoided the injury, was the conduct of the property owner in conscious disregard of the risk of injury to the trespasser.

What happens if the trespasser is intoxicated at the time of injury? This is an important question in many cities. And the answer is favorable to the property owner. If the trespasser is legally intoxicated at the time of injury, or was otherwise affected by drugs or alcohol so that his faculties were impaired, the property owner is immune from liability, except in cases of gross negligence or willful and wanton misconduct that was the cause of death or injury.

RESTRICTIVE COVENANTS

Now that we have discussed leases and purchases of land, there is one other related topic to discuss: land use controls. Land use is covered by numerous issues, with the top three being zoning, environmental concerns, and restrictive covenants. I want to start with the last of these, restrictive covenants, as it is strictly tied to the transfer of the property.

A restrictive covenant is a limitation that actually appears on the deed itself. Generally, a restrictive covenant begins with a real estate developer planning out a multi-unit project. In the planning phases, in order for the development to preserve the ideals of the developer, the developer sets out certain restrictions on the various properties. As the units are built and sold, the deeds are drafted to include these restrictions. These restrictions that appear in the deed are called restrictive covenants.

A restrictive covenant may include many issues. It may limit what the property owner may use the land for (As an example, it may state that the property is only to be used for residential purposes). It may state that none of the buildings may be more than one story in height. It may state that all yards must be fenced. It may state that the owners shall not allow their grass to grow in excess of two inches. These are just some examples of what restrictive covenants can include.

The covenants do not have to be actually stated in the deed; the deed may simply state that it is subject to certain restrictions that are listed in another document. Some restrictions may be implied through a common scheme in a building subdivision. Restrictions may be stated in the plat as designed by the developer. These restrictions in the plat will then remain inactive until the developer sells the individual parcels at which time the restrictions shall take effect.

One of the general purposes of restrictive covenants is to preserve the property in such a way as to stabilize the values of all property in the project. If one homeowner was able to change the design or use of his property, it may affect the values of neighboring properties in a negative manner. Some property owners see this as an imposition on their rights as property owners, however, the restrictions are to protect them as well. Further, they agreed to the covenants when they purchased the property.

Restrictive covenants are contracts; they shall be interpreted like contracts and enforced like contracts. Where the wording is clear, the Court will uphold the exact wording of the covenant, so long as it does not run counter to public policy. Where the wording is vague, the Court will look to the intent of the parties to determine the meaning of the covenant. The Courts will generally read restrictive covenants very strictly as the law favors free use of property. The Court will generally consider the covenant as narrowly as possible to give the property owner the greatest latitude of use with his property. If the covenant violates a state or federal law, the covenant will become void and unenforceable.

Covenants are generally enforced with injunctive actions. If a property owner in a subdivision is using his property in a manner contrary to the restrictive covenants, the other property owners in that development project have the ability to go to Court and get an order demanding the offending property owner cease the improper use of his property. If the owner has constructed an addition on his building in violation of the covenant, the Court can order the addition to be demolished.

Restrictive covenants can disappear if they are not enforced. When the owners in a subdivision fail to seek enforcement of a covenant, it may be deemed that the covenant has been waived and is no longer enforceable.

ZONING

Another form of land use regulation is zoning. Public zoning is the method by which local governments control the development of their communities. Zoning laws have the same effect as restrictive covenants, but rather than coming from a homeowners association or developer, they are issued by local City and County governments.

Zoning can have many purposes. It can be used to restrict growth in a certain area; to reduce density; to protect natural resources; to control the design of neighborhoods, or to protect the safety and rights of residents. So long as a zoning ordinance is properly drafted and has the public health, safety or welfare as it's foremost reason, it will likely be valid.

Zoning is a legal infringement on a person's use of property. In some cases zoning rules can prevent a person from using a property in the manner they intend. For example, a person may purchase land in a commercial area intending to open a warehouse and then find that the land is zoned for retail stores only. Or they may purchase land in a residential area to open an apartment complex but find that the property is zoned for single family houses only. These zoning regulations would prevent the owner from using the land in a way that they intended. This is not to say that the person cannot use the property at all, and it does not mean that the government has any obligation to pay the property owner for their land. A zoning restriction that limits the use of the land is not considered a "taking" as defined by the law. In a "taking", the government prevents a property owner from any feasible use of their property. Under the "taking" rules, the government must reimburse the property owner for the value of their land. With a mere zoning restriction, the owner simply needs to find another use for the land.

What can an owner do if their plans for the property conflict with the zoning rules? The agency that sets the zoning rules may allow for a variance to those rules. A variance allows a property owner to use the land in a manner that is inconsistent with the zoning ordinance. Generally, before a variance is granted the agency asks for input from the neighboring property owners. If the neighbors object to the variance, there may be reluctance by the agency to grant the variance as it may defeat the purpose of the ordinance. Often there are special considerations that the agency must look at before granting a variance. For example, to apply for a variance, the governing body may require that they find that 1) there are special circumstances peculiar to the property, 2) that the conditions were not created by the applicant, 3) that granting the variance will not give the property owner any special privilege that has been denied to others, 4) that a literal interpretation of the regulations would impose an unnecessary and undue hardship on the property owner, 5) that the variance is the minimum necessary to allow the use of the property, 6) that the variance will not be injurious to the public, 7) and that the non-conforming uses of neighboring properties is not the basis of the variance.

If the zoning ordinance changes so that a property owner existing use is now in violation of the new code, it is deemed a "non-conforming use". Generally, when the rule changes, the non-conforming use is allowed to continue. As example, if a building is constructed and then the ordinance changes so that the setback requirements are not met, the building does not have to be torn down. It may remain, even though it does not comply with the new ordinance. However, if the non-conforming use ceases, any future use must comply with the new code; you cannot later return to the non-conforming use.

ENVIRONMENTAL LAWS

The last area of land use we are going to discuss is environmental laws. This is a large and still emerging area of the law. Indeed, as our society has grown and become more urban, the government has passed several laws to prevent pollution and to preserve the environment. As this is such a large are of the law, I will not be restricting it to only those laws that affect land use, but will discuss all major environmental laws.

Environmental laws come from state, federal, and local governments. On the local level, many environmental laws are found in the zoning ordinances. Local governments will often set aside portions of land as unbuildable to preserve protected properties. They can also limit the number of houses that can be built in an area so as to make the least impact on the environment. On a state level, there are numerous laws enforced by the state's environmental protection agency. As an example, every state has a hazardous waste law and an agency to handle environmental matters. In Florida, our Hazardous Materials Act is handled by the Division of Emergency Management, of the Department of Community Affairs, and the Pollutant Discharge Prevention and Control Act is enforced by the Department of Environmental Protection.

Florida has a rich environmental history, going back to

the passage of the Bulkhead Act in 1957. This Act set out the limits to where Florida counties could fill land. The next major environmental law wasn't until 1967 when the legislature passed the Randall-Thomas Act which required environmental surveys to be done before any dredge or fill project. During the 1970's, while our federal government was making great strides in environmental laws (which we will discuss next), Florida was making great strides as well. In 1972, the legislature passed the Water Resources Act, which created five water management districts, the Land and Water Management Act, which gave the State the authority to create areas of critical state concern and to set guidelines for development in those areas (the State immediately named the Florida Keys, Green Swamp and Big Cypress as critical care areas), the Land Conservation Act which authorized the issuance of bonds to buy environmentally endangered lands, and the State Comprehensive Planning Act. In 1975, the Legislature passed the Environmental Reorganization Act which created the Department of Environmental Regulation.

In the 1980's the State saw a flourishing of environmental laws. In 1981, Governor Graham passed Save our Coasts program, followed by Save Our Rivers in 1982 and Save Our Everglades in 1983. Also in 1983, the Legislature passed the Water Quality Assurance Act, followed by Warren S, Henderson Wetlands Protection Act in 1984.

Today, numerous state environmental rules still actively assist to preserve the environment. The Department of Environmental Protection enforces Florida's air pollution control act, the quality of our drinking waters, the surface and ground water quality, and the industrial wastewater facilities. They act to restore our beaches and reclaim land disturbed by mining activities (It should be remembered that Florida has a large phosphate mining industry).

However, if it is believed that DEP is against business, it is a mistake. In 1990, the Clean Air Act created the Small Business Assistance Program, specifically to assist small business work their way through the myriad environmental regulations. While the SBAP is primarily geared towards air control issues, they also provide additional information on other Florida environmental laws and agencies. To qualify for their assistance, the business must have less than 100 employees, release less than 75 tons of all registered air pollutants and less than 50 tons of any one pollutant.

FEDERAL ENVIRONMENTAL LAWS

Although the federal government has been issuing environmental laws for well over the last 50 years, the strongest environmental push came during the 1970's. Currently, there are over a dozen laws that are enforced by the Environmental Protection Agency (EPA). These laws include the following:

The National Environmental Policy Act of 1969- This law sets forth our nation's policy on the environment and created a Council on Environmental Quality.

The Occupational Safety and Health Act (OSHA) (1970)- Congress passed OSHA to protect employees from workplace hazards including toxic chemicals and unsanitary conditions. While OSHA is enforced by the Department of Labor, the EPA takes on a training role, teaching employees and employers about the dangers of lead based paint products, and training workers and their families about the dangers of hazardous materials that may be transported home on the worker's person or clothing.

The Clean Air Act (1970)- This law was actually first enacted in 1955, but was rewritten in 1970 and amended in 1977 and 1990. The law was an attempt to create a comprehensive law that regulated the air emissions from our cars, workplaces, and other stationary and mobile sources. The Clean Air Act originally required each state to reach certain National Ambient Air Quality Standards by 1975. As many states did not reach this goal, the Act was amended in 1977 to extend the target completion dates. The Act now also includes issues such as acid rain, ozone depletion, and air toxins.

Chemical Safety Information, Site Security and Fuels Regulatory Relief Act- This is actually an amendment to the Clean Air Act that passed in 1999, that requires certain business facilities to provide to the EPA a Risk Management Plan in regards to fuels and chemicals held on site. Flammable fuels sold for retail use are exempt from this law, as are those flammable fuels held for the businesses own use. This law is enforced not just by EPA but also by the FBI and carries a criminal penalty of up to one million dollars for violations.

Clean Water Act (1972)- Officially known as the Federal Water Pollution Control Act, this law regulates the discharge of pollutants into our nation's waters. This law gave the EPA the authority to set and implement certain water control standards, such as wastewater levels for various industries. It also granted them the authority to set water quality standards for contaminants in surface waters and made it unlawful to discharge pollutants into navigable waters without a permit.

Federal Insecticide, Fungicide and Rodenticide Act (FIFRA) (1972) - controls pesticide sale distribution and use. The EPA requires users of pesticides to register when purchasing them, and must take exams for certification as applicators. All pesticides in the United States must be registered.

The Endangered Species Act (1973) - This Act provides a conservation program for threatened and endangered animals, plants and their habitats. As of October 28, 2012, there were over 2000 animals listed as endangered or threatened worldwide. The Act prevents any action that would result in a taking of a listed species, and also prevents any adverse action to their habitat. The law also prevents the importing, exporting or interstate or foreign commerce of listed species.

The Safe Drinking Water Act (1974)- This law was designed to protect the quality of drinking water throughout the United States. It authorizes the EPA to set safe purity standards and to require all operators of public water systems to meet certain health related standards.

The Toxic Substances Control Act (1976)- Known as TSCA, this Act gives the Environmental Protection Agency the authority to track over 60,000 industrial chemicals that are made or imported to the United States. It governs over the manufacture, use and disposal of these chemicals. If they determine that the chemicals present too great a danger, they may ban their manufacture or importation. The Act also allows the EPA to review other chemicals and add them to the list of dangerous chemicals if they deem necessary.

The Resource Conservation and Recovery Act (1976)- Passed along with the TSCA, RCRA gives the EPA the authority to control hazardous waste from the day of its creation to the day of its disposal. This includes not only the generation and disposal, but also the transportation, treatment and storage of hazardous waste. The Act also allows the EPA to evaluate underground storage tanks that are used to store petroleum.

Comprehensive Environmental Response, Compensation, and Liability Act (1980)- Most of us know this act by its more common nickname-Superfund. The Act was passed in response to Love Canal, New York; a Niagara Falls suburb that was built on a closed landfill. Seeping hazardous wastes resulted in an increase in deaths, miscarriages and illness. The Act creates a tax on petroleum and other chemical manufactures and allows the money to be used to cleanup sites where hazardous wastes have been located. The Act allows for prohibitions and requirements for hazardous waste sites and penalties for those dumping hazardous wastes. The Act also allows for the development of guidelines and procedures for the disposal of hazardous wastes. As an example, this Act controls the disposal of car batteries and the cleanup of gas station sites where fuel may have leaked into the ground, even if the gas station has been converted to another use.

The Emergency Planning and Community Right to Know Act (1986)- This Act was designed to help local communities protect their citizens from chemical hazards. The Act requires each state to create a State Emergency Response Commission, composed of fire fighters, health officials, local media members, government officials and local citizens to develop plans for emergency situations.

The Pollution Prevention Act (1990)- The PPA is designed to reduce pollution by improving cost effective methods for production, operation and raw materials usage. The Act focuses on conservation by developing practices that create more efficient uses of water, energy and other natural resources.

Federal Food, Drug, and Cosmetic Act requires the proper labeling, manufacture and record keeping of food products, drugs and cosmetic products. It allows for inspection of plants and records, and outlaws false labeling (including trademark infringements), or intentional damage to labeling.

Oil Pollution Act (1990)- OPA strengthened the EPA's ability to prevent and respond to catastrophic oil spills. The Act creates a tax on oil to create a trust fund for cleanup efforts when the guilty party refuses to cleanup the spill themselves. The Act also requires oil storage facilities and vessels to provide plans to the EPA on how they will respond to large oil spills.

LAWYERS' SOURCES OF LAW

Throughout this book I have talked about many issues and cited many laws and court cases. I have tried to demystify some of the issues of the law. While for many, lawyers are a regular part of business (and truthfully, I don't think any business should be started without consulting an attorney and an accountant), others prefer to do basic research for themselves. Thankfully, the internet has made legal research easier. Most statutes, rules and codes are available online if you know how to find them. Also many cases are available online. However, for more detailed legal research you must subscribe to a legal research provider like Westlaw or Fastcase.

While I can't teach legal research in this column (law schools have entire courses dedicated to learning about legal research, and the skills needed are developed only through years of practice), I will attempt to give a thumbnail sketch.

First, the books. When dealing with Florida law, if you don't have access to the internet, there are five sets of books to be intimately familiar with. First are the Florida Statutes (Annotated if possible- the FSA). The Annotated Statutes is a series of books that detail the Florida statutes in numerical order (There are over 900 chapters in the

Florida Statutes and each Chapter has numerous statutes). After publishing the statute, the book then lists a basic history of the current version of the statute and provides a thumbnail sketch of some cases that have interpreted it. The FSA is very easy to use and comes with a very comprehensive set of index books. The statutes and annotations are updated annually in what is referred to as a "pocket part" which is a booklet that is inserted into the back cover of the book. After reviewing the statute, you should be sure to look in the pocket part to see if the law has been modified or deleted. While the annotation may be helpful in clarifying the law, you should never trust the annotation to be correct. When doing research you should always read the complete case to ensure that it says what the annotation indicates. Occasionally, the annotation will be incorrect.

The second set of books are called "Southern Reporter". There are actually three series of Southern Reporters. The first covers two hundred volumes covering cases before 1941; the second series covers cases from 1941-2008 and the third series covers cases after 2008. These books hold all of the reported cases from the Florida Supreme Court and the Florida Courts of Appeal. This is where most of Florida law comes from. The books are not easy to use unless you know what case you are looking for. While the books have small topic references in them, there are other books which we will discuss shortly that are better for looking up topics. The Southern Reporters are best used once you know which case you want to read. Cases are cited by the book and page number where they are located along with the Court and year they were decided. For example, a citation that reads: <u>Key West Polo Club Developers, Inc. v Tower Const. Co. of Panama City, Inc.</u>, 589 So.2d 917 (Fla. 3DCA 1991) tells us that the case involved the two parties Key West Polo Club Developers, Inc. and Tower Construction Company of Panama City, Inc., that it was decided by the Third District Court of Appeals in 1991, and that a copy of the case can be found in volume 589 of the Southern Reporter, 2nd Series, at page 917. These cases tell you what the Courts have said about the law. The Courts rulings are binding on all lower Courts in the same district (the Circuit Courts must follow the rulings of the District Court of Appeals, which must follow the rulings of the Supreme Court). However, just because a case says what you want it to say, it may not be the law.

The third set of books is the Shepard's Citations. Shepard's is little more than a book full of numbers and abbreviations, but those abbreviations tell what the current status of a case is. For this reason, Shepard's is one of the most important research tools available. Shepard's Citations lists every case that has been reported in Southern Reporters (all three series) and then lists every subsequent case that has mentioned it, indicating which portion of the first case was discussed, whether it was in the main opinion or a dissenting opinion, whether the original case was followed or overruled, and which Courts have addressed the case. Without showing you the books, it is difficult to describe, but I will make an effort.

Referring to the case <u>Smetal Corp. v West Lake Inv. Co.</u>, 172 So. 58 (Fla. S.Ct. 1936). This is a very old case and has been mentioned at some point by every appellate court in Florida. Under Shepard's Citations, I looked this case up, first based on its book and page number. Occasionally, there will be two cases published on the same page, and Shepard's will indicate this as well. In my example case, it was the only case on that page. Shepard's then lists by book and page number all of the cases that cited <u>Smetal</u>, starting with those cases from the Supreme Court, then the Florida Appellate Courts in numerical order (1st, 2nd, 3rd, 4th, and 5th), and then the Federal Circuit Courts in numerical order. Next to some of the cases will be a letter. These letters tell how the following court referenced the cited case. The letters are as follows: a (affirmed), cc (connected case), D (dismissed), m (modified), r (reversed), s (same case), S (superseded), v (vacated), c (criticized), d (distinguished), e (explained), f (followed), h (harmonized), j (dissenting opinion), L (limited), o (overruled), p (parallel), and q (questioned). These letters are crucial as a case that has been reversed or overruled may no longer be good law. Also a case cited in a dissenting opinion may conflict with the controlling decision. In the <u>Smetal</u> case, 8 court decisions had distinguished the case, two had followed it, and one had mentioned it in a dissenting opinion. Also next to the listed cases may be a comment such as "note 1". This refers to the "Headnote". At the beginning of the cases as published in the Reporters, you will see a group of small numbered paragraphs, summarizing the major points of the case. These are the headnotes. Often, you will only be interested in one particular point of the case. Shepard's lets you see which cases referred specifically to that headnote, so you don't have to look up other cases that are irrelevant to your issue. The <u>Smetal</u> case had over 24 headnotes. Every case that is looked up should be Shepardized, if for no other reason than to ensure that it has not been overruled.

The reason for headnotes isn't simply to give you a summary of that case, but to allow you to find other cases that address the same issue. Each headnote is preceded by a topic and what is referred to as a "key number". Key numbers are assigned to each topic and subtopic, to group cases together that cover the same points. Key numbers are issued by the West Publishing Company.

Not only does West publish the Southern Reporter series of cases, but also a series of books called West's Digest. The Digest is a collection of the headnotes listed according to key number. In other words, if you find a case that refers to the necessity of obtain personal service on a party to a lawsuit, it will give a keynote of "48" under the topic of "Process". This keynote refers to the subtopic of "Nature and Necessity in General". To find more cases that address this same issue, you would refer to West's Digest, look up the section on "Process" and then turn to section 48. Here would be a listing of headnotes from other cases that refer to the same point. Each headnote states the citation of the case it comes from, allowing the reader to locate other cases that may benefit their position.

To keep the Digests updated, there is a small pouch in the back cover of each issue. Here is inserted a booklet called a "pocket-part" which contains new headnotes issued since the last edition of the book was released. It is helpful to review the pocket-part after reviewing the digest itself to get the more up-to-date cases and to see if there are cases that seem to reverse prior holdings.

Of course, as we mentioned before, you cannot rely on the headnotes alone. Occasionally, a headnote itself will be incorrect. It is crucial that the actual case be fully read to ensure that the headnote is correct. After the case is reviewed, you must again "Shepardize" it (as described last week) to ensure that the case has not been overturned, questioned, or reversed.

The last major book series to be familiar with is Florida Jurisprudence Second Series (referred to as Fla. Jur. 2d). This is a great book for summarizing general legal points. Fla. Jur. 2d is divided into various legal issues, and then each issue is subdivided into various points and sub-issues. Rather than simply list cases or headnotes, Fla. Jur. 2d is written in narrative style so that it is reader friendly. Those interested in learning the state of the law can simply read sections of Fla. Jur. 2d as if they were reading any textbook. As a research tool, Fla. Jur. 2d is a great asset. Throughout each narrative paragraph, Fla. Jur. 2d has numerous footnotes, citing to the cases that they relied upon for their information. However, as with the headnotes, it is important not to simply take Fla. Jur. 2d at face value, but to actually read the cases. They may not actually state exactly what Fla. Jur. 2d says they do. And like with the Digests, Fla. Jur. 2d is updated routinely with pocket parts.

It should be noted that neither the Digests nor Fla. Jur. 2d are actual statements of the law, but should be used as reference material to find the law.

A final series that I want to mention are the Florida Law Weekly series. This is not actually a book set, but a series of booklets which contain those cases that were published by West Publishing Company during the previous week by the Supreme Court and all District Courts of Appeal. Because they are printed on a weekly basis, it is difficult to research through Fla. Law Weekly, but it is important that these cases be reviewed because at any time, a new case may overturn an older one. The last thing anyone wants to do is to give the judge a case that has been overturned.

PRESS STATEMENTS

Occasionally, a news item arises that illustrates a point perfectly. Many years ago I saw a news report that showed issues regarding a lawyer's action in representing their client. While the item regarded a criminal act rather than a business act, the policy is the same on both. A videotape emerged from Los Angeles, California that showed a police officer throwing a handcuffed black teenager against a car and another officer punching the teenager in the face. I don't want to address these actions, as reprehensible as they are. I like to believe that most police officers are doing their job lawfully and in the best interest of the public. What caught my interest were the comments made by the officer's attorney. The officer's attorney stated that this handcuffed teenager "took action which required that he be punched".

Often attorneys make public statements on behalf of their clients, whether criminal defendants or corporate activities. There may be several reasons for this. The main reason is to turn public opinion towards the attorney's client. While a jury is supposed to be unbiased, in truth, when there is a major case, it is likely the jurors will have some advance knowledge of it. If they have a positive view of the client, or at least a questionable view as to the other side, it may benefit the lawyer's case. Similarly, in business, if an attorney can put a positive spin on his clients' activities, it may lead to increased merchandise sales and stock purchases.

A second reason is to clarify mistakes in the facts as they have been reported. The media initially report the facts as they have been given them. If the attorney feels the facts are incorrect, he may provide the media with another version of the facts that may adjust the way the story is reported.

Third, the attorney may simply be seeking media attention for himself. Heavy media attention never hurt a law firm's revenues, even if they don't succeed in the end (Many famous lawyers today actually lost their main cases).

In Florida, public statements by attorneys are addressed in the Florida Rules of Professional Conduct. Rule 4-3.6 states: "A lawyer shall not make an extrajudicial statement that a reasonable person would expect to be disseminated by means of public communication if the lawyer knows or reasonably should know that it will have a substantial likelihood of materially prejudicing an adjudicative proceeding due to its creation of an imminent and substantial detrimental effect on that proceeding". Unfortunately, some lawyers ignore this rule.

For whatever reason an attorney chooses to make a statement, the first consideration should be what is best for their client, followed by what is best for justice and society. This is what the attorney in Los Angeles may not have considered. While it would have been simple for him to state that "the footage did not show all of the details, which will be forthcoming at trial" (a statement that puts a positive spin on his client while giving prospective jurors questions as to the other side), he made a statement that was likely to anger the community and hold his client up to ridicule. In a situation that has already become racially strained, the attorney stated that the officer was justified in hitting a handcuffed teenager and that, essentially, the teenager deserved to be hit. This statement is likely to inflame the passions of those already angered by the situation and may lead to revolts over the officer's actions.

Rarely should an attorney allow his case to be tried in the press. This attorney's statement may have the effect of so tainting the local citizenry that any case brought against his client must be moved to a new county. This does not benefit the ends of justice. As attorney's, we are required to be zealous advocates for our clients, but not at a cost to justice.

LAWYER'S OATH

Since we are discussing lawyers, I would like to set a few issues straight regarding lawyers and their practices.

Not all attorneys are required to be licensed in their states. To practice in the State Court system (including County, Circuit, Appellate or Supreme Courts), an attorney must either be a member of the state Bar or must apply for special permission from the Supreme Court to make a special appearance in a state court matter. However, many lawyers do not practice in the state court system and therefore do not need to be a member of the state Bar. Attorneys who practice strictly Federal law matters, such as tax law, immigration, or bankruptcy, only need to be members of the Federal Bar (Likewise, an attorney who only handles state court matters does not need a federal license). Also, in-house corporate counsel are exempt from state Bar membership if their position is strictly an advisory, negotiating or drafting position. House counsel may not make appearances in Court for the corporation. Also, surprising to some, law school professors, although attorneys teaching state law, are not required to be state Bar attorneys (One of my professors who helped draft part of the Florida Statutes took the Florida Bar Exam years after he started teaching here, simply because he felt that it was inappropriate to teach about the Florida Bar if he wasn't a member of it).

To become an attorney, law students must sit for their state bar exams. In Florida, this is a multi-day event, including essay questions and multiple-choice questions. In addition, there is a separate ethics exam that must be taken. All students must also apply for admission and undergo a rigorous background check. The background check in Florida is one of the most comprehensive in the country and includes an investigation of nearly every aspect of the applicant's adult life (and some juvenile issues as well). The applicant must submit fingerprints which are checked in the FBI files and, if necessary, Interpol. Only if the applicant passes the background check (which can take up to 2 years), can the person be sworn in.

Each Florida lawyer must take an oath to become a lawyer. The oath reads: "I do solemnly swear: I will support the Constitution of the United States and the Constitution of the State of Florida; I will maintain the respect due to courts of justice and judicial officers; I will not counsel or maintain any suit or proceedings which shall appear to me to be unjust, nor any defense except such as I believe to be honestly debatable under the law of the land; I will employ for the purpose of maintaining the causes confided to me such means only as are consistent with truth and honor, and will never seek to mislead the judge or jury by any artifice or false statement of fact or law; I will maintain the confidence and preserve inviolate the secrets of my clients, and will accept no compensation in connection with their business except from them or with their knowledge and approval; I will abstain from all offensive personality and advance no fact prejudicial to the honor and reputation of a party or witness, unless required by the justice of the cause with which I am charged; I will never reject, from any consideration personal to myself, the cause of the defenseless or oppressed, or delay anyone's cause for lucre or malice. So help me God."

In addition to the above Oath, Lawyers also have a "Creed of Professionalism" quoted below: "I revere the law, the judicial system, and the legal profession and will at all times in my professional and private lives uphold the dignity and esteem of each. I will further my profession's devotion to public service and to the public good. I will strictly adhere to the spirit as well as the letter of my profession's code of ethics, to the extent that the law permits and will at all times be guided by a fundamental sense of honor, integrity, and fair play. I will not knowingly misstate, distort, or improperly exaggerate any fact or opinion and will not improperly permit my silence or inaction to mislead anyone. I will conduct myself to assure the just, speedy and inexpensive determination of every action and resolution of every controversy. I will abstain from all rude, disruptive, and abusive behavior and will at all times act with dignity, decency, and courtesy. I will respect the time and commitments of others. I will be diligent and punctual in communicating with others and in fulfilling commitments. I will exercise independent judgment and will not be governed by a client's ill will or deceit. My word is my bond."

Once the oath has been sworn, the lawyer has other rules which govern their behavior. Lawyers have adopted Rules which govern The Florida Bar and all lawyers licensed through the Florida Bar. This list of rules is quite extensive (nearly 100 pages long) and covers a multitude of areas. The portion that is of most interest to the general public, however, is Chapter 4-The Rules of Professional Conduct. The Florida Bar takes professional responsibility very seriously. Chapter 4 of the Florida Bar Rules makes up one-third of all the rules (There are a total of 20 Chapters). These rules tell lawyers what they are allowed to do, what they must do, and what they must not do. Unfortunately, the rules, like much legislation, can be vague and must be interpreted in many situations. For this reason, the Florida Bar has established an Ethics Hotline phone number where lawyers can call anonymously and obtain advice on whether their conduct is within the rules.

It would take weeks to discuss all of the various rules, but the one that seems to occur more than others is the conflict of interest. Under the Florida Rules, a lawyer may not represent a party if that representation will be directly adverse to the interests of another client, unless the lawyer reasonably believes the representation will not adversely affect the lawyer's responsibility and the clients waive the conflict after being consulted about it. What this means is that there is no conflict simply because a lawyer represents two people in the same business (as an example, there is no conflict just because a lawyer represents two Italian restaurants in the same neighborhood). In addition, although not necessarily a smart move, it is not a violation of the rules for a lawyer to file a lawsuit against a person they have previously represented, if they are not using special information they obtained in the prior representation. If the new lawsuit involves a separate issue from the prior representation, there is not likely to be a conflict.

Another place a conflict can arise is in the corporate setting. A lawyer representing a corporation does not automatically represent the individual shareholders. In fact, in a corporation with more than one shareholder, representation of any shareholder against another may be a conflict for the corporate attorney. The Florida Bar Rules state that a corporate attorney may represent the individual shareholders, however, if the corporations consent is required, it must be given by an officer or director of the company other than the one seeking his representation. This is of crucial importance when a majority shareholder seeks to use the corporate counsel to act in their best interest, but against the best interest of the minority shareholder.

When a client feels a lawyer has violated one of the rules of professional conduct, a complaint may be filed with the Florida Bar. Lawyers are self-regulating; that is, complaints are reviewed, judged and punished by the Florida Bar. While some feel this is a conflict of interest in itself, the Florida Bar takes its investigations seriously and several attorneys are sanctioned every month. Nearly every issue of the Florida Bar News contains descriptions of lawyers who have been sanctioned, including a statement of what their violations were.

The Florida Bar Rules can be found online at the Florida Bar website. When hiring a lawyer, you may enquire with the Florida Bar's website to see if the lawyer has been sanctioned in the past 10 years. You may also check their Martindale Hubbell rating which includes a rating on ethics. If you have any questions about your attorney's behavior, start first with the Rules of the Florida Bar.

TV COURTS

The People's Court, Texas Justice, Judge Hatchett, Judge Joe Brown, Judge Mathis, Judge Judy – these are the mainstays in the current lineup of television courtrooms. While many people try to ignore such frivolities as these, there is a benefit for the businessperson watching these shows. What you find in TV Court is an instruction manual on how to present a claim or defense in small claims. While Court TV (now truTV) displays lawyers trying cases, the trials they show are generally lengthy, complicated events. While informative, they offer little in the way of basic court instruction. The television courtrooms on the other hand, provide short, simple matters where the basic rules are applied routinely and sometimes wrongly.

All of the courtrooms on television handle what are known as small claims cases. These are cases where the claim is for a small amount of money (In Florida, the small claims limit is $5,000). Under Florida law, small claims is the one place where a corporation may represent itself without the use of an attorney. In fact, small businesses find themselves in small claims court much more frequently than County or Circuit Court. This is because most disputes in small business are for small amounts, and because Small Claims Court is more user friendly than County or Circuit Court.

This is where the television courtrooms are a benefit. Most of the time, these judges, while trying to be entertaining, also try to explain the rules of law that they use when determining their cases. They often explain not only the particular state law that governs a particular case, but general legal principles and evidentiary rules that will help the parties prevail on their case in other jurisdictions. Probably the best example of this is Judge Marilyn Milian, a Miami judge who now hosts "The People's Court".

The cases that appear on these shows are typical of the cases that usually appear in small claims cases, although the proceedings are much less formal than you would find in a real courtroom. Also, the mistakes made by the people appearing on these shows are typical of the mistakes that occur in small claims cases. By watching the shows and studying the proceedings that occur, a businessperson may strengthen their ability to proceed and prevail.

The most frequent mistake made by the parties in small claims court is the lack of proper documentation. If you are in business, you are expected to keep records, such as invoices, receipts, work orders, etc. If these are required to prove your case, have them available at the hearing. Do not bring copies. Copies can be faked; the Court wants originals. If the business uses a receipt book, it helps to keep the carbon copies in the book so the court can see the sequence before and after. Do not bring a check book register to prove a check was written; bring the cancelled check. Also, do not tell the judge that you forgot the record or that you didn't think it was important. As a party to the lawsuit, you will not know what may become important at trial. It makes sense to have more than you will need, rather than not enough. If a document is even tangentially connected to the case, bring it.

Another mistake is asking for things that cannot be granted. One of the most common errors here is asking for lost time from work to appear in court, or asking for pain and suffering in a breach of contract case (pain and suffering are rarely awardable and only in specific types of cases-not breach of contract). Study your available remedies before filing your case to ensure the Court can legally award what you are asking for. Similarly is not being able to prove your damages. If a plaintiff comes to Court and cannot document their actual damages, the Court cannot create damages for them. The court cannot award speculative damages or possible damages. They must be provable.

Courtroom television shows often display best the wrong way to do things. This is especially true in the parties' level of respect for the courtroom process. Routinely, parties on the courtroom television shows interrupt each other and talk over the judge. Often the Judges admonish them for such behavior. In a real case, a party should only interrupt the other to object based on specific legal grounds. Shouting "He's lying!" is not a specific legal objection and will not endear the judge to your position. The judge realizes that you don't agree on what happened or you wouldn't be in court. Let your opponent have their say and then the judge will give you your chance. It should be noted that the Court can proceed without the parties' presence, so if a party refuses to stop interrupting, the judge can have them removed from the courtroom and still proceed with the case.

One of the greatest mistakes television courts make compared to the real thing is in the area of hearsay evidence. Hearsay evidence is almost anything that is said by a third party outside the Courtroom (This is a gross oversimplification. Law school evidence classes spend weeks discussing what hearsay is and what the exceptions to it are, but we don't have that amount of space). The essential rule of thumb is this, if your proof involves the written or verbal statement of another person, the person who said it or wrote it must appear in Court. If they do not appear, their statement or the written document is not admissible. This includes written repair estimates and police reports. These are not admissible unless the police officer or person making the estimate is present in Court to testify. There is a reason for this rule: under our system of law, each party has the right to cross-examine all witnesses. You cannot cross-examine a piece of paper. If a party is attempting to show the Court a written estimate, the other side has the right to question the person making the estimate to determine if they have the necessary skill, knowledge, or ability to make the estimate or if they had all the pertinent facts in making it. The same is true for police reports (A major problem arises when a party tries to introduce a police report from an accident to prove the cost of repairs, since officers are not trained to give accurate repair costs). In order to introduce a document written by a third party, or any statement made by a third party, you have the right to subpoena that person to appear in court and testify on your behalf. If they do not appear, after being subpoenaed, the Court may continue the case to give them an additional chance to appear. If they still don't appear, they can be brought before the Court on contempt charges.

Under the current state of the law, the Courts hands are often tied in small claims cases. While TV Judges ask a lot of questions and try to guide the parties in developing their cases, this is not allowed in most real courts. The Judges in real courts must allow the parties to present their case as best they can without assistance. If the parties fail to prove essential elements of their case, the judge must rule against them rather than coach them on how to present their case. While this does not seem fair in a system where we are trying to do justice, the judge's hands are tied by the law.

Lastly, remember that TV Courts are there for entertainment. The real cases can be just as entertaining, and the courtrooms are generally open to the public.

BUSINESS VALUATION

What is the value of your business? That is a difficult question and a confusing answer. Business valuation is a combination of an art and a science. While many may tell you that there are quick and easy formulas to obtain a value, that is simply not the case. To obtain an accurate value for a business, the employment of a professional business appraiser is highly recommended. While there are real estate and business brokers who may provide an estimated value for a sale, unless they have specific training in valuation (and preferably an accounting background), their estimate is just that- an estimate. It will likely not stand up in court if there is a challenge to it. It is recommended that an appraisal only be done by a Certified Business Appraiser, Master Certified Business Appraiser or Accredited Senior Appraiser and that the appraiser be a member of Institute of Business Appraisers or American Society of Appraisers.

There are several types of business valuations.

First is the Replacement Cost Analysis. Using this valuation method, the appraiser can tell you how much it would cost to replace the assets of the business. The assets can include just the plant, property and equipment (PP&E) or it can include all the assets, including intellectual property such as trademarks, copyrights, logos and client lists. This value does not represent the true value of the business; it could easily be much higher, or much lower, than the true value based on condition of equipment, reputation of the business, length of time the business has been in operation and experience of the owners. This valuation method does not take into consider such intangibles as location, environment, and legal issues.

Second is the Asset Appraisal Analysis. This value comes from a determination of how much the company could sell all assets for if the company was liquidated. This usually produces a lower value for the company as an operating company is usually more valuable than one in liquidation.

Third is a Discounted Cash Flow Analysis. This method calculates what portion of the business' cash flow is needed to pay the debts of the business to determine a return of equity. This return of equity is then calculated over a period of time to obtain a long-range return. From this, the appraiser can calculate a present cash value for the long-term return.

Fourth is a Comparable Public Company Analysis. The value of a publicly traded company is easily calculated on a day-to-day basis (actually minute to minute) by following the sales on the stock exchange. When a private company has similar attributes to a publicly traded company, an appraiser may be able to calculate the value of the private company by comparing it to the value of the publicly traded company.

Fifth is Comparable Transaction Analysis. This method simply compares the company to that of a similar private company that has been recently sold.

Each of the above valuation methods gives a partial picture of the true value of a business. None provide a true value. The appraiser will want to complete as many of the above valuation methods as possible and then compare those values to obtain a definitive fair market value (Some values must be weighted based on their accuracies or upon the specific requirements of the business). A true valuation should provide the owner with a comprehensive opinion of the fair market value of the business, the economic and market conditions, and the conditions of the business at the time the valuation was complete. The report should also provide the types of valuation methods used, the weight of each, and any information used regarding comparable companies or transactions. A valuation report done properly by a trained professional should stand up in later litigation regarding the value of the business.

CIVIL RIGHTS DECEMBER HOLIDAYS

December is the culmination of many holiday festivities. With Christmas, Chanukah, and Kwanza, many religions are in full celebration. As much as people with strong religious belief want to participate in these celebrations, and while many people believe the law requires them to be allowed to celebrate, this is not the case.

The First Amendment of the United States Constitution states that "Congress shall make no law respecting establishment of a religion, or prohibiting the free exercise thereof". This is what guarantees all of us the freedom of religion. Each of us is granted the right to believe in the God of our choice, or the freedom not to believe in any God. The purpose of this amendment is not to guarantee our right to worship whenever we want; it is to prevent government from trying to promote one religion over another. The government cannot tell us what to believe or how to believe in it. The amendment is not an absolute right to believe how you want. Some followers of Santeria have tried to interpret the law to allow ritual sacrificing of animals. Similarly, some Rastafarians have tried to interpret the law to allow the routine smoking of marijuana. Both of these practices have been struck down as violating the laws of the various state governments. This seems like a conflict, but a conflict that is easily explained.

While the Constitution prevents the government from restricting our religious practices, it does not restrict them from passing general laws for our safety. The legislatures have determined that certain activities are illegal, and preclude anyone from performing them, regardless of religious belief. Smoking marijuana is illegal for everyone, not just Rastafarians. Therefore, the law does not discriminate against a religion.

What about practices that are legal in all other means? What about simply attending church for midnight mass? Of course this is legal, but it doesn't mean it will be allowed. Surprised? Let me explain.

Under the Civil Rights Act, employers are precluded from discriminating against employees on the basis of religion. Employers must take reasonable steps to protect their employees' religious beliefs and practices. Many employees over the years have tried to interpret this law to require their employer to give them time off of work to worship. It has been widely held that this is not the case. While many practicing Christians feel their religion compels them to attend Christmas service, the employer is not required to give them the time off if it is not reasonable to do so. If the employer will be left short-handed or if there are other over-riding concerns (such as other employees with more seniority requesting the time off) the employer can require their employees to work, even through the holiday. While the employer should make some effort to honor his employees' religious beliefs and practices, the employer has no obligation to make more than a reasonable effort. If the religious practice would create a hardship on the employer, the employer may lawfully refuse to allow the employee to exercise their practice. Also, if the religious belief would interfere with the religious beliefs of other employees, the employer need not accommodate it.

The religious belief or practice must be valid. An employee cannot create a religion just to get time off of work or to create rights that they otherwise would not have.

YEAR END PAPERWORK

Happy New Year! For many businesses, this is the busiest time of year-not because business is up, but because there is much to do to end the old and start the new. This is a period to close old files and open new. But the first step is to know what to keep and what to discard.

Hopefully, the business files have some organization. If not, now is the time to organize. Separate the files into basic categories: correspondence, contracts, client files, employee files, payroll, receipts, billing records, safety reports, etc. If the categories are too general, it won't aide organization much; if they are too detailed, they can be unwieldy. Set aside as many financial records as you can. These will be crucial as the tax filing deadline (March 15, for businesses) approaches. This is also a good time to consider purchasing a computer if the business isn't using one yet. With software such as QuickBooks, bookkeeping is made much easier and at year-end, the computer provides a detailed summary for your accountant with just a couple of keystrokes. The savings in taxes and time will likely set off the cost of the computer over time.

Once the files are organized, you can determine what to keep and what to throw away. Start with some common sense. If the file has to do with an existing matter that you are currently working on, don't throw it away. Keep it in an active folder where you can access it for later use.

There is no law requiring you to keep receipts, however, again common sense says not to throw them away. Even if your bookkeeping system is computerized, once you have input the amount into the computer, place the receipt into a file (some highly detailed people choose to subdivide their receipt file by vendors. This provides certain advantages, but also increases file space). These receipts may become necessary later in the event the Internal Revenue Service decides to audit your account. The IRS has a period of seven years to audit a return, so a good rule of thumb is to keep all income and expense records for seven years.

Next, turn to the contracts file. Of course, if a contract is still active, keep it available in an active file for future use. If the contract has expired it should not be discarded for a period of five years. Under Florida law, parties may file suit under a verbal contract for four years and under a written contract for five years.

The next category is employee records. The Immigration and Reform Act of 1986 requires employers to keep all employee records for a period of three years or for one year after termination, whichever is longer. Failure to comply can result in fines up to $1,000 imposed personally on the business' record keeper.

Employee retirement plans and records under ERISA (Employee Retirement Income Security Act), must be kept for a period of six years. Whenever the plan changes, the six-year period starts anew.

Next turn to your payroll records. Of course, as stated above, there is a seven-year period for IRS purposes, however, there are other requirements as well. Under the Civil Rights Act, payroll records, as well as job applications, resumes, and personnel records must be kept for a minimum of six months, or until disposition of pending legal actions. However, under the Equal Pay Act, employee records regarding wages, hours and other terms of employment must be kept for two years. This also applies to any records that would support employment decisions. Finally under the Age Discrimination Act, employee records must be kept for one year, but payroll information and personal data must be kept for three years.

As a rule of thumb, employee records should be maintained for at least three years, and then review them to destroy those records that are irrelevant or immaterial.

These are not the only retention requirements, but provide a good foundation. For further information on what records to retain and discard, talk to your attorney or accountant.

CLOSING

Hopefully this book has provided you with some information on starting and operating a business. As mentioned at the outset, the information being provided in this book is not designed to be specific legal advice. It is offered for information purposes only. If anything you have read here has created questions regarding your business practices, contact an attorney in your area who is well versed in business law. If you are not familiar with any, contact your state Bar Association for a list of local attorneys.

Thank you for reading.
Please review this book. Reviews help others find Absolutely Amazing Ebooks and inspires us to keep providing these most helpful books.

If you would like to be put on our email list to receive updates on new releases, contests, and promotions, please go to AbsolutelyAmazingEbooks.com and sign up.

ABOUT THE AUTHOR

ALBERT L. KELLEY, is an attorney, author, book publisher, film producer, traveler and adventurer located in Key West, Florida. His law practice concentrates primarily in the areas of business, corporations, contracts, copyright, trademark, and entertainment law, as well as foreclosure defense. He graduated cum laude from Florida State University College of Law in 1989. He served for years as an adjunct professor for St. Leo University in their Business Administration program, teaching courses in business, employment and administrative law. For five years Al wrote a weekly business law newspaper column and has authored a book on business law. He has also been a featured panelist at Florida State University's College of Law's Annual Entertainment Art and Sports Law Symposium. Albert L. Kelley serves as legal counsel for the world's largest offshore powerboat race promoter as well as museums, art galleries, television stations, performers and newspapers. On the business side, Albert is corporate counsel to over 150 corporations, and has filed over 60 trademark registrations and countless copyright applications. Albert has negotiated contracts with numerous national companies including Apple Computers, Harley Davidson, and Ralston Purina. Al has given numerous seminars on trademarks, copyrights, film licensing and financing, and foreclosure defenses. He is a licensed skydiver, hang-glider pilot, and scuba diver.

www.ingramcontent.com/pod-product-compliance
Lightning Source LLC
Chambersburg PA
CBHW060947220326
41599CB00023B/3621